A New Green Order?

A New Green Order?

The World Bank and the Politics of the Global Environment Facility

Zoe Young

Pluto Press

LONDON • STERLING, VIRGINIA

First published 2002 by Pluto Press
345 Archway Road, London N6 5AA
and 22883 Quicksilver Drive,
Sterling, VA 20166–2012, USA

www.plutobooks.com

British Library Cataloguing in Publication Data
A catalogue record for this book is available from the British Library

ISBN 0 7453 1553 4 hardback
ISBN 0 7453 1548 8 paperback

Library of Congress Cataloging in Publication Data
Young, Zoe.
  A new green order? : the World Bank and the politics of the Global
Environment Facility / Zoe Young.
       p. cm.
  ISBN 0–7453–1553–4 (hb : alk. paper) — ISBN 0–7453–1548–8 (pb : alk.
paper)
  1. Global Environment Facility. 2. Environmental policy—Political
aspects. 3. Environmental policy—International cooperation. 4.
Environmental policy—Evaluation. 5. World Bank. I. Title.
  GE170 .Y685 2002
  363.7'0526—dc21
                                                          2002008632

10   9   8   7   6   5   4   3   2   1

Designed and produced for Pluto Press by
Chase Publishing Services, Fortescue, Sidmouth EX10 9QG
Typeset from disk by Stanford DTP Services, Towcester
Printed in the European Union by Antony Rowe, Chippenham, England

Contents

LIST OF FIGURES

Preface

In the early 1990s, I was a student and occasional green activist when international discussions about the risks of climate change and biodiversity loss finally led to the United Nations agreeing to set up conventions to protect these aspects of the global environment. But like most people on Earth I knew nothing of the Global Environment Facility (GEF), established in the World Bank to pay the costs of implementing these new environmental Conventions in the global South. Ten years later, I came to write this book as an academic researcher employed on a study entitled 'The Functioning of the Global Environment Facility – a Political Analysis',[1] and interested in the uses made of power, knowledge and international institutions in the name of the global public good.

The GEF was charged to protect natural biological and climatic systems that are complex and self-organising – like the political and economic milieu into which the new financial institution was born. Both environmental and social complexities can be understood as emergent properties from systemic evolution 'at the edge of chaos', and it is at the intersection of these two sets of complex ecologies that GEF people have been appointed to save nature for the public good, and I have tried to understand what they are actually doing.

This book explores how an unprecedented experiment in global resource management has worked behind its public face, and also what this experiment has been like to work with. Aiming to challenge what Rosaldo (quoted in Hertz and Imber, 1995) calls the 'cultural invisibility' of the powerful, this book is a report back to

1. In this book I report on findings gathered while working as research assistant and part-time PhD student in the Department of Geography, University of Hull, UK, also briefly in the Science Policy Research Unit, University of Sussex, UK. The research project and subsequent documentary on the GEF were financed by the UK Economic and Social Research Council under its Global Environmental Change Programme (grant no. L320253193). This assistance is gratefully acknowledged. The grant holder bears no responsibility for the final content of this book.

readers whose taxes probably pay for the GEF, and whose shared natural environments its experts and investments are supposed to save.

The text aims to betray no confidences but to convey understandings developed largely through anonymous, in-depth interviews.[2] I visited people in GEF's constituent governing, advisory and secretarial bodies; national ministries providing and spending GEF finances; units of the World Bank, International Finance Corporation, UN Development Programme and UN Environment Programme implementing GEF projects; secretariats of the United Nations Convention on Biodiversity and (to a lesser extent) Framework Climate Change Convention; interested non-governmental organisations, consultants, scientists and academics; as well as communities affected by a GEF project in India.[3]

Overall, interviewee responses ranged from the heart-opening to the downright deceptive, with a lot of reserved cooperation in between. When my questions inevitably 'ventured into a political minefield', some interviewees preferred to offer an 'institutional view', and several declined to respond altogether. More than one said my questions were hard to answer because, like a marriage, GEF work is 'lived everyday and moves forward bit by bit, so it's very hard to step back and make a one-off judgement' (interview, GEF secretariat, 1997). In fact I found that, like me, nobody involved is able to be fully objective – to the extent that, for some, 'it doesn't matter what actually happened, so much as how you present it'. Over lunch, this international civil servant suggested that I could have made a deal: promising the GEF that my research would not be harmful, in exchange for greater access. But I aimed to tell the truth as I found it – not as it suited the institution under investigation.

For reasons of space I assume that if readers are interested in details of GEF's own published reports, facts and figures, they can follow them up elsewhere (see, for example, the GEF's own extensive website: <www.gefweb.org>). If I give less space to official versions of events

2. I conducted over 80 interviews mostly in the US in 1997 and India in 1998 and 1999, and have learned from innumerable informal conversations and e-mails since 1996.
3. Thanks to Ian Bacon for permission to adapt his report of research in Zimbabwe in 1996 (see Bacon, 1998).

than to the difficulties, protests and elevated gossip, it is mostly because the GEF and the World Bank etc. already publicise the official story, while the perspectives gathered here might not otherwise reach an interested audience.

Acknowledgements

Thanks –

To nature for being alive; my parents for getting me going; friends, family, writers and teachers for making me think; Sonja for leading me to the GEF; Dylan for persuading me into film; everyone at Pluto for putting me into print; Kazimuddin Ahmed for the title; Ian Bacon, Sonja Boehmer-Christiansen, Mary-Jane Dance, Lucy Ford, Wendy Gregory, Joyeeta Gupta, Dylan Howitt, Korinna Horta, Andy Jordan, George Makoni, Simon Mitchell, Sarah Sexton, Neena Singh, Jake Werksman, Alex Wilks, Elizabeth, Wayland and Louisa Young, and numerous others for help, advice and encouragement; Flook for the company; Rustam Vania and the Centre for Science and Environment for the cartoons; Conscious Cinema for the images; the Global Environmental Change Programme of the Economic and Social Research Council for funding the research; the Universities of Sussex and Hull for hosting it; and last but not least the many kind people both inside and out of the GEF system for sharing their time, information and thoughts. Thank you all.

Apologies –

To the friends, family and compadres whom I have been avoiding to get this book done; to anyone whom at any stage in this research and writing I have misunderstood, missed out or misled; and to my readers who deserve clearer social science and story-telling about this exotic ecological organisation existing on the edge of chaos. Since I live there too, I accept responsibility for my omissions and mistakes.

This book is dedicated to everybody with respect.

List of Abbreviations and Acronyms

CBD   UN Convention on Biological Diversity
CEO   Chief Executive Officer
CITES   Convention on International Trade in Endangered Species
COP   Conference of the Parties (to a UN Convention)
CSD   UN Commission on Sustainable Development
CSE   Centre for Science and Environment (Delhi NGO)
CSERGE Centre for Social and Economic Research on the Global Environment
ECOSOC UN Economic and Social Council
EDF   Environmental Defense (US NGO)
FCCC   UN Framework Convention on Climate Change
FEU   Fundacion Ecologica Universal
FP   Focal Point
GATT   General Agreement on Tariffs and Trade
GEF   Global Environment Facility
GEFOP   GEF Operations Committee
GNP   Gross National Product
ICFP   International Conservation Financing Program
ICSU   International Council of Scientific Unions
IDA   International Development Association (soft-loan arm of World Bank)
IEPP   Independent Evaluation of the GEF Pilot Phase
IFC   International Finance Corporation (private sector arm of World Bank)
IMF   International Monetary Fund
IPCC   Intergovernmental Panel on Climate Change
IUCN   World Conservation Union (international scientific NGO)
MIGA   Multilateral Investment Guarantee Agency (arm of World Bank)
MoU   Memorandum of Understanding
MSG   Medium-sized Grants (pathway for GEF funding)

NGO	Non-governmental Organisation
NSC	National Steering Committee
OECD	Organisation for Economic Cooperation and Development
OPS	Overall Performance Study (of the GEF)
PMU	Project Management Unit
PRINCE	Program for Measuring Incremental Costs for the Environment
PVMTI	Photovoltaic Market Transformation Initiative
RDB	Regional Development Bank
RESOLVE	Center for Environmental and Public Policy Dispute Resolution
SAP	Senior Advisory Panel (of the GEF)
SGP	Small Grants Programme (run by UNDP)
SME	Small and Medium Enterprises (Program) (run by IFC)
STAP	Scientific and Technical Advisory Panel (of the GEF)
TWN	Third World Network (Southern NGO)
UNCED	United Nations Conference on Environment and Development (Rio, 1992)
UNDP	United Nations Development Programme
UNEP	United Nations Environment Programme
UNESCO	United Nations Educational, Scientific and Cultural Organisation
USAid	United States Agency for International Development
WBCSD	World Business Council for Sustainable Development
WCED	World Commission on Environment and Development
WEOG	Western European and Others Group
WRI	World Resources Institute (Washington DC NGO)
WSSD	World Summit on Sustainable Development
WTO	World Trade Organization
WWF	World Wide Fund for Nature (international NGO)

1 Greening the New World Order?

'The Future of the Earth ... in our Hands'; The GEF in Context; Establishing the GEF; The GEF in Practice; Understanding the GEF; Outline of the Book; Conclusions

'THE FUTURE OF THE EARTH ... IN OUR HANDS'

Each of you is preoccupied with issues at home – important issues, sometimes urgent issues. But let me submit to you that none of these will be nearly as important to the future of your people as the issues here ... The future of the earth as a secure and hospitable home for those who follow us is in our hands. (Maurice Strong speaking to assembled world leaders at the United Nations Earth Summit[1] in Rio de Janeiro, Brazil, June 1992)

Ten years on from the Rio Earth Summit and 30 years from the UN Conference on the Human Environment in Stockholm, the world's governments, corporations and 'civil society' are once again being roused from day-to-day political and economic survival to talk about the future of all our people, our home planet, and the other species we

---

1. Popularly known as the Rio Earth Summit, this event is formally referred to as the United Nations Conference on Environment and Development (UNCED).

share it with – at the 2002 World Summit on Sustainable Development (WSSD) in Johannesburg, South Africa. But the indications are that just as in Stockholm and Rio, reordering the international economy – or even securing corporate accountablility – is off the agenda, so, despite all the global hype and new initiatives, nothing much will change.

I make this prediction on the basis of not only reports from WSSD's preparatory processes, but also the findings presented below. The subject of this book is the Global Environment Facility (GEF), a publicly funded multi-billion-dollar[2] green aid fund created in the World Bank by Western governments in 1991 – just in time for Rio. The GEF was charged with financing protection of the 'global environment' and, thereby, 'sustainable development', and has supported thousands of international conservation projects, mostly justified under the UN Framework Convention on Climate Change (FCCC) and the UN Convention on Biological Diversity (CBD). Yet as an avowedly 'non-political' body, the GEF's governing Council does not challenge the often anti-environmental priorities for international extraction of and investment and trade in natural resources of its donor governments or the World Bank, International Monetary Fund (IMF) and World Trade Organization (WTO).

In fact, the growing environmental movement challenging the World Bank and IMF in the late 1980s was partially headed off at the pass with the help of GEF's new conservation money. Billions of additional aid dollars promised for conservation projects eclipsed Southern and radical Northern environmentalists' claims for global ecological justice, environmental regulation on international trade and full and fair cost-benefit analyses of economic investments to ensure the polluter always pays. Suggesting that governments were, after all, willing to commit to environmental action, the GEF's additional green aid was also intended to bring in new partners and co-ordinate existing international institutions to respect the global environmental commons. Thus the World Bank could turn its critics into consultants – accepting their advice within limits, offering project contracts and promising participation in the catalysis of global capital's evolution towards sustainability.

A publicly funded experiment, the GEF was intended to generate lessons for a mission in which – as the UN Environment Programme (UNEP), created 20 years earlier, had already found to its cost – there are no easy answers. So far little known and less understood, the

2. Unless otherwise specified, all $ signs refer to US dollars.

story of the GEF may shine a light on conservation and colonialism, capitalism and complexity, compromise, co-option and commodification in a rapidly transforming world. It may even suggest things that could be done differently – more fairly and effectively – in future innovations for global environmental security.

THE GEF IN CONTEXT

Despite early talk of a 'peace dividend' after the end of the Cold War benefitting the world's poor people and natural environments, official aid has generally declined while weapons spending and hot wars for resources have continued apace since the announcement of a US-led New World Order by George Bush I in 1991.[3] The same year, the GEF entered into operation: an adaptation to the institutions of this emerging global 'order' in response to the rise of environmental movements which were becoming a geo-political force.

In the 1980s the green movement, growing internationally and especially in the US, faced intense resistance from powerful established interests: firms, bankers and politicians profoundly irritated – and sometimes partly convinced – by multi-pronged ecological challenges to business as usual. The GEF was a strategic response by some of 'those who claim maturity and legitimacy' in the global 'centres of political life' (Walker, 1995). While financing the UN multilateral environmental Conventions (see below) the GEF also served to draw the aspirations of a growing environmental movement into running discrete conservation projects and reforming the World Bank – one of the Bretton Woods[4] 'family' of global financial institutions that includes the IMF and latterly the WTO.[5]

3. Foreign Direct Investment (FDI) in 49 'least developed countries' increased from $600 million in 1990 to $5.2 billion in 1999, although their share of global FDI remains at 0.5 per cent. Over the same period, official development assistance to these countries declined by $5 billion (more than the GEF's 'additional' aid) to $11.6 billion, see <www.unctad.org/en/pub/poiteiiad3.en.htm>. For arms trade figures see <www.caat.org>.
4. The World Bank and IMF were created at Bretton Woods, New Hampshire, US, in 1944 – see Chapter 2.
5. Effectively controlled by Northern governments' treasuries, these strictly 'economic' Bretton Woods institutions are meant to help the global economy to function, although as lumbering and unaccountable bureaucracies they do not always do so effectively and have widely been held responsible for financing environmentally destructive developments across the South (see, for example, Rich, 1994). The World Bank makes loans to Southern governments for development projects including roads, dams, mines, forestry, agriculture, schools, hospitals and sectoral reform programmes.

Created in 1945, the World Bank and IMF intervene in the inter-national economy primarily in the interests of their major shareholders – the US and Western European economic powers. Since the 1980s these institutions, joined by the WTO in 1994, have also promoted the 'Washington Consensus' of neo-liberal policies, which make life easier for big business, if not always the people and places affected (see Chapter 2). For example, in promoting fisheries 'development', the Bank may offer a government credit to buy large boats, refrigeration and processing factories to serve global markets, but takes next to no responsibility for the resulting decline of fish stocks and local markets and immiseration of artisanal fishing communities, let alone damage to marine ecosystems and spawning grounds by industrial-scale fisheries. Opening some middle-income countries' economies and resources to ever more foreign investment may have created a degree of economic advancement for some, but damaging environmental consequences combined with displacement, hunger and recurrent resource riots across the South, along with economic collapses from East Asia and Argentina to Enron, suggest that all is not well with the model – even if the long-term decline of so many African countries under neo-liberal policies is ignored, as is so often the case.

As this book is completed in 2002, the GEF's official evaluators cannot advertise any serious impact on the rate or causes of global environmental change – indeed, they lack the time, resources and remit to examine the details of grass-roots situations where change may or may not be occurring. At the global level, despite isolated green achievements (for example, the growth of the hole in the ozone layer may be slowing), most forms of pollution are still rife, the climate still seems to be changing, countless plant and animal species and varieties are still going extinct, landscapes, water bodies, fertility and ecosystems are still being degraded or destroyed through ill-considered and unsustainable exploitation – according to the UNEP's scientists as well as the various environmental non-governmental organizations (NGOs).[6] Despite ten years of the GEF's reforming efforts (not to mention 30 years of the UNEP's), fierce critiques and mass demonstrations are again gathering against the very legitimacy of the international financial institutions, opposing

6. NGO has become a generic name for non-profit bodies since it was first used in the UN Charter of 1946 to designate the groups allowed access to the UN Economic and Social Council (ECOSOC).

the ecological as well as social consequences of the policies they enforce (<www.indymedia.org>, <www.schnews.org>).

As banks, corporations and their allied professional classes try once more to pacify popular ecological concerns and separate them from resistance to the capitalist system itself, what further institutional reforms – and difficulties – are likely? Will available funds, expertise, attention and political initiative be used more effectively for environmental protection in future? If governments were unable to come up with an effective solution when there was mass popular interest in conservation in the late 1980s and early 1990s, what hope is there for less compromised solutions now that international attention has largely moved on to focus more on hunger, trade and war?

With US military ambitions for 'full spectrum dominance' of the globe and the bleeding of a so-called 'war on terror' into something like a war on dissent, most of the biggest and especially Washington-based environmental NGOs are working with the World Bank and/or the GEF, and are politically wary of seeming to attack what now passes for the US government's 'national interest'.[7] Whatever their aspirations, hopes and promises, can real-world solutions to widely distributed environmental problems really all be channelled through a largely Washington-based community of environmental professionals whose jobs depend, in the final analysis, on the surplus and favour of the US' and Western Europe's globalising corporate empires?

ESTABLISHING THE GEF

In a world of *realpolitik* the assumption that states signing ever more demanding treaties could solve global environmental problems becomes 'inadequate and politically naive' (Paterson, 1995).[8] Treaties and conventions facing crises of implementation require financial as well as political support if they are to approach the desired impact. The GEF therefore inspired new hopes in some environmental and diplomatic circles because, unlike other global environmental initiatives, it had the powerful World Bank behind it and billions of

---

7. The Sierra Club is among several green US NGOs who called off campaigns that challenged the White House agenda in the aftermath of 11 September 2001 <www.counterpunch.org/giombetti.html>.
8. For example, despite numerous marine and conservation treaties, fisheries continue to be over-exploited for international markets.

dollars of real money to spend. But, for reasons explored further below, the same facts also invited pessimism and mistrust.

The GEF was initially created by World Bank staff and a few officials in Western European government ministries as a 'green window' of the Bank, intended to finance projects supportive of the United Nations Conventions on Biological Diversity Climate Change. These major UN Conventions were due to be signed, by governments, at meetings associated with the Rio Earth Summit in 1992,[9] having been negotiated in response to intense environmental pressure on especially Northern governments. Some sort of fund was needed to persuade Southern governments to agree to the conservation and the constraints on their national development implied in the Conventions. The Northern donors did not however want to become liable for all the potential costs arising from the treaties, nor to put more money into the United Nations system – with its relative accountability to Southern governments[10] and 'inefficient' political debates and processes. The rich Northern governments also wanted to reform existing international institutions to be more efficient – but without alienating their allied banks and corporations by regulating the terms of global trade and investment for the sake of environmental protection.

The 1987 UN-hosted Multilateral Fund for the Montreal Protocol (to counter depletion of atmospheric ozone) had set a precedent for global environmental finance that was not welcomed by the major donor government treasuries, because it allowed all governmental participants in the Protocol a say in the spending of its funds. The Climate and Biodiversity Conventions involved far more politically loaded and complex issues to deal with than ozone. Therefore, when it came to financing them, donors ignored the Montreal Protocol's precedent. Instead they established the GEF to keep the implementation of the new Conventions under the World Bank's legal authority. Building on a reputation for political conservatism, the Bank promised its major donors a 'business-like' approach to 'valuing the environment' and financing 'sustainable development'.

9. With the exception of, most famously, the US, along with a few others.
10. The World Bank and IMF are controlled on the basis of 'one dollar, one vote', giving effective control to Northern governments' treasuries, particularly that of the largest shareholder, the US. By contrast UN agencies are governed on the basis of 'one country, one vote', giving influence to the more numerous governments of the South.

In the lead up to Rio, the quietly established GEF attracted opposition from Southern governments and non-governmental organisations mistrustful of an opaque entity, a *fait accompli*, based in a World Bank accountable to 'donor' rather than 'client' governments, let alone to environmental science or popular movements. In the light of the World Bank's past investments and unfavourable experiences with the GEF so far, some said giving the Bank responsibility for global conservation was like putting a fox to guard chickens.[11] They argued instead for reparations for the damage done to Southern and global environments by Northern expansionism, as well as help for the billions of people whose environmental priorities are more immediate, for example clean water to drink and air to breathe.

The donor governments, however, would not prioritise such local and domestic ('brown', rather than 'green') environmental issues – which attracted relatively little interest from their attendant community of vocally global 'green' NGOs. Rejecting what they called 'rhetorical issues', the donors designed the GEF to pay neither the costs of environmental damage from earlier 'development' nor all the possible costs of implementing the Conventions on Climate Change or Biodiversity in the South.

Nonetheless, for all its consequently limited appeal to those with more immediate problems, the GEF was the only new source of multilateral aid on offer at Rio, and, in response to its many critics, the donor governments promised to review and restructure the GEF to operate more openly, accountably and participatorily. It was made nominally independent of the World Bank and charged with supporting the 'national development priorities' of recipient governments, while making global 'partnerships' – not least with green NGOs and the private sector. A sufficient number of Southern governments and international environmental interests therefore accepted the promise of funds, innovation and access, for the GEF to be refinanced in 1994 and designated 'interim financial mechanism' to implement the Conventions on Climate Change and Biodiversity.

Nevertheless, despite the fact that the UNEP and the UN Development Programme (UNDP) were brought in to help the World Bank implement GEF projects, the Bank remained institutional parent and trustee of GEF funds. Publishing a 'GEF glossary',[12] it literally defined

11. Korinna Korta, Environmental Defense Fund (EDF).
12. <www.gefweb.org/gefgloss.doc>

the terms under which experimental global environmental aid was made available in the 1990s. Through its effective control of the GEF, the World Bank has been able to bring its economistic vision of development into what was previously UN territory of global environmental protection.

THE GEF IN PRACTICE

Raising and Spending Money

GEF funds promised to be 'additional' to other aid flows, but would finance only the 'incremental costs' of achieving 'global' environmental benefits through actions taken under the Conventions. Essentially, the GEF pays only for the extra costs of development projects that protect international waters, atmospheric ozone, biodiversity and the climate system: environments deemed to be of 'global' value.

In the ten years since it was created, the GEF has channelled $4.1 billion from mostly North American, Western European and Japanese treasuries to over a thousand projects in over 150 Southern[13] and former communist countries. To put its work in context however, GEF funds constitute less than 1 per cent of total international aid flows to the South, and offer the equivalent of one day's global spending on military 'defence' for each year of protecting the global environment.[14] Even so, the Washington DC-based GEF currently has about three times as much money to spend each year as the UNEP – based faraway from donor treasuries in Nairobi, Kenya. The GEF's well-funded arrival on the international scene therefore led one UN official to liken the Facility to 'a new wife for the donor governments, favoured over old, tired UN bodies'.

---

13. The capitalised terms 'South' and 'Southern' are used here to refer to countries that are targets for multilateral development aid funds including the GEF. 'Northern' governments made the major contributions to GEF funds, and are sometimes referred to as 'donors'. To simplify the GEF picture, I use the generic term 'South' to refer to former communist areas as well as countries in Central and South America, Africa, Asia and the Pacific region which, if they sign up to the Conventions, are eligible to be 'recipients' of GEF funds. On occasion I also refer to the 'G77 (and China)', a grouping of Southern governments, which emerged in the 1960s to counter the dominance of the 'G7' (North American, Western European and Japanese) governments in international negotiations.
14. Banuri and Spanger-Siegfried (2000) and Imber (1994).

The initial, 'pilot' phase of GEF funding ran from 1991 to 1994; it was promised $1.6 billion. Major donors to the pilot phase were the French and German governments with nearly $150 million each;[15] the US and Japan contributed similar amounts indirectly through 'co-financing' (see Chapter 3). A small group of Southern governments also paid up to $6 million each at the start – their 'fee' to join a new conservation 'club' and share in the $733 million actually spent on GEF projects in countries with a per capita GNP below $4,000 in 1989.[16] For the 1995–8 GEF 'operational' phase, which promised to 'build on the lessons' of the pilot phase, donors promised a total of $1.8 billion – but again, only about half the promised sum was spent, on mostly quite large development projects: for example, for renewable energy technologies and protected areas, the mapping of genetic resources, sources and sinks of 'greenhouse gases' and preparation of plans for their management. The rest of the money was carried over in 1998 when the GEF was replenished with an advertised $2.75 billion to last until 2002.

Though the total sum promised had risen again, it was in this context that some people from the South described the GEF as 'a con'. The longer time period and a carry-over of about $860 million, much of it not yet even raised from late paying donors, meant the real contribution from these governments would quite possibly decline – making careful distribution of precarious funding all the more important.

Governing Access

Agreement on what exactly to fund with limited project aid is always difficult to secure when there are conflicting agendas and interests at stake. This has been especially true in GEF negotiations, in which ministries, including those concerned with environment, foreign affairs, technical assistance and overseas development, all have roles to play alongside numerous other interested bodies. The GEF is formally governed by a 32-strong governing Council, divided more

15. France offered $142 million, Germany $147 million, Italy $66 million, the UK $60 million and the Netherlands $53 million.
16. The reasons for GEF underspend (explored in Chapter 5) include the complexity of funding requirements and the snail's pace of processes through which project proposals were agreed to be politically and technically acceptable.

or less equally between donor and recipient government representa-tives and officially overseen by a three-yearly Participants' Assembly of all the governments involved. The Council receives guidance from and reports to the governing bodies of the UN treaties on Climate Change and Biodiversity but, just as UN bodies cannot effectively challenge trade and investment policies agreed in the more powerful Bretton Woods institutions,[17] Conferences of the Parties (COPs) to the UN Conventions cannot override GEF Council decisions.[18]

Despite complex voting arrangements having been negotiated, the Council makes decisions by consensus, guided by the chairman and chief executive officer (CEO) of the GEF, Mohamed El-Ashry (see Appendix I for biographical details). Appointed from the World Bank's environment department, he also heads the GEF's 30-strong administering Secretariat (see Chapter 4). In Council meetings El-Ashry treats Southern representatives 'like kings' (interview, CBD secretariat, 1997), but cannot offend the GEF's major donor govern-ments who, in the end, pay his wages. Aware of these dynamics, most other people and organisations involved in the GEF seek less to upset this balance than to use it, lobby it, attract funds with minimal strings attached and find employment in the GEF system for their people.

The GEF's unprecedented openness to 'civil society' means these interests include civil society organisations of many hues: from the big Washington-based policy groups such as the World Resources Institute (WRI), the scientific World Conservation Union (IUCN) and others interested in tapping new environmental finance, to the more critical and Southern organisations including the Climate Action Network, Third World Network (TWN) and Delhi's Centre for Science and Environment (CSE) who watchdog GEF policies and projects, drawing attention to common and serious problems (see Young, 1999 for profiles of key NGOs interested in the GEF). Also represented are UN agencies with a sustainable development remit, the organised transnational private sector, and myriad consultants: technical experts, environmental economists, international lawyers, and others with the skills to advise on protecting the global environment.

GEF programmes are supposed to be science-based, guided by the Scientific and Technical Advisory Panel (STAP) managed by the

17. In 2001 an IMF representative stated that the IMF was not subject to international human rights law (Bretton Woods Update, Oct/Nov 2001), see Chapter 2.
18. Governments become 'Party' to a Convention when they have formally ratified it domestically.

UNEP. Many environmental scientists therefore have an interest in the GEF, some for kudos or rent seeking, others just to see their insights applied where it counts. But with the UNEP's interests sidelined in the GEF by the World Bank's (and increasingly the UNDP's) dominant 'development' agenda, scientists' high hopes for the GEF have in general not been met. Beyond some consultancies and financial assistance for research in Southern countries to complete global data sets, scientists' inputs have seemed to legitimate as much as effectively guide project funding decisions made on political and economic grounds by Northern donor governments who, logically enough, while paying for most of the GEF, have sought to control its strategic directions.

Simplifying Tools

To partially disguise this fact and minimise the political complexity of having divergent values, goals and cultures represented within the GEF Council, GEF work has officially been as far as possible 'technical' and 'businesslike' (interview, Southern Council member, 1999). The GEF uses monetary values to measure all costs and benefits, with 'benefit to the global climate', for example, assessed as the cost of reducing carbon dioxide emissions. Though ostensibly technical, this is hardly the most scientific way to deal with the complexities of a global climate system affected by at least six different 'greenhouse gases' each released in multiple and disparate situations, let alone the complicating factors of particulate matter released in vehicle exhausts and unpredictable feedback mechanisms.

A member of the GEF's low profile Senior Advisory Panel (SAP) may be right in thinking that using simplistic, economists' language is the only way to get environmental concerns recognised where it counts in today's global context but, as a result, both real-world ecosystems and the livelihoods of people based on non-acquisitive values lack representation in official processes. For as one critical student of the GEF observed, 'reduction of non-linear and complex human situations to the simple sums and choices of neo-liberal and managerial thinking removes decision-making further from the detail of other people's lived environments' (McAfee, 1999).

Many conservationists conclude that people who interact daily and directly with nature need to participate fully in decision-making if conservation of local, interlocking and transcendent ecologies is to be assured. The GEF's self-descriptions seem to promise this kind of conservation with language of transparency, accountability and participation, but in practice the political negotiation of 'efficient' solutions to faraway problems has implied reductionism – democratic as well as natural and social scientific. In the GEF, as in many international bodies, much of the real deal-making takes place behind closed doors. Politically loaded issues are easier when treated as 'technical' matters and 'solved' from above without too many conflicting values and perspectives engaging in the discussion on equal terms.

In creating a mechanism that sought both to define and to protect 'environmental value' effectively through money distributed 'from above', donors empowered small groups of bureaucrats and technical experts to manipulate legal guidance, political hostilities and institutional alliances to ensure that nature would be defined and protected only on their terms. They have little opportunity to listen to local realities even when they know how, because time and funds are limited, and sustaining the GEF's public image, institutional framework and financial flows – without which the GEF would be unable to function – takes precedence.

Management of both the inevitable internal conflicts and the public face of the GEF has benefitted from the forceful charm and persuasiveness of its chairman/CEO and his political, personal and institutional allies. Overall, democratic inputs to the GEF's direction have effectively been limited by a variety of factors, among them the use of green rhetoric as moral persuasion: the GEF promises to deliver environmental benefits, transfer technology, assist sustainable development in poorer countries, so any criticism can seem anti-environmental and/or anti-poor. The terms of the GEF's promises generally represent 'fuzzy concepts' that can be agreed upon in principle but are usually applied with difficulty, even bias; they include 'transparency', 'participation', 'country-driven', 'mainstreaming', 'guidance', 'sustainability', 'prevention of climate change' and 'conservation of biodiversity'.

Shaping the translation of these terms into real-world impacts are ideological as well as practical constraints which limit the scope of debate, for example commodification and business values as norms defining economic 'efficiency', and econometric formulae disguising the politics underlying 'sustainable development' or carbon emission reduction (see Chapters 4 and 5). Among other factors limiting democratic access to the terms and products of global environmental debates is the use of well-known NGOs (rather than local democratic structures) for advertised participation of and account-ability to 'civil society', despite the fact that many big NGOs lack accountability even to their own members. Finally, the language in which most GEF discourse is conducted must be mentioned: whether platitudinous or technical and legalistic, it is daunting to all but the most dedicated, providing fewer clues for disinterested researchers than for interested groups seeking information on GEF funding opportunities.

UNDERSTANDING THE GEF

This book brings together some of the diverse experiences of people involved in shaping, promoting, rejecting, accessing and embodying the GEF, as well as those affected by it and those who have watched it unfold from a distance. To suggest their range, here follow some conflicting descriptions of the GEF's nature and mission from people who know it well:[19]

A work in progress. (Mohamed El-Ashry)[20]
An enormous con. (international civil servant)
The only practical thing to come out of Rio. (several other inter-national civil servants)
A green virus in the Bretton Woods software. (World Bank envi-ronmental lawyer)
Peanuts. (another World Bank environmental lawyer)
Crumbs from the table of the rich North. (Indian NGO)
Greenwash for the World Bank's destructive practices. (Northern NGO)
Helps the World Bank to externalize environmental costs. (critical historian)
Sweetener for international loans adding to Southern debt. (German researcher)
Green subsidy for transnational science and investment. (North American researcher)

19. The last definition listed is taken from an official GEF document, but most are unofficial personal views, often expressed 'off the record'. In general the interviewees quoted in these pages are not identified unless they spoke as the public face of an institution.
20. Writing in *The GEF – A Self Assessment*.

A mechanism for international cooperation for the purpose of providing new, and additional, grant and concessional funding to meet the agreed incremental costs of measures to achieve agreed global environmental benefits in the areas of biological diversity, climate change, international waters and ozone depletion. (GEF Operational Strategy)

Unresolved questions lie at the heart of these conflicting accounts of the GEF. Is it a beneficent science-based 'green virus', propagating environmental values inside the institutional edifices of a benevolent Anglo-Saxon-led New World Order – announced in the US the same year the GEF entered operations? Or is it more like 'greenwash', sustaining an unjust and unsustainable economic system by distracting environmentalists from tackling the unaccountable power of banks, corporations and governments – whose obsession with expansion and domination of international trade at all costs produces so many environmental, and political, problems in the first place? As with so many other questions about the GEF, the answer here is that maybe one, or the other, or neither, or both of these suggestions may be correct – for 'where you stand depends on where you sit' (Athanasiou, 1997).

For many environment professionals, the unprecedentedly participatory, science-based GEF remains the best hope for funding conservation in a globalising world. The UN Conventions on Climate Change and Biodiversity justify a degree of environmental optimism at the superficial (formal, international) level where vaguely-worded treaties and promises certainly mark a degree of progress. Yet their authority barely permeates through the fine words of formal documents and institutional aspirations to 'the ground' where change must take place – and is so often absent. In many cases this is because environmental action is constrained at every level by the reluctance of treasuries' to pay for activities that are not obviously in their immediate national economic interest.

Countering the GEF's own claims (see <www.gefweb.org>), many NGOs and academics fiercely criticised the GEF in its early days, and often complaints were echoed by the GEF's own independent evaluations – see Chapter 4. Essentially, the problem was that, at least to start with, the GEF hardly lived up to any of its promises. Other critical observers of the GEF have seen its real-world effects less as feeble than, with all the Facility's globalisation of environmental management, as 'green developmentalism' (McAfee, 1999). For example, besides buying the partnership of selected environmental NGOs with access to project funds and policy, the GEF's investments can subsidise Northern firms and consultants exploring Southern resources and potential new markets for 'green' expertise and technology.

With implementation of the Conventions demanding centralised acquisition and management of data about relevant natural resources in the South, GEF investments could also help to develop infrastructure enabling access to information about resources of value to bioprospectors, energy investors, ecotourism operators and so forth. In addition, scientific data on Southern landscapes and ecologies entered into geographical information systems feeds global electronic information databases, including those used by the US military to inform their operations 'in theatre' (interview, World Bank, 1997). In this light, the GEF can perhaps be seen as a bribe for Southern governments to give up a degree of sovereignty over resources found within their territory to professional armies of environmental economists, experts and administrators in search of benefits accruing only 'globally'. The World Bank largely defines the terms of the environmental economics justifying GEF projects, providing 'technical' tools with which selected consultants can reach more or less preordained conclusions (see Chapter 5).

Finally, Caufield (1996) is not alone in noting that while advertised as 'additional' money for environmental protection, the existence of the GEF actually allows development institutions like the World Bank to 'externalise' their own environmental costs – making their loans seem more economic by getting the GEF to pay the costs of any green components required. Thus using free (or 'concessional') funds to 'leverage' other investments into environmental projects in already highly-indebted countries, it seems that the GEF funds can sweeten the terms of World Bank loans that are unlikely directly to generate the foreign currency that borrowing governments will need to repay the increased debt.

Even if only some of these claims are partially true, in the GEF, as sociologist Leslie Sklair has observed, 'ecological demands were problematically translated and drafted into the service of the transnational capitalist class' (Sklair, 1991). And whatever the GEF has done, it has not interfered with the expansionist dynamic of US-led corporate capitalism and its allies in the 1990s. For, as Nicholas Hildyard put it in 1998,

Whose environment gets degraded and whose protected is never the outcome of rational policy making – of weighing up costs and benefits and reaching a decision. It is the outcome of the balance of political forces at any given moment – and of the cunning use of political space by a range of contingent alliances amongst political, economic and social actors.[21]

OUTLINE OF THE BOOK

This chapter has introduced the GEF as an intelligent response by the Northern-led 'international community' to the challenges of global resource management and mass environmentalism, and suggested some of the institution's resulting powers, allies and flaws. Chapter 2 steps back from the GEF to examine the world into which it was born: sources of political influence over globalisation, problems and institutions of global resource management, also the environmental movements channelled variously into direct resistance to the processes and causes of ecological destruction, international treaties and World Bank reform. Readers familiar with the issues and history may want to skip much of Chapter 2.

Chapter 3 follows the development of a multilateral fund to support the Rio environmental Conventions from a banker's idea in the mid 1980s to a 'pilot' GEF formalised in the World Bank in 1991 – a fund with projects underway in time to head off more expensive and radical alternative funds proposed from the South in the lead up to the 1992 Earth Summit. Chapter 4 reports on independent reviews of the GEF and how intergovernmental negotiations to make it more permanent initially fell apart under the pressure of conflicting political ambitions – before the promise of new money overrode other concerns. Even after the Facility's restructuring with 'expedited' processes, clearer priorities and governance, problems of the Council's accountability remain – especially to the expectations of the Climate Change and Biodiversity Conventions.

Chapter 5 leaves the narrative framework to explore how tranches of GEF money were raised, administered, allocated and spent, mostly in the Operational phase of the GEF (1995–8), leading to critical questions of interest, efficiency, accountability and risk. Chapter 6 considers what the operational GEF has meant – less for the 'global

21. 'The EU: Protecting Whose Environment?' Nicholas Hildyard at the Conference of Socialist Economists, London, 6 June 1998.

environment' than for the people, institutions and interests embroiled in its official conservation. It seems that over-centralisation, turf wars and culture clashes have helped to sustain incommensurable distances between implicated institutions, policy and practice, professionalism and participation, decisions and their impacts. The resulting lack of feedback seems to undermine the GEF's limited official missions as well as its implied greater promise.

Finally, Chapter 7 steps back to look at our Global Environment Facility in the light of recent global politics, asking questions about 'sustainable development' and whose values, initiatives and lifestyles the GEF can sustain. Touching on other possible ways to achieve the goals lately entrusted to this so far obscure fund, I conclude that if only it was better known and understood, the GEF might yet be of value in generating lessons for others trying to rein in neo-liberal 'development' for the sake of a living environment for all.

CONCLUSIONS

At the UN's World Summit on Sustainable Development in 2002, there will doubtless be formal declarations of sustainable intent by governments and corporations, some new international institutions may be created or old ones reformed, some new money may even be promised from the world's richer countries to the poorer. Meanwhile the values of global capital are so entrenched in the international institutional ecosystem that the worlds most likely to be saved at such a meeting are those understood and valued by its managing, advisory – and beneficiary – elites, for many of whom 'the environment is not what is around their homes, but what is around their economies' (Lohmann, 1993).

The lifestyles and values of the elites that Maurice Strong (see Appendix I) works with may be on the same planet as the places and communities affected by their decisions, but for most of those who lose immediate land and livelihood to ever more mobile and extractive capital, they (and I: warm and well fed as I work at a computer in London, England) are a world away. And for all the power and ambition in the hands of global elites, any reforms which do not start from the needs and knowledge of people suffering now from unsustainable and unjust developments can hardly hope to save their worlds for them. But before exploring the GEF's real-world potential and limitations, the following chapter turns to the situation giving rise to this unique fund in the first place.

2   Global Enclosures and their Discontents

Globalisation and its Institutions; Shaping Development from Above; Integrating Environment and Development; Multilateral Environment Agreements; Conclusions

The GEF was devised and promoted initially by officials in the World Bank and its major Northern donor governments, acting under political pressure from environmentalists, scientists, private interests and others able to 'think global' – if not 'act local' – in managing natural resources. This chapter sets out the 'globalising' context into which the GEF emerged – a time of political change and 'new enclosures', nearly 50 years after the British and US governments' creation of international economic institutions. In the process, the chapter explores why donor governments chose to channel new multilateral environmental finance through the World Bank, an economic 'development' agency widely criticised by green campaigners, rather than through the United Nations system, traditional home of environmental management initiatives at the global level. The World Bank was lined up for the task both to sustain itself and to help its guiding elites face off resistance to capitalist expansion from people seeking sustainability for their own livelihoods, cultures and valued local environments. But before turning to the World Bank and the kind of development assistance it can offer, it is worth glancing at the roots of the power behind such institutions for the sake of any readers new to the field.

GLOBALISATION AND ITS INSTITUTIONS

Enclosure, Colonisation, Globalisation

The practice of enclosure lies at the heart of the growth of the currently dominant capitalist economic system. Not least in Britain, the original 'inclosures of the commons' by rich and powerful people in the Middle Ages was a kind of privatisation, centralising land ownership and economic production. Depriving poor and landless people of access to common land usually left hunters, herders and gatherers with only their labour left to sell when the industrial revolution came around. Meanwhile powerful figures in Britain and other European powers invested the resulting surplus in exploring a wider world – and enclosing lucrative parts of it as colonies.

Initially the liberal British justification for colonial adventures abroad was to 'civilise savages', but soon intervention was also to spread the benefits of rationality as embodied in Western science (Grove, 1995).[1] Francis Bacon was not alone in characterising nature as female, in need of taming, shaping, and subduing by the scientific mind (Ford, 1995), and many of his contemporaries in the 'Enlightenment' saw colonised peoples in similar terms. In the hands of the 'gentlemen' who benefitted from enclosure, scientific rationality could be a potent tool to inform and justify reorganising relations between classes of people and their environments for the sake of economic 'productivity'. Even centuries later, after most countries of the South have gained their freedom from direct colonial rule, the discourse of 'rational' resource management has remained strong, and 'science' ranks alongside commerce as a key driver of the North's

1. For example, the 'green revolution' of the twentieth century promised to end poverty through better seeds, and around the world diverse lands and communities were subjected to 'scientific' management. But the inputs required to make the new seeds thrive left subsistence farmers and minority tribes sidelined, along with biodiversity and traditionally sustainable practices, to marginal land – or without any at all (Lipton and Longhurst, 1989).

interest in the natural resources of the South – not least as a factor in the recolonising process commonly known as 'globalisation'.

The GEF is a 'global' facility. Its roots are in a kind of globalisation that includes high-speed communications and decline in the power of nation states relative to highly mobile corporate entities. With the help not least of the World Bank, this process is often accompanied by the spread of British and American – Anglo-Saxon – media, language, finance, business culture and neo-liberal doctrine, particularly into the economies of the South. Many aspects of such globalisation are of course welcomed by people on the receiving end, but even developments which are not welcomed by democratic Southern governments can often be secured with the stranglehold of debt conditionality – backed up on occasion by CIA intervention and more (Bello, 1994; Chomsky, 1993).

Politicians in NATO's member governments tend to speak of economic globalisation as if it were a force of nature, an awesome development which cannot and must not be tamed – thus obscuring how their own policies shape the phenomenon, largely according the priorities of corporate sponsors and lobby groups such as the European Round Table of Industrialists.[2] Authors like Vandana Shiva (1993) meanwhile refer to the 'globalisation of a particular local' – that is, mostly male, technocratic, 'Western' and commodifying – culture of international resource management. From this perspective, the World Bank has effectively been a key agent of corporate recolonisation ever since Europe's Southern colonies began to break free from direct rule in the mid twentieth century.

Building Financial Institutions at Bretton Woods

In 1945, African leaders meeting in Manchester, England, declared that no longer would they tolerate European colonisation of their much-abused continent (Dunbabin, 1994). As the Second World War ended, India was rising and the UK was too war-weakened to suppress indigenous resistance indefinitely across a worldwide empire. Instead they joined with US plans to use political and economic advantage to set up a new financial system for indirect, non-military influence over stabilised international trade and investment. At Bretton Woods, New Hampshire, in 1945, the soon to be victorious Western 'allies' created a set of institutions – the World Bank, IMF and General Agreement on Tariffs and Trade

2. <www.monbiot.org>

(GATT) – through which they could shape the post-war economy without directly governing any 'client' countries. Instead of guns and bombs, the tools were to be the global manipulation of capital, credit, legal and allied expertise.

The British John Maynard Keynes is traditionally credited with shaping the institutional framework finalised at Bretton Woods. In practice, however, Harry Dexter White, representing the US (which in economic terms benefitted enormously from the war), was the one to offer actual finance for institution-building. While these two men reached their conclusions more or less bilaterally, White insisted that Latin American governments at least should be invited to the negotiations so that any conditions attached to multilateral loans would look less like the impositions of a 'rich man's club' (Oliver, 1972). In addition, White felt that if borrowers had 'a voice, however small,' in determining the general policies of the new institutions, they might be expected better to live up to the obligations attached to specific investments. Voting power, however, would still be based on contribution, with the US government the major donor. The US government remains the only member of the Bank's governing board with the power to veto changes to the Bank's articles of agreement (Caufield, 1996), and the Bank's president has been 'by tradition' an American.[3]

Overall, US priorities for the planned international financial system were, as Henry Morgenthau put it at the time, for a world 'in which international trade and international investment can be carried on by businessmen on business principles'.[4] Even before the controversial World Trade Organisation took over from the GATT in 1994, the World Bank and IMF had 'become the centre of institutional power on the world development scene and the extension of the national policies and ideologies of their major shareholders'. (Gosovic, 1992)

The Limited Impact of the United Nations

The United Nations was negotiated separately from the international financial institutions, by officials mostly from different ministries. With many more governments involved from the start, UN

---

3. Current president James Wolfenson was born Australian and took on the job after changing his nationality (Alex Brummer, the *Guardian*, 23 January 1999). The IMF meanwhile is traditionally led by a European.
4. Senate Committee on Banking and Currency, Bretton Woods Agreement, quoted in Kolko, 1972. Morgenthau was Secretary of the US Treasury in 1945.

governance was formalised as 'one country, one vote', giving more power (or at least speech time) to governments from the South – sometimes known as the 'majority world'.[5] 'Non-governmental organisations' were represented at early meetings of the UN Economic and Social Council (ECOSOC), and ever since the UN has generally been perceived as more open and accountable than the Bretton Woods institutions. Finding it hard to engage with the World Bank and IMF even if they have understood their importance, most people – including government officials – keen to regulate for peace, culture, the environment, human rights and social development, have tended to turn to the UN. The results include international action under all these headings – and a degree of success under most.

However, more could certainly have been done had the UN been able to intervene in the international economic affairs already covered by the World Bank and IMF. Some also say that the UN was designed to be less efficient than the Bretton Woods institutions – certainly unnecessary bureaucracy on top of inevitable politics tends to hold up even urgent action in the UN's fields of operations. Meanwhile, as Keohane (1998) observes, 'institutions dominated by a small number of members – for example, the IMF, with its weighted voting system – can typically take more decisive action than those where influence is more widely diffused, such as the UN General Assembly'. With their legal foundation established earlier, the World Bank and IMF boards are not subject to subsequent UN agreements on protecting human rights, the environment, and so on (interviews, GEF Secretariat and World Bank, 1997).[6] This book therefore pays less attention to the UN than to the World Bank, largely because the GEF was created within the World Bank and has taken on many of its characteristics, if not all its powers.

The Work of the World Bank

Initially the World Bank was supposed to invest in rebuilding war-shattered Europe, but the free money of the US Marshall Plan soon

5. Named for its vastly larger human populations and increasingly numerous countries. The UN is not, however, numerically representative – tiny Tuvalu and Togo have nominally the same voting power as China and India's billions of people.
6. In 1947 the World Bank and IMF were officially made specialised agencies under the umbrella of the UN system (Sand, 1994) but they remain functionally independent.

usurped this role. The Bank then turned to newly independent Southern states, planning and financing projects for infrastructure development and sectoral reform in transport, mining, energy, agriculture, forestry, education, etc., to the benefit of transnational firms and national elites, if not always of the avowed goal of steady economic growth in host countries (George, 1988; Rich, 1994). By the end of the 1990s, nearly half of the $25 billion-odd paid out annually as World Bank loans had been disbursed directly to Northern corporations contracted to carry out projects in the South, and $2.5 billion in consultancy contracts privately distributed (Draffan, 2000). In a two-year period in the late 1990s, US corporations received nearly $5 billion in contracts with the help of former World Bank staff in their employ.

Sometimes the World Bank has effectively served as an agent of US foreign policy. Though it has reaped hostility from the US Congress over the decades for seeming to prop up socialist regimes (Caufield, 1996), more characteristically it has, for example, recently reduced Pakistan's debt burden in return for General Musharraf's help in the Afghan war. In earlier decades the Bank and IMF also supported Suharto's murderous anti-communist regime in Indonesia, and withheld loans to the democratic regime in early-1970s Chile, then supported General Pinochet after his US-backed right-wing coup.

The World Bank is made up of several parts. Besides the International Bank for Reconstruction and Development which loans to governments for approved projects and purchases, it encompasses: the International Finance Corporation (IFC) created in 1955 to finance initiatives undertaken by the private sector; the more recently established Multilateral Investment Guarantee Agency (MIGA) to underwrite overseas investors' risks;[7] an International Centre for Settlement of Investment Disputes; and, since 1960, the International Development Agency (IDA) which makes highly concessional loans and grants to the world's poorest countries – initially set up in response to complaints that the Bank ignored poverty. Unlike the rest of the Bank (but like the later GEF), the IDA has to be replenished every three years, at which time it is tested by the fire

7. A practice later proposed for the GEF by its unit in the IFC – see Chapter 5. Meanwhile both IFC and MIGA have been under attack from NGOs for underwriting the risks of severely environmentally damaging investments (see, for example, *Bretton Woods Update*, October–November 2001 at <www.brettonwoodsproject.org>).

of donor country parliaments, who must approve each new tranche of funding.

In 1982 Sheryl Payer found the World Bank to be not just an instrument of its donors' interests but a dangerously introverted bureaucracy, highly resistant to scrutiny and change. Others observed that once World Bank projects were identified and given a name, they seemed to take on momentum, almost a life of their own (Plater, 1983), and staff were rewarded for moving money, then promoted before any feedback came in (Rich, 1994). Authors like Susan George extended the critique and in 1992 an unusually well-publicised assessment, conducted by former Bank vice-president Willi Wapenhams, reviewed nearly 2,000 Bank projects in 113 countries, for which the Bank had lent $138 billion, and damned their high level of failure (World Bank, 1992). As we shall see below, nearly ten years later many of the same complaints were made about GEF's investments. But instead of wondering why the World Bank finds it so hard to do this kind of work effectively, it is worth noting what it does do so well.

Adjusting Structures

Together with the IMF, the World Bank is both a creator and manager of what is popularly known as the 'Third World debt' – 'the elephant in the corner that everybody's ignoring'[8] in discussions of individual project and policy performance. With its massive donor subscriptions and treasury guarantees to cover any liabilities, the Bank uses its 'triple A' credit rating on the global bond markets to raise finance cheaply. Placing strict conditionalities on the loan of these funds, it ensures that its own and allied debts are repaid as a priority, or at least the interest is financed. This 'superior debt service' from its debtors creates a 'positive externality' for the transnational private sector[9] – in such ways do the World Bank and IMF 'play a profoundly political role in the national development of developing countries', says Gosovic (1992, quoted in Gupta, 1995), 'under the facade of technical impartiality'.

8. Mike Rowson of MedAct at a workshop on 'Understanding the World Bank', organised by BOND and the Bretton Woods Project, London, April 2002.
9. Said under Chatham House rules, 1997. Statements made in meetings under the aegis of Chatham House, a private foreign policy thinktank in London formally known as the Royal Institute for International Affairs, may be quoted only without attribution.

In the wake of the 1980s international debt crisis, the World Bank and IMF have together imposed 'one size fits all' Structural Adjustment Programmes on debtor governments[10] in return for bail outs with new loans. Lending terms have generally been based on classic 'new-right' neo-liberal policies: privatise state agencies and open up domestic economies to foreign investment; reduce public spending and social and environmental regulations while promoting exports of raw commodities to earn foreign exchange. The overall goal has been to officially eliminate economic inefficiency and generate foreign currency with which to repay creditors in international banks (Bello, 1994) but, despite two decades of structural adjustment, 'no country has ever succeeded in discharging the debts it owes to the IMF/World Bank/commercial banks on money borrowed for development'. For when all 'client' governments promote the same cash crop exports, gluts occur and prices for raw materials go down – at the same time cuts to welfare, health and education undermine national development. With the 'international economy ... riddled with monopolies and near-monopolies, application of a deregulated free trade agenda was bound to lead to the enrichment of powerful nations and progressive impoverishment of the poorer nations' (Rowbotham, 2000).

Most Southern governments continue to play along with the Northern-led 'free trade agenda', despite its manifestly sloped playing field, because they see no alternative to taking the offered dollar to finance deficits and development. In addition, corrupt elements in collaborating elites can take a cut of any new loans and privatisation deals for personal use and/or distribution among their political allies, while buying Western-made luxuries and weaponry with which to repress the inevitable 'IMF riots' (Caufield, 1996; Palast, 2002). An extreme example is Indonesia's General Suharto who presided over the death of a third of East Timor's population and by the end of his reign had the same number of dollars in his personal bank accounts as the country had borrowed from the Bretton Woods institutions during his reign.

Despite being relaunched in the late 1980s 'with a human face' and more recently with added debt- and poverty-reduction, the World Bank and IMF's economic 'reform' programmes have been widely opposed in the South as not only unjust and undermining democracy

10. Except the biggest state debtor of all: the US government (*International Herald Tribune*, 27 February 2002).

but also failing in their avowed goal of enabling debt repayment (Walton and Seddon, 1994; Chossudovsky, 1999[11]). But banks can live with a level of debt, and without a Southern 'debt crisis' to manage, alliances of Northern investors would have less purchase on governments sitting on natural resources ripe for enclosure.

SHAPING DEVELOPMENT FROM ABOVE

Elite Social Movement Organisations

Global cooperation between powerful interests from industrially-advanced countries underlies the creation of the GEF, as it did the World Bank. This kind of cooperation takes place in relatively public fora like the Organisation for Economic Cooperation and Development (OECD) and the G7 gathering of finance ministers; and also more privately in fora like the Bilderberg Group, Trilateral Commission, Club of Rome and other elite groupings (Gill and Law, 1988).

Rumours abound about the network that Prince Bernhard of the Netherlands first brought together at a Hotel Bilderberg in the 1950s – members still meet yearly in different locations with full state protection. They allow no media access and release no publications,[12] but one thing certain from attendance lists is that participants 'would, on most definitions, be regarded as members of the "ruling class" in Western Europe and North America ... important figures in most of the largest international corporations ... leading politicians and prominent intellectuals (in both academia and journalism)' (Peters, 2001).

Determined that corporate capitalism should survive the political upheavals of late-1960s radicalism and the early-1970s oil crises, 'Bilderbergers' Zbigniew Brzezinski and David Rockefeller worked to set up the somewhat more public Trilateral Commission in the 1970s. This brought Japanese business elites into discussions with Europeans and North Americans (Sklar, 1980). Trilateralism is one aspect of 'the project of developing an organic (or relatively permanent) alliance between the major capitalist states, with the aim

11. See <www.transnational.org/features/chossu_worldbank.html> for Chossudovsky, 1999.
12. <www.bilderberg.org>

of promoting (or sustaining) a stable form of world order which is congenial to their dominant interests' (Gill, 1990).

One early initiative of the Trilateral Commission was to invite senior commentators from the three regions to team up and produce a report on the governability of their countries' populations. Published as *The Crisis of Democracy* (Crozier et al., 1975), the report's three authors identified an 'excess' of democracy or 'democratic surge', threatening class and other hierarchies in the 'liberal democracies' of the Trilateral axis, countries where stability so far had depended on stratification in society and 'institutionalized non-communication'. The authors cautioned that

> A value which is normally good in itself is not necessarily optimised when it is maximised. We have come to recognise that there are potentially desirable limits to economic growth. There are also potentially desirable limits to the indefinite expansion of political democracy.

Suggesting that 'Western-style democracies' can function only if a good proportion of marginal groups remain apathetic and uninvolved, the report concludes that 'experts' must henceforth dominate the formation of public policy. For, according to a speech attributed to senior Bilderberger David Rockefeller, 'The supernational sovereignty of an intellectual elite and world bankers is surely preferable to the national autodetermination practiced in past centuries.'[13] As we shall see below, in effect the GEF seems to have applied this principle to international resource conservation much as the Bank applied it to resource exploitation.

Propagating Values for Development

With help from the World Bank, a class of Northern-oriented technocratic experts and managers (or 'managerial bourgeoisie', (Sklar, in

13. Attributed to David Rockefeller, speaking at the June 1991 Bilderberg meeting in Baden Baden, Germany; a meeting also attended by then-Governor Bill Clinton. In ostensibly democratic nations, however, this work needed to be kept subtle, so Rockefeller expressed his gratitude to the 'great publications whose directors have attended our meetings and respected their promises of discretion for almost forty years ... It would have been impossible for us to develop our plan for the world if we had been subjected to the lights of publicity during those years' <uk.indymedia.org/display.php3?article_id=10435>.

Becker et al., 1987)) has long been emerging in many Southern capitals. When newly independent nations – abandoned by many of their professional classes and lacking funds for government – sought help from abroad for infrastructure and institution building, the World Bank was able to offer not just funds but staff, training and advice consistent with the Western allies' post-war agenda for international business. For example, since 1956 the World Bank has had an 'Economic Development Institute' based on the thinking that 'If people came into association with the Bank through studying here, they would carry with them ideas that were more congenial to the Bank when they went back to their own country' (EDI's first director, Alexander Cairncross, quoted in Caufield, 1996). In strategically important nations born in the 1950s and 1960s, it seems that politicians, managers of corporate and parastatal companies, entrepreneurial elites, as well as members of the learned professions who spoke the World Bank's language were rewarded with their cut of international aid and cheap 'development' loans (Langdon, 1979).

With the help of such allies, the World Bank has encouraged the development of legal and bureaucratic systems based on the 'Western liberal model' (Williams and Young, 1994). Back in the early twentieth century, Antonio Gramsci had recognised what he called 'transformismo', the 'co-optation of elites in particularly the more powerful semi-peripheral states ... into the hegemonic structure and processes of the capitalist world system' (Gill, 1990). These elites' 'incorporation helps to guarantee politically the rule of transnational capital', and as a British insider observed,

> It benefits the US government to have an 'honest broker' like the World Bank advancing certain views. 80 percent of World Bank economists have graduate degrees from universities in the UK, Canada or USA, and the World Bank is an articulator of the Anglo-American way of seeing states and markets. It does not usually produce innovative research but legitimises opinions shaped by a certain set of assumptions about the world.[14]

The World Bank employs over 10,000 economists, engineers and other technical professionals – 'more PhDs than a major university' (interview, World Bank, 1997) – with tax-free salaries in 1995 averaging $144,000 inclusive of benefits (Caufield, 1996).

14. Chatham House rules, 1997.

Despite having only one social scientist to every 28 economists and technical people (interview, GEF Secretariat, 1997), World Bank staff and consultants produce numerous authoritative reports on the state and practice of global development. Whilst superficially impressive, these outputs mostly refer to other Bank publications and treat as given the need for economic growth and liberalisation,[15] neglecting much of what is said, done, thought and discovered in the rest of the world. The Bank's analyses are distributed, often for free, around the world – spreading a politically acceptable view to people who either use the information appreciatively or even if they would question it, rarely have the language, skills and resources to challenge the Bank's 'professional' account of development.

As Kardam (1993) argues, people working in the Bank can only really deal with new ideas, issues or partners in ways that fit with the institution's existing goals and their own professional norms. This is not unusual in a development institution – examining official 'development' practices from an anthropological perspective, Hobart (1993) reveals that professional representations of underdevelopment generally require intervention, 'usually by the party doing the depicting'. Yet in theory, universal 'human rights requirements ... insist on freedom for people to articulate their needs and interests, to state what development means for them, and to carry it out by and for themselves' (Tomaševski, 1993).

The chasm between these principles and the approach to development taken by the World Bank seems wide indeed. When any community finds its values overrun by the practices of a more powerful people, even one promising the benefits of 'development', it can be as difficult to defend meanings and values as it is to defend land and resources from elite enclosure. Acselrad (1996) observes how territorial appropriation takes place in both material conditions and cultural contexts. Agents creating large dams, for example, reduce people affected to the 'milieu' of the dam: hegemonic interests impose onto others their own conceptions of how environment and development should be viewed and managed. In this

---

15. Robert Wade, an academic who formerly worked for the Bank (1997), tells how it repackaged the fairly protectionist Japanese version of capitalism as a success story for free trade policies in a World Development Report (WDR) on the 'East Asian Miracle' – thus supporting its own 'paradigm' of development. WDRs are produced annually by the Bank, each covering a selected issue of international development – for example, environment, poverty, knowledge.

context, 'Political ecological conflicts are thus as much struggles over meaning as they are battles over material practices' (Bryant, 1998).

Aid as Charity – and Tool

In general, writers on official international aid can be split between those who do not challenge the donors' given purpose of help for the poor as enlightened self-interest but point to how it could be better spent, and those who see the apparent moral imperative of official altruism masking more profit-focused and Machiavellian agendas. Lumsdaine (1993), for example, argued that the moral injunction to 'help the poor', later also to 'help the planet', effectively drives much official government-to-government aid. Cassen (1994) meanwhile asked *Does Aid Work?* to promote development and help the poor – and decided more or less that it does not, but perhaps could do so if commercial and political objectives were not allowed to override development objectives, if the policy environment in recipient countries was appropriate, and if donors would co-ordinate and learn from mistakes (both their own and others'). However, Hayter (1971), for example, more critically analysed *Aid as Imperialism*, and John R. Bolton, former US attorney general and general advisor to the United States Agency for International Development (USAID), described the agency as 'a subsidiary of the CIA which serves to promote political and economic interests of the federal government' (quoted in Carey, 2002). Yet given the complexities of human nature, culture and politics, perhaps both points of view may be 'true'.

In many cultures, the powerful give to the powerless because they can, to persuade them to do, feel or think certain things, and to confirm and enhance the donors' own status (Strathern, 1988). 'Big men' in a traditional Papua New Guinean culture hold parties known as *mokas* where they hand out goods with a high local value: more or less a case of the more and bigger gifts, the 'bigger' the man, and each successful *moka* reinforces the culture in which the gifts hold value.[16] Similarly, in Western society, powerful people hold sumptuous parties, establishing the hosts as members of society endowed with values worth cultivating. Charitable events and donations paint patrons as confident enough to share the spoils of power, and place their recipients in moral – if not financial – debt.

16. See, for example, the ethnographic film *Onka's Big Moka*.

So if the international community is just another group of individuals with a shared belief system sustaining their culture, then international aid confirms Northern government treasuries as the 'big men' of the international economy.

The business of international 'developmentalism' began partly as a component of the Western anti-communist agenda. The richer governments sent food aid, advice and technology to friendly Southern governments, handing out grants and cheap loans to be spent largely on goods or 'know-how' which donor country industries supplied. Often aid was therefore not just strategic alliance building but an 'invisible' subsidy for domestic firms, and/or simple dumping of surplus goods in far off lands where they would not affect prices at home – whether or not these products were useful to the recipient countries. With evidence of, for example, food aid undermining local producers and donated tractors rusting across Africa's farmlands for want of appropriate parts and skills, a growing number of researchers and NGOs working in 'development' began to demand a new approach to official aid.

In response to such critiques, the goals of international aid have shifted in the last 50 years through a range of narratives from 'global capital stability' through 'basic needs' and 'entitlements' to 'poverty reduction' and 'sustainable development' (Fairhead and Leach, quoted in Bryant, 1998). But throughout these changing times, the World Bank's economic analysts and educators have continued to treat labour, capital and natural resources largely as mere variables on a graph, or externalities to equilibrium models of idealised economic development – structurally neglecting the evolving complex reality.

The Uses of Commodification

The World Bank measures countries' economic development in terms of their annual dollar per capita income, on the assumption that quality of life can be measured thus – whatever a person, family or community's non-monetary income or values. Economists working in the World Bank largely define development in terms of growth in satisfaction derived from consumption of food, clothing, housing and experiences obtained with money through the global market. Such simplistic economic models are clearly easier to manage than pluralist politics, and they enable the creation of convincing 'facts' from unproven theories by masking political choices and assumptions behind complex formulae, baffling to all but the initiated. In the words of the *Ecologist* magazine's report 'Whose Common Future?' (1992), 'measurement thus replaced discussion', and, as another commentator observed,

> It would be hard to manage the Bank effectively if a wider range of views were represented. Defining the debate in simple terms, with free market theory the source of 'rational' solutions, saves lots of time and money by avoiding the need for specific studies and complex cost-benefit analyses. (Chatham House rules, 1997)

The resulting 'anti-pluralism' or even 'intellectual fascism' (Hodgson, 1988) of certain assumptions and values creates a kind of 'autistic' economics.[17] Mainstream economists tend to focus all their attention on maximising impersonal measurements of growth, pushing away the insights into humanity of other social sciences and removing themselves from the conflicting rationalities and emotional detail of democratic feedback and discussion.

While such an approach may be superficially 'efficient' for its professional managers, some of the resulting contradictions of capitalist economics were effectively outlined by Hirsch in *Social Limits to Growth* (1978). He pointed out that maximising production and consumption without fully considering the implications can undermine the social, moral and environmental resources necessary for capitalism to succeed in the long term. For the towering edifice of global capitalism is built on a flow of subsidies from voluntarism and the ecological commons – ranging from (mostly) women's work raising new workers and consumers to the 'ecological services' of the Earth's raw materials and waste absorption capacity – and it cannot grow without them. In this context the Midnight Notes Collective (1990) labelled the actions of World Bank and IMF as strategic agents of the 'new enclosures', bringing ever more knowledge, science, governments, workers and resources into sustaining capitalist expansion.

Conserving Common Heritage

While many senior scientists happily take on the kind of technocratic role called for by the Trilateralists (above), supporting science

17. See <www.autisme-economie.org> and, for English text, <mouv.eco.free.fr/movementtext.htm>.

has proved a double-edged sword for senior capitalist advocates and investors. Usefully identifying potentials for profit, throughout the twentieth century independent scientific enquiry also contributed to popular concern in Northern societies about the impact of growth in extractive industrial development on natural environments worldwide.

Environmentalists with the ears of governments have tended to be concerned with conservation of the 'global commons' (Commoner, 1971; Ostrom, 1991) – aspects of the Earth not fully understood, enclosed or managed by private ownership and techno-science, but nonetheless affected by pollution and other physical impacts of 'development'. Much environmental thinking in the North has been informed by Thomas Malthus' fear that the needs of a growing human population will soon outstrip available resources, and by the Tragedy of the Commons theory, which assumes that each individual exercises what mainstream economists call 'rational self-interest' and maximises their own exploitation of a common resource at the expense of others, with the result that all lose out when the resource is run down. The obvious solution for many is to entrust these threatened lands to expert management.

However, at the local level in many Southern cultures, especially those living without much in the way of technology or money, much of the 'common' property to which people need access to live (including water, land, wood, wildlife) has actually been managed through local regimes securing a degree of both fair access and con-servation (for example, 'water priests' of Bali control farmers' access to water in a complex traditional system).[18] Problems can therefore arise when well-intentioned outsiders misunderstand the threats to a given environment, and disrupt stable arrangements when they come to save it.

When conservation of 'the common heritage of all mankind' means scientists and bureaucrats creating national parks in Southern countries with Northern money and treating the people living there as threats to the 'animal totems' of 'western wilderness lovers' who come in jeeps, it breeds resentment of 'authoritarian biologists' claiming a monopoly on the wisdom to manage nature (Guha, 1997). Local people often turn against nature reserves when 'con-servation' measures that they might otherwise support turn out to involve eviction and injustice (Neumann, 1998). Meanwhile, newly

18. <www.wadsworth.com/humanity/ch18/>

unemployed and/or landless people pushed out of nature reserves often have little option but to join in the environmentally destructive developments continuing unhindered outside park gates. Realising the limits of this approach, environmental groups both North and South have diversified in the attempt to bring environmental concern to the heart of economic development.

INTEGRATING ENVIRONMENT AND DEVELOPMENT

The Environment in International Politics

By the late 1960s, Northern governments were strengthening links with mainstream and scientific environmental groups like the World Wide Fund for Nature (WWF), the IUCN and the Sierra Club, and International Parliamentary Conferences on the Environment, founded to build awareness and pressure for worldwide governmental action on the environment, led in June 1972 to the UN Conference on the Human Environment in Stockholm. Attended by representatives of 113 nations, one outcome of the summit was the creation of the UNEP to catalyse, initiate and co-ordinate environmental policies throughout the international institutional system (Strong, 2000). Another outcome was the World Bank becoming the first international aid agency to declare that environmental and development goals could be complementary (Fox and Brown, 1998).

The Stockholm conference was organised by Maurice Strong, a Canadian businessman who later convened the Rio summit, sat on the GEF chief executive officer's private Senior Advisory Panel, coordinated UN reform, advised the World Bank President and held 'roundtables' of 'eminent persons' in the run up to the 2002 World Summit on Sustainable Development in Johannesburg. Describing the Stockholm conference, Strong said that

> The most important single event in this process was the informal meeting we convened in a motel in Founex outside of Geneva with some 30 leading experts and policy leaders ... The meeting ... certainly had a profound influence [on] the evolution of the environment–development relationship ... [and] called for an expansion of the entire concept of environment to link it directly to the economic development process and the priorities of developing countries.[19]

19. The Hunger Project Millennium Lecture 'Hunger, Poverty, Population and Environment', by Maurice F. Strong, Chairman, Earth Council, 7 April 1999, Madras, India.

But a small group of high-level experts and politicians meeting in a Swiss motel could not wish away the inherent divergences between ecological and economic priorities, let alone dissolve abiding North–South political tension over control of natural resources. In the years following Stockholm, G77[20] demands at the UN for a redistributive 'New International Economic Order' (Marchak, 1991) coincided with the budding of radical environmental movements seeded in the 1960s. And despite the creation of the UNEP and many national environment ministries around the world, Northern governments could not effectively face down an increasingly politically engaged environmentalism.

Strategies of Environmentalism

The 1980s were a decade of polarisation between rich and poor on the ground, and in politics between grass-roots activists and scientists, and their higher paid professional counterparts working as part of what would later come to be known as the New World Order. Throughout the 1980s, the environmental movement grew in political strength worldwide but especially in the US, and its eco-centric and social justice wings began to challenge more fundamentally the patterns and politics of mainstream global economic development (Rich, 1994). By the mid 1980s a group of ten, mostly Washington-based, environmental NGOs gained greater access to the ears (and funds) of donor governments by suggesting that economic growth was not only compatible with environmental protection, but necessary to generate sufficient money to pay for it.[21] Devall (1990) listed their proposed principles: sustained economic growth is good for environmental quality; regulation is good for both the economy and the environment; and NGOs should adopt rhetorically radical but practically conciliatory strategies. Distanced from

20. To counter the power of the G7 leading industrialised nations at the first UN conference of UNCTAD, Geneva 1964, G77 was established as 'an avowedly political organisation … based on common interests arising from the unequal nature of the international economy' (Williams, 1997). (China has not joined but often acts alongside the grouping, which now has many more than 77 members.)
21. These US-based NGOs included the Sierra Club, Audubon, Wilderness Society, Natural Resources Defense Council, National Wildlife Federation, Environmental Defense Fund, National Parks and Conservation Association, and Friends of the Earth.

radical eco-centrics and black movements demanding colonial reparation and environmental justice, such noisy green reformists could then be embraced by Northern governments and big companies seeking PR scoops by making allies out of enemies.

As companies searched for ways to adapt their image and earn the 'green dollar', by the 1990s the Environmental Defense Fund (EDF) were advising McDonald's on its packaging and Greenpeace were advising Shell and BP on green energy; the WWF and IUCN formed working groups with the World Bank. Partly in reaction to mainstream environmentalism seeming thus to 'cave in' and accept the legitimacy of vested interests, more confrontational groupings like Earth First! and the environmental justice movement in the North emerged to raise the stakes in eco-politics.

Refusing to honour capitalist economic credo, many such 'radicals' see mainstream environmental organisations as part of a corrupt establishment, and turn to direct action in support of communities and ecologies whose needs go unheard in the big institutions. As outsiders to capital-friendly institutions they protest, picket, occupy, blockade, lock on, sing, shout, climb and abseil, and get wet, muddy, cold or hot and/or arrested, jailed, beaten, blown up and shot. Meanwhile greens who become insiders, lobbyists and consultants, gain credibility by participating in the reports, meetings, receptions and power-games, wearing suits (including for men the symbolic noose around the neck), flying the world and drinking bottled water in air-conditioned offices while they talk about matters of life and death in distant, bureaucratic language.

Some people do manage to keep feet in both worlds, to represent the 'uninvited' to the global party. They can bring elements of social, local and traditional science and values to bear on global resource management, and keep people stuck outside informed of how things work inside. But to do so these Januses have to make sure they are understood in the mainstream discourses of development, and sometimes, when communing and consuming with the rich and powerful in the name of a better world for all, it is hard to keep sight of the needs and perspectives of other peoples far away (as I found while interviewing people working with the GEF in Washington). But this is a risk that has to be run if greens are to make any urgent changes from 'inside the system', assuming that capitalism will not be overthrown tomorrow. Among those trying to bring green values more effectively to bear today are environmental economists.

Economics Moves into Environment

When it came to integrating environmental concerns with mainstream development thinking, as Andrew Stirling (1995) points out, there was a strong incentive for academics and others to expand the scope of environmental economics. This reflected both socio-political pressure for new ideas to be translated into the dominant discourse of the day, and the entrepreneurial spirit of economists who, willing to adapt their tools and following their own conception of rational self-interest, saw a gap in the market.[22] The market they sought to supply was for new analyses to measure and integrate specific environmental externalities to current models of economic development. However, as Brentin observed back in 1994, 'Attempts to put an economic value on conserving biodiversity have not been particularly helpful to the conservationists' argument.'

Liberal free market theory essentially assumes that environmental values will be expressed like any others, with investment responding to consumer demand. If people value the natural environment and the potential it bears for food, drink and medicine, clean air, climate stability, recreation, spiritual sustenance, genetic material, and so on, then they will pay for it and prices should automatically reflect real values. But efforts to put a price on species or ecosystems through calculation of their marginal use value, the public's 'willingness to pay' to see something conserved or willingness to accept compensation for its loss, have floundered. Even one person saying a wetland is priceless would render any honest calculations of its value to zero, and environments valued by the poor tend to be unfairly given lower values because poor people cannot afford to pay to conserve them and/or show more willingness to be paid to lose them. But even if this approach really worked, the economic value of conservation may never outweigh the value of continuing exploitation – given economic practices like discounting the future in the drive to short-term profit.

North–South Conflicts on the Environment

Despite any amount of cost-benefit analyses, collaborative strategies and official responses to protests worldwide, by the late 1980s there

22. See, for example, David Pearce's Blueprint Series, e.g. *Capturing Global Environmental Value* (Pearce, 1995).

was little effective environmental action at the global level. For the most part, global negotiations for environmental protection and economic development have been conducted separately – lacking common interests, institutional relationships, sometimes even language. Resentful of treasury and other constraints on their policy ambitions at home, officials from environment ministries have taken their aspirations to UN environmental negotiations at the international level – where many of the misunderstandings and battles familiar from domestic politics are played out again when possible regulations and budgets come up.[23] Evolving multilateral institutions therefore embody the tensions of not only traditional North–South inequalities, but also the ongoing divides between ecology and economy, regulation and profitability, long and short-termism, public and private interest.

Overall, governments have been much less interested in environmental issues than in economic ones; and even where ministries within one government have agreed on policies, Northern and Southern governments have differed on which environmental issues were most important for 'the globe'. In the North, the global environment has meant essentially stratospheric ozone, climate change, seas and biodiversity, basically in terms of rainforests, exotic animals and useful genes for biotechnology. Southern governments' environment ministries tend to have more concern for deforestation, soil erosion, poor air and drinking water quality – threats to national economies and the immediate health and livelihood of already impoverished communities (Moiseev, 1996). G77 countries were 'adamant that their "right to development" should not be sacrificed in order to protect the environment when, in their view, it was the economic growth patterns and "footprints" of the current industrialised countries which are responsible for environmental problems' (Williams, 1997).

In addition, when Northern environmentalists aspire to teach the South principles of wildlife preservation and sustainable development that they have been unable to implement at home, the global green discourse only contributes to pre-existing resentments. By 1997, Guha was not alone in fearing that 'the three Cs of Empire' – Christianity, Commerce and Civilisation – had been joined by a fourth: Conservation.

23. Brentin (1994) wrote in terms of the 'traditional internal struggle between the economic and environmental sides of the [US] administration'.

But this did not mean that people all over the world were not eco-logically aware and active, only that they were more interested in managing local conservation locally, with advice and help on tap, than in having it imposed by international experts and investors. With a more equal and participatory approach, constructive con-nections could be made between ground-level scientists, communities and organisations and international expertise and finance, to enable a grass-roots, bottom-up and sustainable version of development – if governments could be persuaded to support it. Or even if all governments were not convinced, the World Bank invests public money officially for the public good and needs to improve its public image, so perhaps it could be persuaded to add these new elements of conditionality to its lending.

Reforms for 'Sustainable Development' in the International Institutions

Towards the end of the 1980s, the US Congress came under unprece-dented pressure about the World Bank's record from Washington-based environmentalists, particularly over projects like Polonoroeste in Brazil, which opened up large areas of rainforest to roads and logging. Sometimes working in 'unholy alliance' with right-wingers opposed to aid altogether (Rich, 1994), these NGOs eventually persuaded Congress to impose environmental conditions on new money granted to the Bank.[24]

The World Bank gained a specialist environment department in 1987 and started sending all staff on weekend courses in environ-mental awareness. It was soon describing itself as a 'conservation bank'. As their environment business grew, staff were also expected to hold wider consultations on projects, especially with NGOs critical of the Bank's approach. With many such groups possibly interested in showing how large-scale public finance could be better used, the Bank's management saw a chance to improve performance and buy new friends. But when it came to effective environmental criteria, they were imposed on Bank staff from the top down, without effective internal incentives for change or accountability for environmental impacts. The new expectations left Bank staff in a

24. At the time the Bank was seeking extra funds to protect the US banking system from 'the hazards of Latin American debt default' and had to accept environmental conditionality in return (Wade, 1997).

difficult position, having to jump through complicated new environmental hoops, while still required to move big money swiftly (Wade, 1997).

When environmental conditionality for aid hove into view, 'greenmail' was a term used by both Northern and Southern politicians, with the North accused of imposing its own development priorities for the South via environmental threats, and the South refusing to recognise common problems unless paid for doing so and given access to the latest Northern technology (Jacobs, 1991). Exploring the possibilities of 'sustainable development' as defined in the Brundtland Report of 1987 (see Chapter 3), an increasingly intricate dance began in the corridors of power – between professionals in environment and development. But while the World Bank and its development mission remained on the floor throughout, environmental dancing partners had to wait to be picked and coached before the major donors would switch on the music – that is, commit large-scale funds to sustainable development. And with Brundtland's version of sustainable development seeking 'a co-optation of the very groups that are creating a new dance of politics … turning them into a secondary, second rate bunch of consultants' (Visvanathan, quoted in Escobar, 1996), legal agreements were needed to establish on what terms each environmental issue could be invited to dance.

MULTILATERAL ENVIRONMENT AGREEMENTS

Funding the Montreal Protocol

As mentioned in the previous chapter, the GEF ended up supporting UN Conventions to counter climate change and protect biodiversity and the ozone layer, as well as agreements on international waters and, indirectly, land degradation. Each of these agreements took years, sometimes decades to achieve. The first of the truly international environmental treaties was the Partial Test Ban of 1963, resulting from the public's horror at radioactive particles from nuclear weapon tests being found in human milk. Numerous other treaties followed, from the Law of the Sea to the Convention on International Trade in Endangered Species (CITES). But for all the apparent progress, this piecemeal approach was leading to convention overload (known to some of its sufferers as 'conventionitis') for governments with limited funds for international travel and policy development.

In the face of this problem, a network of international environmental lawyers, many at the IUCN and WWF in Switzerland working in alliance with the UNEP, in the mid to late 1980s began discussing the creation of a few major new multilateral environmental conventions. The aim was to bring together some of the smaller agreements – both those already established and those still to come – under one legal 'umbrella'. As work began to identify issues and draft framework texts for climate change and biodiversity, mounting evidence of a hole in the atmospheric ozone layer over the Antarctic drove governments to agree in principle on the Vienna Convention to conserve the ozone layer by cutting the use of certain chemicals particularly in refrigeration, propellants and air conditioning.

This was a fairly fast moving process thanks to the relatively non-political implications and 'near universal appeal of the discourse of precautionary action' (Litfin, 1994). The Montreal Protocol to the Vienna Convention, signed in 1987, provided challenging schedules for participating countries to phase out technologies emitting CFCs, HCFCs, methyl bromide and other chemicals found to deplete atmospheric ozone. As we shall see below, the fairly effective way in which the Montreal Protocol was financed would generate lessons for the FCCC and CBD then still in development – though not perhaps with the result that all those involved may have hoped for.

The Multilateral Fund of the Montreal Protocol was established in 1990 with $240 million for 1991–3 to 'meet, on a grant or concessional basis … the agreed incremental costs' incurred by Southern countries 'cost-effectively' complying with the Protocol's requirements. Governments 'party' to the Protocol decided the Fund's overall policies and level of funding, with equal voting rights and effective veto power for both donor and recipient parties. Chairmanship rotated annually between donors and recipients, and implementation was overseen by an executive committee, supported by a secretariat based in Montreal, Canada.[25]

Some Northern governments involved in the original negotiations wanted the Montreal Protocol Fund to be run through the World Bank, so when it was created 'without baggage' as a new insti-

25. The executive committee sought to ensure streamlined procedures, and used expert-based technical and economic advisory panels – rather than, as some governments would have preferred, a body of individuals politically selected by the governments they represented (pers. comm., Jake Werksman, 2001).

tution outside the Bretton Woods system, they expressed fears that the fund would be inefficient and expensive, involving a 'proliferation of bureaucracy' (Andersen et al., 2001). Partly this reflected donor treasuries' unease about the extent of claims likely to be made on them under the global environment label by a governing body with the UN's more or less democratic international decision-making system.

Yet the secretariat stayed small, donors have not had to pay huge amounts, and the Montreal Protocol is generally felt to have been a success – growth in the hole seems recently to have slowed (see press). Nonetheless, the major donor treasuries were determined that never again would they allow a UN convention to determine its own level of funding, especially given the potentially far greater scope for change to impact on wider patterns of development threatened by newly emerging agreements on biodiversity and climate.

The Climate Change Convention

Where oil companies and others see the UN's Framework Convention on Climate Change as a threat to global competitiveness, its proponents suggest that if it didn't exist, the international community would have had to invent climate change as an issue, because of the need to render development more efficient and sustainable anyway (interview, FCCC secretariat, 1996). This is not the place to go into the scientific or political complexities of climate change, except to say that in the late 1980s governments set up an Intergovernmental Panel on Climate Change (IPCC). Selected scientists from around the world pooled their findings in an attempt to reach consensus on what, if anything, was happening and should be done about anthropogenic climate change. Boehmer-Christiansen (1997) found that at first, the IPCC agreed on little more than the need for more data gathering and computer climate modelling, but eventually the Panel found it politically necessary to come down on one side or the other. Once they decided that on the balance of probabilities, there had been a discernible human impact on the global climate, negotiations began in earnest for a multilateral agreement on climate change. This culminated, as we shall see in the following chapter, in the FCCC being opened for signing in 1992 at the UN's Rio Conference on Environment and Development.

For the purposes of the Framework Convention, the 'climate system' was defined as 'the totality of the atmosphere, hydrosphere, biosphere and geosphere and their interactions'. Yet the IPCC took the position that emission level of carbon dioxide, one of six potential greenhouse gases (GHGs), was an appropriate proxy for measuring performance in combating climate change.[26] As with economic valuations of environmental benefits, in real terms, this approach faces some serious problems:

> [The] six major GHGs ... are produced in different places, by different processes, by and for different groups of people, and for a variety of social purposes. These differences are ignored when the estimated contributions of the various GHGs to global warming are calculated in terms of their supposed equivalence to units of [carbon dioxide]. (McAfee, 1999)[27]

The planned Convention also faced more immediate challenges, since 'the climate change regime ... requires that governments are expected to take actions to reduce [carbon dioxide] emissions that contradict the signals and demands of the WTO and IMF regimes' (Vogler, 2002). As we saw above, the IMF (and by the mid 1990s WTO) regime promotes economic growth and world trade – both currently dependent on fossil fuels.

The Biodiversity Convention

According to Calestous Juma (1989), who later became Executive secretary of the Convention on Biological Diversity, 'the world's

26. The media are often blamed for encouraging scientific reductionism, but interviews with people in the GEF and FCCC secretariats confirm that people dealing with these issues professionally also exhibit such simplifying tendencies. Even environmentally literate academics have spoken unchallenged about the 'CO2 Convention' (sic). Yet in the context of early Joint Implementation (JI) initiatives, Ridley concluded that methane emission reductions were probably a more cost-effective approach to mitigating climate change than focusing on CO_2 (University College London PhD thesis quoted pp. 10–11, *JI Quarterly Newsletter*, July 1997, Groningen, NL).
27. The naturalisation of inequality involved in the FCCC was exposed dramatically in the guiding document for FCCC implementation produced by the IPCC. Using a market-modelled methodology of mainstream environmental economics to estimate the costs of global warming, the Panel estimated the value of an individual's life in the higher-money-income OECD states as 15 times greater than the life of a person living in the global South (Demeritt 1999, quoted in McAfee, 1999).

poorest countries as a group account for some 95.7 percent of the world's genetic resources', and colonial history has meant that relatively 'gene-poor' rich countries have generally had the most benefit from the South's genetic resources. As a result, donor governments negotiating to create the CBD had to deal with the attitude of many Southern governments towards the North's sudden apparent interest in 'global' biodiversity – 'we've got most of it: if you want it; you'll have to pay for it' (McConnell, 1996). Northern governments eventually agreed to pay for some of the Biodiversity Convention through the GEF, an agency given 'broad leeway in translating the Convention's vague mandate into specific projects' (Steinberg, 1998). But before examining how this panned out in the following chapters, it is worth looking more closely at the CBD's origins and ambitions.

First mooted in the early 1970s soon after the Stockholm UN environment conference (Brentin, 1994), international discussions about a possible new convention for conservation and sustainable use of flora and fauna gathered pace again in the late 1980s. They returned with a new buzzword, 'biodiversity', as expressed in, for example, a 500-page report edited by socio-biologist E.O. Wilson for a US National Forum on Biodiversity in 1988. According to Flitner (1998), despite the (appropriate) diversity of its content, this report marked the arrival of biological diversity as 'one coherent thing ... bringing together rainforests and economics ... development aid, technology and ethics'. It also brought two apparent assumptions: one a pervasive neo-Malthusianism and the ubiquity of 'explosive population growth' as the main factor in biodiversity's decline; the other, the importance of economics in conservation and particularly of finding market values for endangered habitats, life forms and their genes.

This tendency to economic enclosure reflected 'both the general ideological shift in the 1980s and its material–scientific realisation – the new technological possibilities through genetic engineering' (Flitner, 1998). The CBD promised to protect 'genetic resources, organisms or parts thereof, populations or any other biotic component of ecosystems with actual or potential use or value for humanity', and has been described as 'a three-legged stool', standing on three basic principles: the conservation of biodiversity, the sustainable use of its components, and the fair and equitable sharing of benefits derived from genetic resources. Yet, as Steinberg (1998) observed, 'The parties to the CBD incorporated a vast array of social and ecological concerns into the text of the treaty, while carefully avoiding any specific regulatory requirements.' So when it came to implementing this Convention, just as with the FCCC, there were clear political limits to what would be financed by governments with strategic economic interests in the resources and processes covered by the Conventions.

With global biodiversity described as 'our biological capital in the global bank' (Mittermeier and Bowles, 1993), the last 'leg' – benefit-sharing – was new for a conservation agreement, and demanded clarity about who would manage and who would be able to sign cheques out of this 'global bank'. Biodiversity is unevenly distributed around the world, it is also unevenly valued and any benefits resulting from its sale would be uneven too. Meanwhile an international agreement with such grand aims inspired all sorts of people with hopes that it would begin to redress injustices in global biological resource management, increase green business opportunities, transfer biotechnology's tools to the South, and conserve rare species and fragile ecosystems for the future generations. In addition, supporters of underfunded conservation treaties like CITES, the Ramsar Convention on Wetlands, and so forth, saw in the CBD a 'backdoor to finance' (interview, CBD secretariat, 1997). As a result, donor treasuries sought tight restrictions on the use of any money made available under the planned Convention.

In this context it might be expected that donor governments would seek the cheapest approach to biodiversity conservation and sustainable use. McNeely et al. (1989, quoted in Fairman, 1996) suggested that the most cost-effective strategy would have been to reform domestic policies: to reduce subsidies on environmentally destructive practices, such as cattle ranching on cleared forest land, and to redraft laws in (for example) Brazil that required settlers to cut down biodiversity-rich forests in order to claim legal title to land. Yet despite treasuries' legendary tight budgets, these options were even more politically difficult than creating a new multi-billion-dollar environmental aid fund.

Finance for the Conventions

Negotiations for the CBD were formally initiated in 1989 by a UN General Assembly resolution, which stipulated that a proposed new treaty should provide associated 'modalities for favourable access to ... environmentally sound technologies [supported with] new and

additional financial resources'.[28] Management of the multilateral
fund of the Montreal Protocol suggested lessons for such financing
of the CBD and FCCC, but while donor negotiators adopted its
'incremental costs' restriction (see above and following chapters),
they rejected the idea of separate funds for each Convention as well
as the Protocol's model of governance. It seems that donor treasuries
would not risk replicating 'one country, one vote' decision-making
with new funds for climate change or biodiversity: highly complex
environmental issues with potential implications for the patterns of
Northern-style development – if dealt with as many Southern governments, let alone environmentalists, demanded.

Increasingly frustrated with what they saw as politicking in the
United Nations, donor governments were also wary of recreating or
strengthening anything along the lines of the UNEP where
management was, in the view of the US Treasury, 'piss poor'
(interview, 1997), and loyalty has tended to be more to the South
and to science than to 'business principles'. Donor environment
ministries were under pressure from their treasuries to ensure that
any additional finance for the planned Conventions would do only
what it was meant to – that is, to protect the global environment –
and not support new bureaucracies or encourage economic or
political irritants. In this context the major donors' influence over
the 'one dollar, one vote' World Bank put it in a good position to
attract new environmental funds.

As we saw above, the World Bank was starting to respond to environmentalist pressure, and in 1987 Barber Conable, president of the
Bank, told the world that 'if the World Bank has been part of the
problem in the past, it can and will be a strong force in finding
solutions in the future'.[29] In the following four years, the number
of environmental staff in the Bank increased from seven to 106, but
when management proposed moves into explicitly environmental
funding, senior staff were divided (Sjöberg, 1994). Some were
reluctant to divert funds from 'development' as traditionally
envisaged, and there was resistance to asking donor governments for
extra environmental money at a time when overall levels of development assistance were falling. Others, however, saw the
opportunity to move the Bank more authoritatively into a new
policy arena, there to actively shape the mandate of any new funds

28. UNGA resolution 44/228.
29. Quoted in Gan, 1992.

available according to the expressed desires of donor country treasuries – and their own institutional interests.

Particularly interesting for Bank management was the potential for any new concessional aid to leverage the Bank's planned loans into countries wary of taking on new debt. Bank operations tend to be limited on the demand – rather than supply – side, and, aiming to diversify where necessary to keep money moving, its staff welcome new incentives for clients to borrow.[30] In addition, new environmental funds could attract a community of green allies who might be willing to commit their skills and expertise, although 'the question of timing and presentation is delicate', as David Beckmann observed in an internal Bank memo in November 1987, 'Environmental organisations in the industrial countries should feel that this is their idea, and they should be the ones to press for it' (quoted in Sjöberg, 1994).

CONCLUSIONS

Wolfgang Sachs observed in 1993 that by the end of the 1980s 'the "international community" was expected to both recognise and act upon environmental issues rendered of "global" importance by the attention of Northern activists'. Wanting to show their public that they were 'doing something' about threats to the rainforests, tigers and the rest, donor governments began to think seriously about shaping the environmental Conventions, helping their national industries learn to be 'green' and assisting their nationals with 'environmental expertise' to compete at the global level (interview, NGO, 1996). When Northern treasuries were persuaded to put forward new funds for the planned Conventions, in an ideological climate favouring the use of private rather than democratically accountable bodies, the international 'community' of self-selected environmental NGOs offered relevant expertise and ideas. However, for all their work effectively as unpaid consultants, as we shall see in the following chapter, the plan that donor governments eventually adopted was put forward by a banker.

30. Chatham House rules, 1997.

3 Creation of a Global Green Fund

The woods are lovely dark and deep
but I have promises to keep
and miles to go before I sleep

The GEF's Initiation; The Institutional Arrangement Created; UNCED and After; Conclusions

The last chapter described the emergence of environmentalism as a geo-political force, with major donor governments signalling that they would be willing to fund new environmental conventions as long there was no new institution, no new money in UN hands, and reform of existing international institutions. This chapter traces how the GEF was devised by a banker (hence the financial term 'facility') and created as a 'global' (rather than 'international') fund by a few governments, selected NGOs and the World Bank. The plan was put into action hastily, in time to be presented at the 1992 UNCED in Rio as an inspired compromise between the needs of North and South, commerce and conservation, United Nations and Bretton Woods institutions, democracy and efficiency. Designed to finance the Conventions while also pre-empting any radical green funds on

a 'polluter pays' basis (Agarwal et al., 1999) proposed from the South
in the preparatory G77 meetings in the run up to Rio, the GEF had
to appeal not just to Northern treasuries and Southern governments
but to environmental NGOs, scientists, the organised private sector
and a range of other 'partners' – actual and potential. So when the
pilot GEF was shaped in practice by a few key Northern governments
(Reed, 1992), their purposes included attracting environmentalist
critics to support their fund and help it work effectively. This chapter
explores how they sought to do so.

Some Important Dates in the GEF's Early History

1982 – UNEP's ten-year review of Stockholm conference
   recommends creation of World Commission on Environment
   and Development (WCED)

1987 – WCED's Brundtland Report suggests funds for sustainable development; UNDP invites WRI to set up International
   Conservation Financing Programme

1989 – GEF proposed by World Bank, supported by West
   European donor governments, WRI suggests international
   environment facility

1990 – after consultations, governments establish a 'pilot phase'
   GEF in the World Bank with over $1 billion

1991 – GEF-1 participating governments start approving environmental projects

1992 – UN Climate Change and Biodiversity Conventions
   agreed at the Rio Earth Summit (UNCED), GEF conditionally
   accepted as their 'interim financial mechanism'

THE GEF'S INITIATION

A Global Environment Fund is Conceived

With environmentalists calling ever louder for more intergovern-
mental cooperation and spending on green issues, in 1982 the UNEP
held a ten-year review of the 1972 UN Conference on the Human
Environment. Delegates (governments, UN agencies, and a few
NGOs, notably the IUCN and the International Council of Scientific
Unions) recommended the creation of a World Commission on
Environment and Development to look further into the linkages
between the issues. The Commission worked under the leadership

of James MacNeill, former head of the OECD's environment department, and in 1987 produced a report named for its public face, Norway's Gro Harlem Brundtland.

Recognising that earlier global environmental initiatives (including the UNEP) had suffered for lack of funding, the Brundtland Report (Brundtland, 1987)[1] registered the need for funding of sustainable development – but it did not mention social, political and cultural consequences of various solutions to environmental degradation (Chatterjee and Finger, 1994). Consequently when the Centre for our Common Future was created to organise a new UN summit on environment and development planned for 1992 (later popularly known as the Earth Summit), Maurice Strong was recalled from his business career to organise the involvement of NGOs in the process. Chatterjee and Finger (1994) observe that, in effect, the NGOs were welcomed mostly for their expertise in management of the issues, rather than for their analysis of ultimate causes or solutions.

The idea of a green financial instrument seems to have been promoted in the mid 1980s by a banker, Michael Sweatman.[2] Also director of the International Wilderness Leadership Foundation (known as 'WILD'), Sweatman was initially interested in an international conservation bank to finance primarily investments in land (Sjöberg, 1994): 'A venture capitalist and businessman, birder and conservationist, one of Mr. Sweatman's primary interests is to promote the private sector role in conservation worldwide, particularly in Africa' (<www.wild.org>).

The idea spread far and evolved fast. The Brundtland Report credits Sweatman as the source of its proposal for a multilateral fund, the goal of which was to persuade Southern governments to cooperate with a global agenda for conservation that otherwise seemed irrelevant to their pressing concerns about national development. Despite its global remit, the Brundtland Report was closely tuned to the desires of key donor governments, and, while stating that the UN 'should clearly be the locus for new initiatives of a global character', specified that 'serious consideration should be given to the development of a special international banking programme or facility linked to the World Bank' (Brundtland, 1987).

1. *Our Common Future*, written for governments by mostly unnamed experts.
2. Sweatman (pronounced Sweetman) was formerly senior accountant with Arthur Andersen consulting, CEO of Barclay's Industrial Finance Company, and director of numerous oil, gas and mineral exploration companies.

Around the same time Maurice Strong noted that

> something in the order of $2.5 billion for the first five years
> [might be available for a] special fund for sustainable develop-
> ment ... making available to developing countries funds they
> require to meet the 'additional' costs of acquiring the most envi-
> ronmentally-sound technologies for particular applications.
> (quoted in Sjöberg, 1994)

With the UN General Assembly also calling for 'new and additional
funding' for the global environment (UNGA 44/228), numerous
proposals soon appeared, 'varying widely in quality, purpose and
political realism. Two proposals came to be of particular relevance:
one from the WRI and the other from the World Bank' (Sjöberg,
1994). It is not clear how proposals were evaluated, but it is notable
that both those deemed 'relevant' came from technocratic organisations based in Washington DC.

Practical Proposals Emerge

The planning process began in earnest when Sweatman persuaded
the UNDP to initiate 'high-level discussions' culminating in 1987
with the creation of an International Conservation Financing
Program (ICFP) based at WRI in Washington. Led by Robert Repetto,
an influential US economist, the team also included an investment
banker, Frederik van Bolhuis,[3] and Sweatman as senior advisor
(Sjöberg, 1994). The ICFP advisory panel included representatives of
other NGOs, private investment banks and major development
agencies (among them two World Bank directors). They consulted
with potentially interested parties internationally and found a
general openness to initiatives for the environment, especially in
Southern countries seeking assistance for institution-building,
national planning, data banks and education (Sjöberg, 1994). The
team also investigated money-raising ideas like ecotourism and a
green venture capital fund.[4]

3. Van Bolhuis later worked in the World Bank's GEF administrator's office
    and went on to serve the GEF Secretariat as financial officer in charge of
    replenishment negotiations.
4. Sweatman went on to help the Overseas Private Investment Corporation
    try to implement such a fund, but it failed (interview, NGO, 1997).

The World Bank meanwhile was responding to donor hints and developing its own proposals, some of which it shared with the World Resources Institute's ICFP team. In 1989 a report, entitled *Natural Endowments: Financing Resource Conservation for Development* (WRI, 1989), set out options including one or more International Environmental Facilities on a model proposed by the World Bank. Although the formal ICFP process eventually fizzled out, there were only two real differences between the WRI recommendations and the GEF which eventually emerged. The GEF was to be a 'global' facility where WRI had suggested 'international', and the GEF was to provide funds for projects itself rather than help existing institutions design projects to move money through certifiably greener channels. As we shall in the following chapters, both of these changes affected the GEF's identity and impacts.

Ten years later, WRI staff remained pleased with the formulation that did emerge, but some felt that a project design facility could have been a more efficient use of funds – especially as a learning tool. It could have tapped directly into mainstream flows of aid, and bankable proposals prepared by this kind of facility might have done more to 'mainstream' environmental values into the Bank's wider programmes (interview, NGO, 1997). However, any such (cheaper) option, even if it were acceptable to the Bank, might have given donor governments an excuse to put in less money and deprived the Conventions of a project fund for their priorities. Initial support for the GEF came mainly from a few European governments seeking financial controls over the implementation of the proposed environmental Conventions, and few observers imagined much of a role for the GEF at all beyond directly financing these treaties (interviews, 1997–9).

Meanwhile the World Bank had other pans in the fire – for example, a pilot programme to conserve Brazilian rainforests; in July 1990 the G7 governments meeting in Houston announced that its funding mechanism, the Rain Forest Trust Fund, was to be part of the GEF framework, but in the end it was left out (Reed, 1992). By the time Rio came around the World Bank had also developed Strong's proposal for an 'Earth Increment' – adding an environmental finance component to the forthcoming (tenth) replenishment of the Bank's soft-loan arm, the IDA. But with the GEF proving successful in winning support in the run up to Rio (see below), donors were not willing to supply any other concessional funding, so the Earth Increment proposal too was quietly dropped.

Money Starts to Move

The scales were finally tipped for a GEF by the promise of funds at a World Bank meeting in Bangkok in the autumn of 1989. The French environment minister, with German and a few other governments' support, offered $100 million that they had left over at the end of a financial year. Other donors soon fell in with their own commitments, and they gave Bank staff something akin to freedom to make arrangements and sketch out a strategy for the experimental green facility under the guidance of Ernest Stern, a very senior figure in the World Bank. Working 'quickly and in secrecy' without even consulting their own environment department (Caufield, 1996), the World Bank's finance people developed a fund which, with technical assistance from the UNEP and the UNDP, they would administer and largely invest themselves. The World Bank's environment department, led by Ken Piddington, had initially sought extra funds for technical assistance in project development, but with Piddington out of the office on compassionate leave during the Bank's preparation process, he had little input to the eventual shape of the facility and on his return criticised its failure to integrate new environmental funding with the Bank's regular development work. The Global Environmental Trust Fund was eventually endowed on the Anglo-Saxon trust model (interview, World Bank, 1997), so what interest has it aroused and whose trust has it rewarded with investments to date?

The GEF's initial mandate was defined vaguely enough to attract widespread support, but tightly enough to make it clear that there would be no blank cheques. As suggested by Brundtland, the new multilateral fund was limited to concessionally financing 'programs and activities for which benefits would accrue to the world at large while the country undertaking the measures would bear the cost, and which would not otherwise be supported by existing development assistance or environment programs' (World Bank, 1990). This proposal was passed by the Bank to donor governments for comment in February 1990, and developed thereafter in small meetings predominantly attended by Europeans and World Bank people. For example, one meeting in Paris in March 1989 was presided over by Ernest Stern.

The GEF proposal initially faced hostility from parts of the US government under pressure from its Congress – which had to approve every item of aid spending. Some congressional representatives were wary of the proposed biodiversity Convention and did not want to stump up extra cash for international agreements, nor to support anything which might hold risks for emerging US-based biotechnology industries. Congress was also being told by some Washington-based environmental NGOs that the Bank should reform itself rather than hive off responsibility for 'the global environment' to a separate fund (Sjöberg, 1994).

In this context the US government wanted to hold off from any new financial institution-building – at least until the new Conventions were up and running. However, over the summer of 1990, the US position changed to match almost exactly that of a vocal group of Washington-based environmental NGOs. They had apparently decided that if a GEF was the best hope for new multilateral green funding, then their government should support it. Thereafter the US government offered support to the GEF, on the condition that it be a pilot programme, allow a degree of NGO participation in both policy development and project implementation, and generate lessons for the World Bank through 'mainstreaming' (see below) rather than evolving into a new institution. In Europe, government proposals for a GEF had similarly attracted big NGOs and parts of the scientific community, for example systematic biologists in the UK (see below) and the UK soon joined the US in cautiously supporting European plans for a three-year pilot GEF programme.

Nevertheless, some governments – notably those of the US, Australia and Switzerland – were still unwilling to participate fully in a multilateral facility. Instead of contributing to the Global Environment Trust's 'core fund', they provided 'co-financing' with bilateral grants or highly concessional loans, thus maintaining direct administrative controls over their funding. These governments preferred to explore their priorities for the environment with a degree of independence, but without directly undermining the GEF's role as a prospective mechanism for implementing the conventions.[5]

5. For example, the government of Norway entered into a $4.8 million co-financing agreement to support World Bank–GEF projects in Poland and Mexico. Part of the deal included an analysis of issues arising if similar projects were used as vehicles of Joint Implementation under proposed arrangements for the climate Convention. This proposed mechanism would involve Northern governments paying for activities to reduce carbon dioxide emissions in Southern countries rather than at home, where it would be more expensive to achieve the same level of reduction in carbon emissions. With help from such Nordic governments, the World Bank seems to have been manoeuvring to use experiences gained with the GEF to corner the market in Joint Implementation and beyond: possible markets of 'carbon trading' under any protocols emerging from the FCCC. As with the GEF, these initiatives were used to create facts and experiment with procedures long before the relevant treaty had been signed by most countries, let alone ratified and protocols negotiated.

Getting the South on Board

Next in turn to comment on the GEF proposal, in the summer of 1990, were a selection of representatives – many of them already affiliated with the World Bank in some capacity – from nine potential recipient governments including Zimbabwe, India and Indonesia. The GEF was presented as a new window for World Bank finance, with no clear connection to the Rio Earth Summit by then looming on the diplomatic horizon.

In early preparatory meetings for Rio, India and China were talking about an alternative 'Green Fund' to make restitution for Northern exploitation of resources worldwide and allow Southern governments control over uses made of the funds. When the Northern donor governments made it plain they would not agree to such terms, the Southern representatives consulted seem to have had to persuade their governments that the GEF, however insufficient, was the best that the donors were likely to offer for the time being. Key recipient governments therefore agreed to pay a minimum of $1 million as a fee to join the donors' new 'club' largely it seems in the hope that they could shape the developing fund better from inside than out.

In particular, the Southern representatives deemed it valuable to get in at the start so as to ensure that donors and the World Bank did not have totally free rein to decide what projects, where, should be funded, and under what guidance.[6] Their other key concern was ensuring 'additionality' – that funds advertised as 'new' would not be taken from other aid budgets. In response, the World Bank's vice-president for finance, Ernest Stern, felt able to say that 'this is an old question, and a solution takes a combination of faith, art and creative accounting' (quoted in Sjöberg, 1994). It is not clear how the Southern governments consulted were convinced of GEF's additionality (on which, as we shall see in Chapter 5, Stern was proved

6. Moiseev (1996) notes that ozone depletion was the focal area for which the GEF had the strongest guidance, yet in the pilot phase GEF only two ozone projects (out of a total of 112 – see below) received GEF assistance. This apparent avoidance of activities subject to clear guidance did little to quell unease in G77 and NGOs about the World Bank being free to manage conservation money largely as it saw fit, instead of helping governments to fund their own priorities and translate environmental policies into action at the local level.

right). Perhaps it was the dilution of the World Bank's dominance, perhaps the innovative claims made for the GEF that convinced waverers. Some have suggested that key Southern governments were offered GEF project finance and jobs for their nationals to smooth the way to agreement (interviews, 1997). Whatever happened in private, as soon as notional agreement had been established between donors and selected recipient governments, the GEF was established by a resolution[7] of the executive directors of the World Bank. The Bank became trustee,[8] and in November 1990 a revised proposal for the pilot GEF programme was approved, with over $1 billion pledged by participating governments.

Nevertheless, while negotiations continued on a draft entitled *Issues and Options for the Future Evolution of the Global Environment Facility*, GEF advocates did not find the run up to Rio to be plain sailing. For example at the Ministerial Conference on Environment and Development held in Beijing in June 1991, where the US and UK governments were particularly active in stressing the suitability of GEF as a green fund, the 40-odd Southern representatives expressed distrust of the World Bank and warned of the dangers of eco-imperialism (Gan, 1993).

With no alternative available however, the GEF was formally approved by participating governments and Implementing Agencies in late 1991 – by which time two tranches of funding were already in place (Kjorven, 1991; Fairman, 1996). By April 1992, when participating governments began to form an operational policy and the GEF's Scientific and Technical Advisory Panel (STAP)[9] completed work on criteria for project selection, 80 per cent of the initial funds promised had already been allocated.[10]

7. Resolution 91.5, based on a paper prepared by the World Bank in consultation with the UNEP and UNDP.
8. The Bank's executive directors maintained the power to amend the provisions of the resolution 'after consultation with the participants'.
9. STAP was intended to contribute to the development of operational programmes in the GEF focal areas, and to selectively review projects prior to approval.
10. Kjorven (1991) observes that the GEF assisted a lot of biodiversity projects at the start because the World Bank's agriculture staff had been looking for an opportunity to try out new ideas that they had been learning from critical NGOs and others.

THE INSTITUTIONAL ARRANGEMENT CREATED

Decision-making and Policy Guidance

The pilot GEF was run on a day-to-day basis from the 'GEF administrator's office' in the World Bank. The administrator was Ian Johnson, a British high-flyer in the Bank, initially assisted (and later superseded) by Mohamed El-Ashry, an Egyptian environmental engineer who had previously come from the WRI to head the Bank's environment department. Funding for projects up to $10 million could be allocated within the Bank, funds above that sum had to be linked to other World Bank loans and referred to the Bank's governing board (Caufield, 1996).

Decisions were made by consensus at irregular 'participants' meetings'[11] of the donor and recipient governments involved in the GEF. Specific decision tools for GEF funding emerged only gradually with the help of the World Bank's technical experts and environmental economists. The UNEP was supposed to provide scientific and technical advice to guide the GEF's work, but its STAP did not even convene until the spring of 1991 – by which time most of the money had already been allocated. The US Treasury held monthly meetings with NGOs, and as Lin Gan (1993) reported, inputs to GEF's early policies came from technical staff working on the GEF (who commented on 63 per cent of projects), donor governments (61 per cent), the scientific community and NGOs (42 per cent); inputs from both the leaders of the institutions involved and Southern governments meanwhile were generally deemed 'insignificant'.

The GEF's first operational policy took the form of eight 'principles' (which remain at the heart of the GEF in much the same form today). GEF was to:

- provide additional, concessional grant finance to meet the incremental costs of creating global environment benefits
- support activities that benefit the global environment in four focal areas: climate change, biodiversity, international waters and ozone depletion; also land degradation 'as it relates' to the focal areas
- be financial mechanism to planned multilateral environmental agreements

11. The first twice-yearly participants' meeting was held in May 1991, chaired by Mohamed El-Ashry.

- be cost-effective
- fund activities that are country-driven and fit with national policies for sustainable development
- operate through Implementing Agencies (World Bank, UNDP and UNEP) and require no new bureaucracy
- be transparent and accountable to both donor and recipient governments
- be innovative and flexible.

Interestingly, these principles contain no mention of local environments or institutions, nor of how democratic input and scientific assessment at the ground level was to be ensured. Only the fifth principle – projects financed by the GEF were to be 'country-driven' – emphasised the role of national contexts and commitments. This principle required the GEF to fund activities consistent with recipients' national priorities for sustainable development, but, in practice, few countries had meaningful policies for this, so projects were usually designed by international agencies and a few in-country allies to meet their own priorities first. Similarly hard to achieve, as we shall see below, were the GEF's aspirations to transparency, innovation,[12] and efficiency.

The Involvement of UN Agencies

Partly in response to Southern governments' wariness of the World Bank, donor governments agreed to let the UNDP and UNEP help run some of the new Facility's projects. Essentially, while the World Bank ran major investment projects, the UNDP was to provide technical assistance and capacity-building and the UNEP a Scientific and Technical Advisory Panel (see Chapter 4). Overall, these agencies' task was to identify and support development projects including energy, conservation and capacity-building in the South as the most 'efficient' and 'cost-effective' use of green aid money.

Some donor ministries hoped that an emerging 'inter-agency synergy' would contribute to Bretton Woods and (more so) UN reform – they said the GEF could act as a catalyst, 'co-ordinating the

---

12. Even the World Bank's own GEF newsletter, *GEF Watch*, of February 1992 notes that both technical reviewers and task managers deemed the criteria used to measure innovation 'inappropriate', and that 'innovation boils down to semantics'.

environment' in the UN system, while rationalising activities according to comparative advantage and 'mainstreaming' environmental activities into international development programmes (interviews, various Northern governments, 1996–7). However, any real synergy would probably have needed a more equal partnership, and more mutual understanding between the agencies. When the GEF came along with more money for three years than the UNEP's environment fund had received since its inception in the early 1970s,[13] some UN agency staff resented the better-resourced World Bank moving onto their 'environmental' turf. Perhaps surprisingly, UNEP people did not initially object strongly because at least the GEF promised to bring some money to their cash-starved programmes (interview, GEF Secretariat, 1997). The UNDP, based in the UN headquarters in New York, is not as cash-starved as the UNEP but runs offices in many Southern countries and works hard with what it has – at least compared with the World Bank where for all their protestations of overwork, staff seemed more relaxed about their mission to bring environmental protection into development administration.

As 'trustee for the environment' in the UN system, the UNEP sought to 'plan priorities' for the GEF. Writing from inside the agency, Sheila Aggarwal-Khan (1997) expressed the hope that the GEF would be used less as an 'add on' to development projects than a transformative facility ensuring that loans for the 'least cost option' would be decided on the basis of '*total* costs to society'. The optimistic hope was that with the GEF's limited funding, it would help to solve global environmental problems by reforming the lending process of development institutions to take account of non-economic social and ecological costs and benefits.

As we shall see in later chapters, feelings that the UNEP's hopes were 'pie in the sky' were only partially defused by the Bank's redrafting the joint declaration of the heads of agencies before it was approved in New York in November 1990 – initialising the GEF with the support of 28 governments (twelve of them recipients). The UNEP seems to have been 'tolerated' in the GEF as a 'give-away present' to its supporters (interview, NGO, 1997)[14] because the major donor governments' priority by then was to have something up and

13. Between 1973 and 2001, the UNEP's environment fund received just over a billion US dollars from governments.
14. UNEP supporters were to be found in its East African host region, environment ministries, NGOs and scientific bodies.

running in time for the Earth Summit in 1992. They wanted to show delegates that they were willing to act, and to set a precedent with some Southern support before the new Conventions could make explicit demands of any new funding. As soon as formal agreement had been reached therefore, the GEF's administrators began devising projects and spending money.

GEF Projects

Overview of GEF's Spending in the Pilot Phase

Countries were initially eligible for GEF assistance if they could borrow from the World Bank (that is, they had an annual per capita income of under $4,000) and/or received technical assistance grants from the UNDP through a country programme.[15] Altogether 112 projects worth $712.1 million were endorsed by GEF participants during the pilot phase (IEPP, 1994), leaving unspent much of the $1.13 billion contributed by member governments.

GEF funds in the pilot phase were distributed fairly evenly across the world's regions, though the Asia–Pacific region gained most. Fifty-five projects were focused on biodiversity, 42 projects on climate change, 13 projects on international waters and two projects on ozone depletion (IEPP, 1994). Projects ranged from environmental components integrated into bigger (usually World Bank) development projects, to 'stand alone' initiatives funded exclusively by the GEF. To get some GEF money to NGOs and the grass roots, a Small Grants Programme (SGP) was established in the UNDP with around 1 per cent of the GEF's funds for things like bicycle paths in Poland, a solar cooker recipe book in Belize and an electric fence in Botswana (Caufield, 1996).

One of the few outsiders to examine the GEF's pilot phase projects[16] was Alex Wood of the WWF, who found more emphasis on speedy project approval and implementation than on a coherent rationale guiding which projects should most usefully be funded, or how they should be funded (pers. comm., 1997). Another close observer, David Fairman (1996), reports that both the GEF's strategies and its projects therefore suffered in the rush for Rio.

15. Inclusion of the UNDP criterion seems to have been part of a deal between donors and G77 negotiators to allow more governments to benefit from the GEF than if World Bank criteria were used on their own.
16. Documents were not then publicly available.

The spread of GEF projects in the pilot phase reflected a desire on the part of the participants to distribute funds widely amongst supportive governments as well as between the focal areas. Many environmentalists and others argued that funds should be targeted to ecosystems deemed most 'at risk' and should not be distorted by politics. Others complained that projects devised by international agencies ignored local environmental needs, initiatives and expertise. In an effort to make them better, over 200 NGOs participated in 156 pilot phase GEF projects, mostly concerned with biodiversity. The projects mentioned below were initiated in the pilot phase, even if some did not get going until after the restructuring in 1994.

Biodiversity Operations

By April 1995, 46 per cent of GEF funds had gone to biodiversity, including $7.8 million for national biodiversity surveys of 29 countries (Caufield, 1996). Most projects were concerned with research, capacity-building and geographically specific protected area management: for example, $5 million was given to Egypt for *Red Sea Coastal and Marine Resource Management*.

The goal of the $4.5 million Poland/Belarus *Forest Biodiversity Protection* project in the Bialowieza National Park was to conserve an endangered ancient forest populated with lynx and Europe's last wild bison, as well as to provide institutional support for conservation in the Ministry of Environment, Natural Resources and Forests. The plan claimed innovation with the establishment of a gene bank and arboreta to protect genetic diversity and to provide plants for reforestation in areas degraded by pollution. Yet critics like Friends of the Earth International lambasted connections between this project and a logging project and roadbuilding initiative in the same virgin forest.

A Congo biodiversity conservation project meanwhile was said by Bruce Rich (1994) to leverage or sweeten a much larger World Bank forestry project, itself intended to open up the Congo's forests to further exploitation and 'breathe new life into the forestry sector', according to a project document.

Aggarwal-Khan (1997) suggests that the World Bank's 1986 wildland management policy for Cameroon gave the Bank responsibility for conservation, but by the 1990s the Bank was able to delegate the task to the GEF with the *Biodiversity Conservation and*

Management project, while it got on with promoting timber extraction.

The GEF website states that the World Bank's $6.2 million *Tana River National Primate Reserve Conservation* project in Kenya was intended to assist

> Development and implementation of a management plan for the Tana River National Primate Reserve, which contains the last remaining contiguous area of indigenous riverine forest along the Tana River. The Tana Reserve protects two endangered primate species, the Red Colobus and Crested Mangabey monkeys. (<www.gefweb.org>)

But this ten-year project, run in collaboration with the Kenya Wildlife Service, provoked the ire of 5,000 indigenous Pokomo people unwilling to be evicted from their ancestral lands. As conservationists in the East African Wildlife Society pointed out, the Pokomo had originally alerted scientists to the presence of one of the monkey species, and local cooperation was vital to their conservation. Local conservationists also noted that the real threat to the area's biodiversity was a World Bank-assisted dam and irrigation scheme on the Tana River (Caufield, 1996).

In her critical account of the World Bank's history, Catherine Caufield provides several examples of GEF projects being used in an attempt to clean up the environmental damage caused by larger World Bank development projects. For example, she tells of a GEF-assisted $5 million project intended to protect Lake Malawi's biodiversity, largely by persuading local people not to fish in it. This conservation project was originally linked to a larger World Bank project for fisheries development. Aiming to promote commercial fishing in Lake Malawi through the provision of boats, processing factories and the like, this Bank project should have done its own fish species survey (Aggarwal-Khan, 1997) but it featured no environmental assessment. The access roads built for the bigger project would provide access not only to the new factories and shore facilities but also to loggers, whose activities in the local watersheds promote erosion, clogging feeder streams and damaging the lake ecology.

Overall, NGOs' and scientists' verdicts on early GEF biodiversity projects were not very positive (see Chapter 4), essentially because the GEF's approach did not engage with the causes of biodiversity loss. Its climate projects were only slightly better received.

Climate Change Operations

When it came to climate projects, GEF funds were less likely to cover full project costs, not least because the opportunities for private finance were more immediate and obvious in climate change programmes than in biodiversity. Forward thinkers had long realised that 'potential markets for solar (PV) [photovoltaic] technology in the South are huge and profitable, too big to be quantified – if market barriers can be removed. Therefore solar development would need more channels for credit and product distribution (Report of the Oxford Solar Investment Summit, 1996[17]).

Environmental economists eventually found ways to support energy efficiency measures by using GEF funds to remove 'market barriers' (interview, consultant, 1997), but to start with, GEF funds mostly supported the capital costs of World Bank projects directed towards generating more capacity with 'cleaner', non-fossil fuel (but not nuclear) powered technologies. The archetypal GEF climate change project features a Southern government wanting a new power plant and raising international finance to cover the costs of, say, a coal-fired power station, then turning to the GEF for the extra money required to pay the higher costs of using renewable fuel technologies to produce the same amount of energy with lower carbon emissions.

The global benefit of such a project is measured in terms of the carbon *not* emitted. One of the first assumptions justifying GEF finance for projects related to climate change was that the 'global environmental benefit' of reducing the risk of climate change could be objectively measured and then priced in terms of the costs of reducing emissions of carbon dioxide. However, as we saw in Chapter 2, the World Bank was not designed to support diffuse activities on the ground. Its staff – including those employed in the GEF Secretariat – found it easier and more in line with existing practices to achieve 'economies of scale'. Aid would be targeted towards big projects producing a measurable environmental output in terms of reduced carbon dioxide emissions.

The case study in Appendix III, telling of a project for decentralised solar installations in Africa, suggests that even when GEF funds go through the UNDP with its Southern development focus,

17. Organised by Greenpeace, the event was supported by the Rockefeller Foundation, Oxford University and others, and was attended by numerous corporate chairpeople and CEOs.

to electrify rural African communities, an uncomfortable distance remains between local need and global provision.

UNCED AND AFTER

GEF's Role in the New Conventions

In the run up to Rio in 1992, negotiations for Conventions on Climate Change and Biodiversity intensified. G77 countries, better represented in UN environment negotiations than in the GEF processes, still wanted each Convention to have their own fund – like the Multilateral Fund of the Montreal Protocol where all participants decide between themselves how much money is needed, demand it from donors and allocate it amongst themselves. Donor governments, however, insisted on limiting their exposure with a single, World Bank-led fund – requiring G77 governments and the governing bodies of any new environmental conventions to compete for a single pot of new money.

Citing the need for democracy and justice in environmental finance, G77 governments attempted to avoid adopting the GEF as the Conventions' financial mechanism. The donor governments were making it clear that like Southern proposals for a 'polluter pays' 'green fund', proposed separate funds for each Convention would not be made available, however, some Southern government negotiators were still determined that finance for implementation of the biodiversity Convention in the South should be free from the clutches of the World Bank (McConnell, 1996) and accountable to the governing body of the Convention.[18] G77 spokespeople in the CBD negotiations remained firm that they would not agree on any text until the Western European and Others Group (WEOG) of countries agreed to finance all biodiversity conservation activities in 'developing countries' (McConnell, 1996).

With Northern governments determined to have something to show their environmental lobbyists at Rio, this resistance to the GEF in the Convention processes was one of the few bargaining counters held by Southern and environmental officials in their ongoing battles for resources with Northern treasuries. But as we shall see

18. Perhaps FCCC negotiators were less troubled by arrangements for their financial mechanism because they saw that the GEF was unlikely to be the only funding available for implementing their treaty.

below, as Rio loomed, opposition to the World Bank's new Facility was not solid.

The last session of negotiations for a Convention on Biological Diversity began in Nairobi in May 1992, just as negotiations for the establishment in framework form of a UN Convention on Climate Change drew to a close in New York. Several G77 negotiators were unhappy with the outcome of the latter process[19] (Chatterjee and Finger, 1994) and went to the last CBD sessions, determined to win something better for the countries of the South (McConnell, 1996). A stand-off ensued, largely around the issues of technology transfer and finance – areas where donor governments hoped the GEF would play the key role, and Southern governments feared being sold short again. It seems the impasse was broken only when the chairman, Egyptian Mustafa Tolba, stepped in to tell the US, UK and German delegations that he understood the financial constraints on their policy options, but they must offer *some* movement. He also offered these three delegations exclusive access to his own telephone to call their home governments for consultations (McConnell, 1996), enabling a diplomatic flexibility that the Southern bloc of governments could not match.

Southern opposition to the GEF was eventually 'moderated' after the UK delegation led donor calls for a thorough independent review and reform of the pilot phase of the GEF (McConnell, 1996). In the end a fudged solution to the GEF argument was put forward at three in the morning by the Indian delegation – perhaps suggested by the UK delegation who had got clearance for the new phrasing from their bosses in London but could not be seen to propose it themselves. The text of the CBD was eventually finalised after Dr Tolba 'bullied' the delegates, not allowing them to leave the meeting room until agreement was reached (McConnell, 1996), and Article 39 of the legal document confirmed the GEF as 'the institutional structure operating the financial mechanism to the Convention on Biological Diversity on an interim basis' (CBD, 1992). A delegate who remained hostile to the GEF noted presciently, 'these interim measures have a habit of becoming permanent fixtures' (quoted in McConnell, 1996).

19. Where it seemed that aid would be directed to 'low-hanging fruit': the cheapest options for transforming investments, rather than where Southern governments or others saw investment to be most needed (Gupta, 1995).

Hostility to the GEF at Rio

At the Earth Summit, or UNCED, held in Rio in June 1992, the signing of framework Conventions on Climate Change and Biodiversity, as well as a plan for a worldwide 'Agenda 21' – planning sustainable development at the ground level for the twenty-first century – grabbed media attention.[20] It also became clear at Rio that the American lifestyle was 'not up for negotiation', as George Bush I famously put it, and that donor governments would only put new multilateral environmental funds for the Conventions in the hands of the GEF. Though its processes were not part of the UNCED agenda, the GEF's future status was closely tied to the outcome of these more high-profile negotiations – because without Conventions to fund and thereby delimit, there was no reason for it to exist.

Southern governments and ministries not invited in at the start objected to the way in which the GEF had been created by a small club of World Bank-friendly officials in donor governments and more powerful Southern governments. Both the ministries and governments left out and various NGOs and conservation commentators complained not only that the GEF was insufficient for the Conventions and Agenda 21, but that it was a *fait accompli*, secretively controlled by the unaccountable World Bank, and created back to front with strategy trailing finance. Seeing the Bank as ideologically unsuited to the job of financing the Conventions, they still hankered for an alternative 'financial mechanism' with less centralisation and more scope for national priorities to be met (Gupta, 1995).

Nobody involved could deny that especially for the poorest governments, the global investment climate meant that 'In the absence of free (or heavily subsidised) technology transfer, Southern countries will be unable to afford to pursue sustainable development strategies' (Williams, 1997). With the hyped up 'promise of Rio' implying costs as high as $600 billion per year for implementation of the new Conventions and the 'profoundly revolutionary' Agenda 21 – which many said should have been accompanied by wholesale restructuring of the UN (Henry, 1996) – any real-world offer by donors was bound to breed disappointment.

20. Besides the GEF and the Conventions on Climate Change and Biodiversity, the main outcomes of the UNCED were Agenda 21 (which the UNDP also assisted through an allied programme called 'Capacity 21') and the UN Commission on Sustainable Development (CSD).

The GEF's advocates at Rio also faced what some Northern negotiators dismissed as 'rhetorical issues' (quoted in Agarwal et al., 1999):
Southern calls for international justice, abolition of international
debt and quite possibly the institutions managing it, reparations for
colonialism and transformation of power relations in the global
economy.[21] In this context, donor treasuries were self-interestedly
rational to want to limit their additional aid to meeting the incremental costs of limited environmental protection (Gupta, 1995), and
a group of South Asian NGOs was rational to call the GEF 'an illegal
and immoral institution, where the North could not be assessed for
its environmental liability, but the South must beg alms' (quoted in
Agarwal et al., 1999).

Facing up to that fate, the main priorities of most Southern governments at Rio were reduced to simply maximising aid flows and
technology transfer as far as possible[22] – while maintaining their
independence from sometimes unwelcome international experts,
consultants and NGOs also seeking GEF assistance.

Overcoming Resistance from a New Paradigm

The 1992 Earth Summit was the culmination of a long process of
international negotiations inspired largely by a combination of
pressures on global elites from the South and the environment
movements documented in the previous chapter. The Rio
conference came at a time when environmental problems as well as
the 'Third World debt crisis' were drawing popular attention to the
limitations of existing development models. Meanwhile some transformative new ideas – many born as environmentalism was gaining
widespread popularity in the 1960s – were maturing in parts of the

21. One UN observer described the donors' promotion of the GEF in terms
of the Goldilocks story: having stumbled upon a bear family's house and
enjoyed their chairs, beds and hot porridge, Goldilocks was now returning
with a lawyer, complaining that she had burnt her mouth. This
presumably reflects a feeling that the Northern countries (Goldilocks)
have stolen resources from the South (three bears), and are now
demanding that the Southern countries make up for the damage done
with those resources.
22. At least one Southern delegation to Rio, representing a government facing
a financial crisis at home, had been told to return with extra money at
any cost (McConnell, 1996).

Western scientific world. These innovations included the importance of non-linearity and holism in scientific understandings of a world made up of 'autopoietic' self-organising systems evolving 'on the edge of chaos' (Davies, 1992), and they were filtering fast into emancipatory ecological thinking about both conservation and development (Chambers, 1993; Holling et al., 1995).

If such a generalisation can be made, a post-neoclassical 'new paradigm' for real-world science and development extended from maths and physics through biology and psychology to anthropology, social organisation and (back through the mathematical models partly inspiring this new paradigm) the potential of a different kind of development economics (see, for example, Dosi et al., 1988). Going beyond the top-down and mechanistic analyses common to the dominant Anglo-Saxon economic culture, adherents of the new paradigm began to challenge mainstream thinking for failing to reflect the complexities and bottom-up evolution of real-world societies and ecologies.

Despite the potential for the GEF to incorporate some of this new thinking, it was a conservative message that was re-emphasised by governments and their preferred partners at the UNCED in 1992. 'Sustainable development' was to see nature preserved and the poor assisted by more trade and capital flows, by the opening up of the South to Northern technologies, managers and experts still promoting growth and efficient top-down resource managerialism in 'partnership' with transnational capital. This was the message represented in Rio by the World Business Council for Sustainable Development (WBCSD, a result of cooperation between the International Chamber of Commerce and the Business Council for Sustainable Development). The WBCSD was headed by Stephan Schmidheiny: Swatch CEO, board member of Asea Brown Boveri and Nestlé – and friend of the Earth Summit's secretary general, Maurice Strong (Thomas, 1994; Pimbert and Pretty, 1995). Other members include individuals from DuPont, Coca Cola, BASF, BP, Caterpillar, Cargill, GM, Monsanto, Unilever, Rio Tinto, Shell and Unocal.[23] The WBCSD fed directly into the UNCED consultative process and the Summit itself was organised using a North American lobbying model that favoured 'financially potent and organisationally strong lobbyists' (Chatterjee and Finger, 1994).

23. Unocal is closely implicated in the oil developments behind the 2001–2 US Afghan war <www.tenc.org>.

Their solutions cast environmental problems in the language of economic resource management. With measurement replacing discussion, this approach diverted attention from what many greens like Tickell and Hildyard (1992) saw as the real causes of environmental problems: enclosure of development's benefits by the few and externalisation of its costs onto poor people and nature. Additional aid flows may have been welcomed by Southern governments and accepted by Northern governments as the price of Southern compliance with the new Conventions, but new funds would hardly reach the poor, the landless and grass-roots environmentalists, although they might be used to dispossess them.[24] Therefore some saw the GEF as designed for bankers, politicians, executives and business interests both North and South: those with sufficient financial and political power to avoid constraining their own community's development on environmental grounds.

In an article entitled 'Green Dollars, Green Menace', Tickell and Hildyard called the GEF a 'financial monster' with no political conscience. It assumed the availability of capital was a prerequisite for environmental action, while these authors countered that for real-world conservation 'what we need instead is a change in attitude – with the right attitude we could be needing less money, not more' (Jose Lutzemburger, quoted in Tickell and Hildyard, 1992). Though this view did not pervade throughout the non-governmental interests represented at Rio, when combined with abiding hostility to the World Bank among environmentalists it had some power. The GEF therefore faced an uphill struggle to convince global NGOs and scientists as well as Southern governments that it could meet their needs – even though most do seem to think that conservation needs big money.

When the flurry of international meetings died down after the excitement of the Earth Summit, GEF's advocates emerged a little battered and bruised, but essentially victorious. A few Northern government officials and the World Bank had assured their creation's survival as the servant of the Conventions, and with the

24. The question of whether additional funds can actually help the preservation of the environment in the current situation was not even raised at UNCED, and at no time arises in the GEF (which could be said to behave – and is often treated – as sweets to be distributed among those of the international children who win the golden ticket to tour the chocolate factory, but only if they behave exactly as the owner says).

'incremental costs' restriction they could keep the tight leash on funding demanded by donor treasuries. Southern governments grudgingly accepted the GEF as the best they were likely to get on condition that it really was 'additional' to other aid flows and a full and independent review fed into a thorough restructuring for greater transparency, mainstreaming, accountability and democracy. As one Southern government representative told the GEF's donors at Rio, 'we will accept the GEF [in the World Bank] ... but can we not have a little say: can we not have more transparency in the administration of the fund? Surely, this does not amount to the South squeezing the North?'[25]

For all its limitations, the GEF survived Rio largely because its backers' expansive responses to such requests persuaded a broad range of interests that it had at least some potential to be reformed to meet their needs. The institutional bodies interested in the GEF's development after Rio therefore included not just governments from North and South, their constituent ministries and the World Bank but the UNEP and UNDP, assorted NGOs, consultants, experts, lawyers, scientists and former civil servants, all variously seeking work, funding, policy relevance and prestige. And then there were the largely uncounted and unheard millions of people – families, companies, communities, cultures – affected by the projects and policies supported by the GEF.

Lin Gan (1993) reported on a survey of people involved in creating the GEF. He found that 53 per cent registered pressure from the Northern governments, 47 per cent from senior members of the international organisations involved, 42 per cent from scientific communities and environmental NGOs, 32 per cent from the Earth Summit, mass media and popular movements, and 10.5 per cent from Southern governments.

It was later noted by administrators in the Bank that 'the major problems of the GEF come from having various actors and constituencies involved' (interview, World Bank, 1997).

Interests in GEF after Rio

The World Bank Reforming

After Rio, the GEF remained under the effective control of the World Bank, despite widespread doubts about its suitability to handle the

25. Statement of the Malaysian representative to UNCED, Rio 1992 (quoted by Gupta, 1995).

'sensitive and politically explosive interface between the North and the South on environment and development' (Gosovic, quoted in Gupta, 1995). Partly in response, the World Bank reorganised its environment department in late 1992.[26] The 'GEF administrator's office was renamed as the GEF's nominally independent Secretariat, and Mohamed El-Ashry, former head of the World Bank's environment department, became its CEO.[27] Yet still the World Bank held the GEF's cash and exercised legal authority over its spending, which inspired the jealousy of organisations interested in using GEF money for purposes which did not always tally with those of the Bank.

Despite the arrival of the GEF, after Rio the World Bank's values and performance came under renewed pressure from environmental and social activists worldwide. Critical internal reports like that produced by Wapenhams (World Bank, 1992) showed reformers how much needed to be done to make the Bank work even on its own terms, and gave ammunition to more damning opposition embodied, for example, in the '50 Years is Enough' alliance calling for abolition of the Bretton Woods institutions. Mass popular protests – particularly those against the Bank's involvement in the ecologically and socially destructive Narmada Valley dam project in India – undermined the Bank's position in the ongoing propaganda war for the soul of sustainable development. These pressures, fed through into the Bank's major shareholding governments, forced further attempts at reform, for example the hurried creation of a permanent Independent Inspection Panel to investigate disputed projects.

Nonetheless in the US a Republican-dominated Congress remained hostile to foreign aid in general and the Bretton Woods institutions in particular. The Bank therefore needed to be seen to reform further and faster from within in response to less abolitionist critiques coming from Europe, if it was not to risk re- or de-construction from outside. Facing a kind of structural adjustment themselves, Bank staff resented having to prune costs and bureaucracy to meet their financial masters' demands, but knew that the

26. The division previously known as the GEF Co-ordinator was renamed the Global Environment Co-ordination Division, to manage the World Bank's role as a project Implementing Agency under a new vice president for environmentally sustainable development.

27. Worried that the GEF Secretariat might be hosted by the UNEP in Nairobi, he, like all the potential candidates for the CEO's position, had initially held reservations about the job (CSERGE memo, undated). But the GEF stayed in the World Bank, and El-Ashry was able to stay with his employer.

survival of their institution depended on adapting to new contexts and making new friends. They sought further partnerships, including with environmental scientists and others in the upper echelons of global 'civil society' who might argue their case with donor governments. The GEF was becoming a key element of the Bank's mission to create a 'new constituency for international development' (Beckmann, quoted in Sjöberg, 1994, see above). Again, however, it was not their only pan in the environmental fire.

The range of other 'green' plans developed by a 'learning' Bank in the early to mid 1990s included the Global Overlays Program – where environmental priorities are 'overlaid' on development policies for client countries – and the Carbon Trading Initiative – designed to position the Bank for any new developments under the FCCC (Boehmer-Christiansen, 1999). Like the GEF's calculation of incremental costs, carbon trading uses environmental economics to identify prices for pollutants and their impacts on ecological functions. Also like the GEF, the Carbon Trading Initiative could pre-empt any more politically challenging financial proposals liable to emerge from international environmental negotiations (see footnote 5, this chapter).

Governments Find the Silver Lining

Despite wariness in some quarters of economics' commodifying colonisation of conservation, many environment officials, their allies and advisors engaged with the World Bank's new initiatives – trying to wage battles and build up budgets abroad that they could not win at home. Yet the imbalance of power between economic and ecological strategists within national governments is echoed at the international level too. Environment policy has to be passed by treasuries to receive public funds at the domestic level, and with the GEF, the Conventions' global environment policies depend on the World Bank for finance.[28]

Through co-financing, the US government became the major donor to the GEF's work programme, and since European govern-

---

28. Perhaps in light of this successful limitation of liabilities under the new conventions, negotiators from the UK and the Netherlands attempted to shift funding for implementation of the Montreal Protocol to the GEF's remit in July 1992 – without success. (The GEF supports the Montreal Protocol only in Eastern European and former Soviet states that had not participated in negotiations for the Protocol or its fund in the mid to late 1980s.)

ments needed US support to sustain the GEF, American needs and fears needed to be taken into account when restructuring it after Rio. Doubts remained in some parts of Washington over whether the Facility should be continued beyond its experimental three-year pilot phase, especially since the World Bank seemed less to be learning promised lessons than hiving off its environmental responsibilities to the GEF (see Chapter 6).

Recognising the Europeans' political foresight however, some in the US government saw in the new Conventions' 'financial mechanism' a way to exert influence over the implementation of treaties that their own government was unwilling to ratify. Through their representations to the GEF, the US Treasury could ensure the Conventions would not be directed to constrain American policy or way of life, and could even be used to subsidise diverse US interests abroad (see Chapter 4). The US government therefore tried to ensure 'rational' or 'businesslike' processes for environmental management through the GEF (Gan, 1993).

Southern governments remained more divided over the GEF. A few saw large project funds coming their way,[29] but many especially smaller and poorer Southern governments lacked the staff and resources to engage with all of the GEF's obscure language and requirements. Even those who could apply were not always all that interested in aid for the 'global' environment when local development remained a more pressing problem. When it began to emerge that the promise on additional aid was not being kept in practice (after a peak around the UNCED, aid flows fell throughout the 1990s), unease about the GEF's limitations bubbled up often, not least, as we shall see in Chapter 4, in the meetings of the Conventions.

Yet even for some Southern government representatives very opposed to the GEF, 'compared to the UN, it seems like less of a waste of time' (interview, GEF Council member, 1997). This is largely because it promises real money, instead of another ignorable initiative like Agenda 21 or talking shop like the UN Commission on Sustainable Development (CSD).[30]

29. By 1997, Indonesia had three climate projects totalling $30.5 million; India a single one costing $49 million and China three projects totalling $39 million.
30. With an overly wide remit, the CSD was unable to compel governments to report fully on implementation, let alone to enforce policies, and degenerated into a 'talking shop' of little practical use (French, 1995).

The NGOs Move In

With its unprecedented added value to offer, the GEF involved a lot of talking. Having recruited environmental NGOs to support their cause in the run up to Rio, Northern negotiators had to manage their subsequent involvement in GEF processes – making productive use of NGO energies and expertise to channel GEF aid, and keep them supportive where possible.[31] The UNCED forced NGOs to organise and go international, creating new linkages that transcended traditional politics. This effort certainly gave them improved status and bargaining power, but in the process fundamental differences of approach emerged, and the NGOs therefore can be divided into three categories.

The most important NGOs in the Global Environment Facility have been the mainstream environmental organisations such as the IUCN, WRI and WWF, whose scientific work and credibility with governments are good but who are widely seen as co-opted by Southern and more radical Northern environmental groups. For example, they held monthly meetings with the US Treasury Department on GEF related issues, and actively sought access to GEF funds. More politically critical groups like the Environmental Liaison Centre International in Nairobi, Greenpeace, Friends of the Earth, the Third World Network and the CSE in New Delhi aim to link environmental issues of concern to Northern and Southern populations. As a result they have had more ambiguous relations with governments, whose ears and funds they need, as well as the social movements they seek to represent. The other category, with only sporadic interest in the GEF, are single-issue groups aiming to raise awareness and find solutions to particular environmental problems.

In response to their organised demands, NGOs were increasingly used as extra consultants by the GEF to undertake assessments of project impacts on local (human) populations, advise on project design and implementation, and to implement projects – especially for biodiversity projects where local peoples' involvement can be useful. NGOs were also enabled to submit project proposals to the GEF – as long as they had approval from the appropriate focal point

31. All 'outsiders' interested in the GEF were classed as NGOs, whether they were environmental groups, academics, representatives of indigenous people or of private sector bodies.

in a national government. Some participating governments (notably France, Brazil and India) had reservations about the level of especially US NGOs' involvement, but after Rio the GEF began to respond constructively to these NGOs' critiques, increasing the numbers of projects with NGO participation, letting them into meetings and raising a 'voluntary fund' from member governments to pay for Southern NGO representatives to attend GEF consultations alongside their Northern fellows.

Though part of a very diverse community claiming to represent international civil society, the main set of NGOs interested in the GEF wanted, first, to improve global environmental policy and projects – more particularly to persuade the World Bank to be more transparent and to 'mainstream' the environment in its non-GEF lending – and, second, to build up their own and allied budgets by helping to channel flows of the GEF's new money (interview, Steiner, 1997). Some also hoped to represent the 'uninvited': outsiders who would never (or more likely could never) go to Washington and be taken seriously by (mostly) men in suits – because they were too poor, spoke no English, French or Spanish and/or their interests and concerns would not make sense to the diplomatic–economic culture in which GEF deliberations take place (interviews, NGOs, 1997–9). We shall see in later chapters how far they were able to fulfil this mission.

The Private Sector

As we have seen above, by contrast to most other 'global citizens' the organised large-scale private sector speaks the same language as the Bank and its major donors. Incited partly by the hype of Rio and its business friendly 'partnerships', many firms wanted to be seen to be green by engaging with environmental experts and organisations. In Schmidheiny's (1992) words, 'Progress towards sustainable development makes good business sense because it can create competitive advantages and new opportunities.' Yet while many procurement contracts for GEF-funded projects went to international firms via World Bank procedures, for the most part the private sector showed little direct interest in GEF finances. As Schmidheiny observed in his next book (1996), 'there is such a deep cultural rift between business and these big agencies that these working partnerships are extremely rare'.

As we shall see in chapter 5, the GEF's approval procedures were generally incompatible with private sector schedules; furthermore firms were scared off by the pre-eminence in the GEF of government ministries more skilled at 'paying lip service' to the private sector for political reasons than actually engaging with it usefully (interview, UNDP, 1997) – partly because of the risk of inviting protests about the use of GEF money to directly subsidise profit-led companies. Meanwhile, numerous private environmental finance initiatives were underway, for example the Washington DC-based Global Environment Fund Management Corporation which raised $75 million from institutional investors with direct US government support (Schmidheiny et al., 1996). Yet more strategically perhaps than such funds offering direct subsidy for environmental investments, the GEF seemed to hold potential to open new markets and extend credit lines of strategic value to the transnational private sector (see later chapters).

What contact there is between key GEF actors and private sector representatives seems to have taken place mostly 'behind the scenes' especially at international meetings, and decreased after an initial burst around Rio.[32] Several members of the GEF's Senior Advisory Panel have strong links to the private sector – which presumably influenced their strategic advice to Mohamed El-Ashry, GEF's CEO and chairman (see Chapter 4 and Appendix I).

Since Rio, El-Ashry has held meetings with individuals and organisations such as the newly formed WBCSD, but when requested for information on these interactions, a spokeswoman for the latter's president said it would be 'unethical' to respond while discussions continued.[33] However, a 1993 draft GEF document on 'small and medium scale private sector participation in the GEF' indicates that one purpose of meeting with private sector bodies was, not surprisingly, to elicit advice on increasing private sector participation in the GEF. But since the GEF is supposed to spend public money for the global public good, it is not clear why even these meetings should have to be private.

32. A representative of the Global Climate Coalition (an alliance of mainly fossil fuel-reliant companies opposed to international action under the climate change label) attended an early GEF meeting as an NGO, but the 'NGO community' already in attendance would not accept this organisation in their ranks.
33. Letter to Sonja Boehmer-Christiansen from the assistant to the chairman of the WBCSD, 1996.

Research

Besides business people and others, senior scientists were also represented on the GEF's Senior Advisory Panel, and the World Bank expanded both its own and the GEF's new Secretariat's technical staff. With the official GEF Scientific and Technical Advisory Panel (STAP) attracting a range of natural scientists, diverse researchers in fields related to the global environment saw in the GEF a potential user of their insights. It could also provide a new source of funding with which to build up institutional budgets and expand spheres of research, especially in Southern countries where data can be scarce and facilities limited.[34] Scientific research interests were to some extent institutionalised in the GEF, having driven both it and the Conventions with the insights of environmental science. A shifting international community that Boehmer-Christiansen (1997) calls the 'research lobby', acting through networks such as the International Geosphere–Biosphere Programme and the IPCC, quietly sought targeted research funding.

The first mention of the GEF in the UK parliament was in a debate on a report from the Select Committee on Science and Technology on potential sources of research funding for the UK's 'world class' community of systematic biologists (Lord Dainton, in Hansard, 8 July 1997). Based around the Natural History Museum, Kew Gardens etc., these experts have the task of identifying and mapping the taxonomy of every living thing on this planet. There was certainly hope among such scientists that the GEF would support institution-building for global research – as well as the consultancies, project reviews and international meetings that a cynic might call 'scientific tourism'. While such a verdict may be uncalled for, all this scientific work sometimes seemed to legitimate GEF operations as much as to shape them (see later chapters).

Despite it not being a donor government priority, STAP members convincingly argued that targeted, action-oriented research should be funded, and several projects involving elements of research did make it through the GEF's system. Systematic biology benefitted to a limited extent, for example with the $3 million Global Biodiversity

34. Justification for Research Activities that Support the Global Environment Facility, Related Environmental Conventions and International Scientific Assessments, GEF STAP, July 1994.

Assessment.[35] The development of the Program for Measuring the Incremental Costs of Actions to Conserve the Global Environment (PRINCE) in the GEF Secretariat employed a number of mainly UK-educated experts and environmental economists to assess nature's worth and calculate algebraic framework formulae for incremental costs analyses (see Chapter 5).[36] Overall, research interests probably got less than they had hoped for out of the GEF,[37] not least since much of the use made of their expertise seems to have been directed to providing technical inputs to environmental economic calculations.

CONCLUSIONS

The pilot phase GEF, which ran from 1991–4, was meant to be experimental, providing lessons for the World Bank and UN, possible new phases of GEF finance and/or for any new institutions designed to work in the same field. It was also meant to bring together a new partnership of international actors for the global environment, soothing North–South conflicts over liability for the costs of environmental action in the South. Yet one key goal for all involved seems to have been maximising their own influence, as well as the scope of funds and opportunities flowing into their field of work. Wondering if it might be a goose that lays a golden egg, people involved often talked up the GEF in public, while in private they discovered the impossibility of its satisfying everybody. The pilot phase established new turf for wars between the uncomfortably hitched GEF 'family' members.

35. The Global Biodiversity Assessment was edited by Prof. Vernon Heywood of Reading University and the International Council of Scientific Unions (ICSU). Originally a STAP initiative, UNEP hoped the Assessment would give 'start up momentum' to the Scientific and Technical Advisory Body of the biodiversity Convention, and co-ordinate bodies working on bio-diversity within a common agreed framework (UNEP statement to the GEF meeting in Abidjan, 1992).
36. Yet this framework would be very little used, since as we shall see in the following chapters, in practice (and in law), incremental costs had only to be 'agreed' on a case-by-case basis, and could not be calculated in any meaningful sense (personal communication, former GEF consultant, 1998).
37. Bob Watson as chair of pilot phase STAP recommended that 10 per cent of GEF money should go on research, but participants were unconvinced, and after restructuring, GEF's guidance contained no mention of this priority.

Given the structure and power relationships in the GEF family of governments and institutions, tensions were largely traceable to multiple actors with unequal status and incompatible missions competing for a new 'honeypot' of scarce aid resources, under pressure to perform in public by the ranks of critics on the outside looking in. The international effort to eliminate the environmental 'blindspot' noted above had meanwhile adopted a formulation for funding decisions which became the GEF's main 'Achilles heel'. Limited to financing the incremental costs of global environmental benefits, it was essential from the very start for the GEF to define in monetary terms the global as distinct from other environments. Thus the new institution was to pursue its goals economically and more or less separately from the work of other institutions. It was not intended to contribute to sustainable development as understood and valued at the local level, because this would by definition not directly benefit 'the globe'.

The GEF's defining characteristics – its birth in the World Bank, 'global' tag and links to the Conventions – had a formative impact on its history and direction, and provided fertile ground for misunderstandings. Given its global ambitions, complex genesis and restrictions and the turbulence which characterised the GEF's early years, what legal, institutional and personal qualities contributed to making it into something that Southern governments remained willing to accept, donors to replenish,[38] administrators to run, and assorted environmentalists, scientists and business people to try and make the best of?

38. Negotiations for replenishment of the operational GEF began with a meeting in Rome in March 1993.

4 Getting the New Facility in Order

HELLO, I'M 'GEF'!

Review and Restructuring; The New Governance Structure; The New Operational Structure; The New Issues Emerging; Conclusions

Despite early US demands that it be an 'experimental' facility, testing approaches and generating lessons for reforming the institutions involved, poor performance in the pilot phase did not lead to the GEF being abolished, nor to its functions and lessons being reabsorbed into the World Bank. Even though GEF policies were both pre-empting and sometimes incompatible with instructions from the two big Conventions it was supposed to serve (Werksman, quoted in Gupta, 1995), the GEF was restructured and given another chance.

Many of those Southern governments who criticised the GEF so fiercely around Rio remained desperate for additional aid, particularly to pay for clean technology transfer and capacity-building, and to meet the direct requirements of the Conventions. In return for provisional acceptance by the Conventions' governing bodies of the GEF as their 'financial mechanism', the donor governments promised to adapt it to meet some of the demands made by the Southern governments, scientists and NGOs active in the Conventions' processes.

The fact that North–South negotiations to restructure the GEF disintegrated at the end of 1993 demonstrates the incompatibility of many of these demands – especially the demand from Southern governments that donors should not have *de facto* control over how GEF funds should be spent – with the Northern perspective, and the fact that the GEF survived nonetheless demonstrates the determination of powerful actors to sustain a World Bank-led approach to global environmental management, through strategies of political persuasion extending to manipulation and perhaps even bribery.

This chapter follows the GEF as it was reviewed and replenished with $1.8 billion for 1995–8 (GEF-1), restructured and given a 'democratic' governing Council, Participants' Assembly and Secretariat, an Instrument setting out its legal status and an Operational Strategy to guide its spending. According to the GEF website 'GEF was restructured after the Earth Summit ... to serve the environmental interests of people in all parts of the world. The facility that emerged after restructuring was more strategic, effective, transparent, and participatory' (<www.gefweb.org>). Before turning to the veracity of these claims, this chapter explores the arrangements and ambiguities that may have won over the GEF's opponents in the short term, but left many of the institutional bodies involved in a state of diplomatic conflict.

Timeline of GEF's First Decade as a Financial Mechanism

1992 – UN Conventions on Climate Change and Biodiversity agreed at Rio Earth Summit, governments accept GEF as interim finance mechanism in the absence of realistic alternatives

1993 – GEF reviewed critically. Talks collapse at a meeting in Cartagena, Colombia

1994 – Instrument of Restructuring agreed at a meeting in Geneva, Switzerland

1995 – 'Operational' GEF-1 replenished with $2 billion. Operational Strategy circulated

1998 – Participants' Assembly in New Delhi, India, another review completed (OPS-1), GEF-2 replenished with $2.75 billion

2002 – New replenishment (GEF-3) due in time for Second Participants' Assembly in Beijing, China

REVIEW AND RESTRUCTURING

The First Evaluations Come In

As promised at Rio, the pilot phase GEF was thoroughly and very critically reviewed, both privately by donor governments, officially by an independent panel, and by interested NGOs. The usefulness of some of the feedback was however limited by its timing – the Independent Evaluation of the GEF Pilot Phase (IEPP) reported just as the restructuring negotiations were due to draw to a close – and/or participants' political difficulties with some of the findings.

In 1993 the donor governments commissioned an independent panel to confidentially evaluate the pilot GEF. Previewing problems that recurred throughout the 1990s, the report called attention to 'a consistent, biased exaggeration, if not falsification of the amount of consultation and participation with governments, NGOs and affected communities in the project documents' (quoted in Caufield, 1996). Among other fierce (but not subversive) findings, the unpublished report found that the first two years of GEF operations had featured 'unproductive competition and antagonisms' between the World Bank, UNDP and UNEP, and warned that 'the many instances of unsatisfactory practices by the GEF Implementing Agencies point to a need to pause and rethink policies and practices'.

Alex Wood of the WWF came to some similar conclusions. He wanted to know how GEF activities fitted into any larger framework for achieving conservation and sustainable development in the institutions involved. Finding people generally unwilling to talk freely – partly because of their limited experience with implementing GEF projects – he got few real answers, especially from the Bank.[1] He concluded that the GEF needed a pause to establish policies with more coherence, transparency and (perhaps predictably) openness to NGO involvement.

David Reed, author of several reports on the GEF for the WWF (for example, 1992), was concerned that a 'seemingly handsome' portfolio of projects would emerge 'of peripheral relevance to the central development issues that threaten the viability of the biosphere'. He cited the example of a GEF-assisted biodiversity project in Vietnam which aimed to mitigate the environmental impacts of previous development mistakes – rather than transform-

1. Wood based his study on the few project documents then available and interviews with task managers.

ing development policies so as to prevent such problems occurring. Noting that the GEF's climate change projects also did not alter the underlying structure of energy sectors, he felt that the GEF could be seen as more of a palliative than a mechanism for effective inter-nalisation of global environmental costs – as we shall see below, this became a fairly common critique to which the GEF and its supporters realistically had no answer.

A fuller NGO study of the GEF came from Washington-based Con-servation International and the Natural Resources Defense Council: *Reframing the Green Window – An Analysis of the GEF Pilot Phase Approach to Biodiversity and Global Warming and Recommendations for the Operational Phase* (Bowles and Prickett, 1994). Observing that the World Bank's traditional project approach was ill-suited to GEF's promise of innovation, they nonetheless expressed cautious optimism – *if* there could be a pause for 'sincere introspection' and thorough reform. In biodiversity conservation and energy efficiency, they found that GEF projects generally lacked sustainability, inbuilt monitoring, local support and capacity, and adopted a 'technical fix' approach.[2] On the ground they noted a tendency for the Bank especially to be 'too big': its GEF projects tying up local scientific resources and administrative capacity, distracting experts and attention from other important issues and initiatives.

Like Reed and the private reviewers quoted above, Bowles and Prickett demanded that a clearer programme strategy and criteria be in place before any more money could go through the GEF. But this was not the sort of advice that the World Bank, still keen to show the donors how it was reforming and the Conventions how it could spend money fast in their support, was likely to take. Instead, as

2. A later academic study by Fairman (1996) noted that GEF's early interna-tional waters projects did not take a holistic view of marine conservation and failed to ensure that the GEF policy framework was consistent with existing global treaties and action plans like the UN Conference on the Law of the Sea and the UNEP's regional seas programmes. Instead, the GEF merely provided grants for 'end of pipe' solutions to pollution, for example treating ship wastes in new port developments assisted by the World Bank in China, rather than tackling systemic sources of marine pollution. A UNEP statement to one of the early GEF participants' meetings suggested that they had failed to achieve their agenda for international waters because it was a focal area without a supporting constituency equivalent to those pushing for projects in the other focal areas – partly because it was not always clear to which governments funds for international waters should flow.

reviews and restructuring went on around them, they continued to move projects through the GEF 'pipeline'.

The Official Independent Evaluation of the Pilot Phase (IEPP)

The IEPP was requested by participating governments to assess the GEF so far and formally feed lessons into the restructuring. The process of agreeing arrangements and terms of reference for this high-profile and 'onerous task' was described as 'painstaking' by El-Ashry, who by May 1993 was clearly frustrated by the delay.[3] The report was carried out for the World Bank, UNEP and UNDP by consultants conducting field studies and analysis under 'extreme time constraints'.[4]

To assure their independence, the evaluation team reported to a panel incorporating some fierce critics of the GEF, perhaps since any appearance of 'soft-soaping' would have been unhelpful to the GEF in the political circumstances. An analytic and outspoken report however, confirming some oft-heard complaints, suggested that this was a mechanism ready and willing to listen to its critics. On the report's publication in late 1993, several NGOs commended GEF participants for 'insisting on a thorough and independent [evaluation] ... so little affected by the institutional agendas of the agencies that managed [it ... and providing] a focus for a positive, forward-looking contribution from the NGO community'.[5]

The evaluators questioned the pilot phase GEF's success in achieving its avowed goals, and challenged the structures through which tasks were approved and managed. Like the NGOs, it queried the meaning of 'global benefits' and 'incremental costs', why particular focal areas had been chosen and why the GEF had proven so costly, complex and cumbersome, with so little participation and transparency in its decision-making. The report also asked why other agencies could not manage some of the funds, not least since GEF-funded activities to date had hardly followed instructions to support host countries' 'policy, regulatory and institutional framework', while the sheer size of many grants overwhelmed the 'absorptive

3. In 1997 El-Ashry again showed frustration with the progress of the next major GEF evaluation.
4. UNEP statement to the GEF participants' meeting in Cartagena, December 1993. The 2002 report was also pushed for time (OPS-2, GEF 2002).
5. NGO statement to the Cartagena participants' meeting, 1993.

capacity' of local institutions. Echoing the donor governments' private review of the pilot phase (quoted above), the official report found that recipient countries rarely had as much influence as official documents would suggest.

The IEPP also declared that accountability remained too diffuse at policy and programme as well as project level. Since all three Implementing Agencies (the World Bank, UNDP and UNEP) lacked technical capacity for effective programmes and broad participation, and the new Secretariat was not in a position to preserve the integrity of GEF's mission, the fund needed to be managed independently. The GEF units in the Implementing Agencies needed to be 'reinvented', and guidelines produced to help recipients prepare their own projects – without a big agency taking control.

From the start, there had been no articulation of well-defined priorities for the GEF by the 'international community', so the IEPP confirmed a widespread feeling that the pilot phase was characterised by a hurried, agency-driven approach. Organisations treating GEF operations as an 'add on' to normal operations had not 'main-streamed' or integrated GEF priorities into their overarching strategies. In addition, since 'the Facility's main value, at this juncture, lies in its promise', hasty evaluations such as that on which the report was based were deemed to be no substitute for the feedback that a genuinely 'experimental' facility should be generating. Therefore a better method of learning was needed: an independent 'GEF-wide' system to gather and disseminate lessons from experience, to track and monitor strategies, operations and projects.

The authors also suggested that the three Implementing Agencies should reach out more broadly to agencies and NGOs with trial and error experience of working at community level, to regional multi-lateral development banks (RDBs), private and semi-private institutions, and so forth. The evaluators' call for better working rela-tionships between GEF agencies and NGOs went down well in the Washington NGO community whose support remained vital to keep the US government on board with the GEF, but not with those gov-ernments (France, Indonesia and others) who doubted the US negotiators' motives in involving mainly US and Northern European-based NGOs in the GEF.

Unsurprisingly, not all the evaluators' suggestions were welcomed by the agencies and administrators running the GEF. The World Bank complained that the IEPP had been a superficial desk study using incomplete documentation and insufficient consultation –

perhaps ironic in light of the Evaluation's conclusions about the sufficiency of the Bank's own transparency and consultations – and that the evaluators had failed to take account of the amount of work done by Bank staff.[6] While agreeing with the 'overall thrust' of the report, an official response from all the agencies involved disagreed with some of its analysis and conclusions.[7] They saw conflict between the Implementing Agencies as a sign of 'healthy competition' for GEF resources, and felt it would be unrealistic to hold up funding while an all-encompassing strategic framework was developed in a top-down fashion. After all, existing guidelines, criteria, frameworks, procedural checks and balances, and so on, had worked well enough in the pilot phase, and any new overarching strategy should not pre-empt the prerogative of Conventions to guide the GEF in the future. But whatever the possibility of NGO and official recommendations being implemented, or even of the Conventions' instructions directing GEF funds, by the time the IEPP reported, the restructuring negotiations were in their final stages – and at risk of falling apart under the pressure of conflicting expectations.

Negotiations Underway Again

Government representatives meeting in Abidjan, Cote D'Ivoire, in December 1992 agreed that the 70-odd governments by then participating in the GEF – both donors and recipients – should all be represented in further meetings to decide on its structure and governance. In reality only 20–25 took part: those with the resources and interest to do so. Two issues were pre-eminent in the restructuring negotiations: one was the level of any new replenishment – would it approach the amounts promised at Rio for technology transfer and training? – the other the vexed issue of 'efficient and harmonious' decision-making based on a legal framework which would recognise 'the importance of balancing the plurality of interests implicit in universal participation, and the need to give due weight to donors' funding efforts'.[8]

6. World Bank Submission to Independent Panel on GEF Evaluation, 22 November 1993.
7. *The GEF and the Evaluation: Learning from Experience and Looking Forward*, GEF/PA.93/97, Background Note for the GEF Participants Meeting, Cartagena, Colombia, 2 December 1993.
8. El-Ashry's opening remarks on Decision-Making in the Restructured GEF, Beijing participants' meeting, 27 May 1993.

Southern governments continued to fear for their sovereignty in the face of 'global' environmental claims, so they wanted a governance structure which reflected their numerical superiority and the fact that GEF projects would shape their national development. Despite having 'recognised the inevitable' in 1992 by accepting the World Bank's role in any financial mechanism for the Conventions (Matthews, 1995) they also wanted to ensure it was replenished with sufficient funds to begin to meet the promises made at Rio. In this context the UNEP at the next GEF meeting expressed 'the frustration of many developing countries that the high hopes of UNCED have not been realised'.[9]

Some Southern representatives suggested that donors should divert their planned GEF contributions to the UNEP's own environment fund, which emphasised policy interventions to conserve local environments and showed greater respect for power bases in the South. But still the main Northern governments did not favour this approach, preferring to keep their funds for the global environment flowing through an institutional form that they could control. So the frustration of many Southern governments had to be managed, not only in the Convention processes but in the GEF where their demands for control of the little money available had to some extent be met.

Options for Legal Formation

The choice of 'form' for the GEF's legal establishment will determine … the GEF's legal status, and from this status will flow the GEF's legal capacities and powers and the nature of its relations with States and other international entities. (internal World Bank memorandum, 1993)

Naturally enough, World Bank management preferred to maintain its authority over whatever form the GEF took, but this memo also shows the level of realisation that some change was needed to keep the South – and the Conventions' governing bodies – on board:

It should be recalled that developing countries … were reluctant to accept the GEF as a financial mechanism [for the Conventions],

9. Statement by the UNEP's representative to Beijing meeting of GEF participants, 1993.

and demanded that it be restructured [because] they felt marginalised from the Bretton Woods decision-making structure and
were unwilling to entrust the implementation of the Conventions
to a facility dominated by the Bank and its donor countries.
Retaining the status quo by re-establishing the GEF through a
second Bank resolution, would thus seem to go against the wishes
of many of the Participants, the express directives of Agenda 21,
and the legal requirements of the Conventions. Finally, the Bank
resolution approach risks the serious possibility that the COPs,
where the developing countries will have a large majority, will
reject the GEF. (internal World Bank memorandum, 1993)

As we shall see below, the GEF's legal form was established by
compromise, as was its governance. At the participants' meeting in
Beijing in May 1993, El-Ashry registered continuing disagreement
between participants on arrangements for GEF governance and the
role of his planned Secretariat. The proposals on the table at the time
were a participants' assembly with universal membership meeting
every year or two, and a constituency-based governing board of up
to 30 constituencies. Disagreement centred on the relative roles of
the two proposed governing bodies, with some participants wanting
'more compact' arrangements, and the voting system to be balanced
between North and South.

   Meanwhile, the GEF's implementation committee was still
approving finance for projects – with the consensus of the
'adhocracy' of governments involving themselves in the GEF
meetings. They did so in the absence of guidance from the COPs of
the Conventions (which had not yet met to decide what their
guidance should be, see below), and without integrating key
elements of the feedback from which all involved were supposed to
be learning – because if they had, the momentum might have been
lost and a loss of confidence on the part of the donors might have
undermined the chance of any new replenishment.

Tensions Erupt

Following the publication of the highly critical IEPP in late 1993,
actively participating governments met in Cartagena, Colombia, to
resolve outstanding issues and finalise the restructuring of the GEF.
G77 governments were still looking for the new kind of cooperative
environmental aid promised by donors, and with numbers on their

side, held out for final authority to rest in an assembly of all participating governments. Despite accepting donor governments'
arguments that a small governing Council would be administratively
efficient, the G77 bloc sought the major portion of its seats (20
recipient, 10 donor), the right to elect a chair for each meeting from
among the representatives present, and for its work to be subject to
the authority of a universal assembly of all the governments participating in the GEF.

The chairing of GEF meetings was an issue on which the G77
grouping was determined not to budge. With the head of the Secretariat and the chair of the Council embodied in one person, it had
been hard to ensure the Secretariat's accountability. As the IEPP had
just confirmed, the chairman's lack of independence in the pilot
phase interfered with administration and oversight, also distorting
the GEF's 'distinctive identity'. The NGOs active at Cartagena agreed
with G77 governments that the chief executive officer of the Secretariat should be separately elected by any new Council, stressing the
IEPP's recommendation that the Facility be 'organisationally, administratively and functionally independent from the implementing
organisations ... stand[ing] politically apart without creating a new
institution' (NGO statement, 1993). Reiterating common criticisms
– that the GEF had focused on mitigating environmental damage
caused by previous development activities at the expense of tackling
the causes, and that it conflated 'participation' with information dissemination and passive consultation – the NGOs went on to tell the
participants that

> We are familiar with the discrepancies between what is offered to
> the public and what political realities dictate. We would urge you,
> however, not to take too narrow a view of these political realities,
> because the future of the whole facility is at stake ... the manner
> in which the participants deal with the evaluation will be seen by
> us as a strong indication of the character of the new GEF. (NGO
> statement, 1993)

It was in this critical climate that officials from donor governments
– themselves constrained by their treasuries – tried to find a way
forward that did not involve their reducing conditionalities for new
aid, or otherwise work against their national interests. In this
context, what support there was for the GEF among its (potential)
recipients in governments, NGOs, and so forth, reflected the

ongoing decline in aid levels, leading many to feel that it was better to have an imperfect environmental aid fund than none at all. In the end, the temptation of the money they could offer was the ace in the donors' hand when the whole GEF game began to fall apart under the pressure of North–South politics.

The Southern Walk Out

When the G77 delegation walked out early from GEF negotiations at Cartagena in December 1993, some observers said they had taken a moral stand against donors' arrogant manipulation of the process and attempted blackmail (Horta and Hajost, 1993; interview, UNEP, 1998). Some deemed it a result of interference by the personal with the political (interview, Northern government, 2001), others even saw a 'rape of the G77 governments' (interview, World Bank, 1998). The full story remains obscure, perhaps too embarrassing for some of those involved for it ever to be properly told, but here follow two versions compiled from a published account (McConnell, 1996) and various unconfirmed rumours.

The first version is that the French negotiators, supported once again by the Germans, were threatening to reduce their funding for the GEF if they did not get their way over its governance (Horta and Hajost, 1993). During discussions late one evening the French delegate, speaking at the time on behalf of the Western European and Others Group of governments, offered a resolution acceptable to the G77 negotiators. When it turned out that their offer was not actually acceptable back in European capitals, the British delegation – whose turn it was to speak on behalf of WEOG – retracted the offer the next morning. The G77 negotiators took this as an insult, the last straw in the circumstances, and called an end to the meeting in protest at the Northern governments' arrogance.

An alternative story has two of the civil servants active in international environmental negotiations involved in an affair. Between them, the lovers sought to influence outcomes so that one of them could get a new job near the other in the US – rather than having to return to their family in the South. Meanwhile the representatives of other G77 governments, 'hanging together because otherwise they would hang separately', feared their interests as a bloc were being 'sold down the river' for the sake of private lives, and chose to bring the meeting to a close in the hope of reconvening later with a different set of negotiators and chair (pers. comm., 2001).

Either way, the meeting which was supposed to finalise the GEF's restructuring broke down with a G77 walkout – probably the closest the whole process came to outright failure. What exactly happened next is also not clear, but, in order to get negotiations back on track before the pilot phase had to be wound up in April 1994, some say that big projects were privately promised to key Southern governments to break the solidarity of the G77 bloc (pers. comm., 1998).

Whatever actually resolved the situation, government representatives meeting in Geneva in March 1994 completed the restructuring of the GEF with a replenishment of over $2 billion, available for distribution by a 'balanced' governing Council meeting under the co-chairmanship (see below) of the CEO of a formally independent Secretariat. Operations were to be reviewed every three years by a Participants' Assembly where all the governments involved in the GEF would be represented. The South got its universal Participants' Assembly, democratic Council and independent Secretariat; the North kept the Secretariat's CEO in the Council's permanent chair; the World Bank still hosted the GEF both administratively and financially and ran most of its projects – though the UNDP and UNEP were made 'equal' Implementing Agencies.

The GEF 'broke new ground' with its standards for accountability, democratic management, and NGO participation. It was given transparency conditions unheard of in any mutilateral development bank, and while accepting that the complex mechanisms for transparent governance could lead to institutional 'gridlock', interested NGOs hoped the GEF could provide a model of participation and accountability for other international institutions (Bowles, 1996).

The GEF's governance, responsibilities and structures were set out in the Instrument for the Establishment of the Restructured GEF (1994), a legal document adopted by the governing bodies of the World Bank, UNDP and UNEP after participating governments signed an agreement to restructure the GEF in Geneva. In the following sections, extracts from the Instrument are presented in italics.

THE NEW GOVERNANCE STRUCTURE

The Governing Council

The Council shall be responsible for developing, adopting and evaluating the operational policies and programs for GEF-financed activities ... in conformity with the policies, program priorities and eligibility criteria decided by the [governing bodies of the] *Conventions … The Council shall consist of 32 Members, representing constituency groupings … taking into account the need for balanced and equitable representation of all Participants and giving due weight to the funding efforts of all donors. There shall be 16 Members from developing countries, 14 Members from developed countries and 2 Members from the countries of central and eastern Europe and the former Soviet Union.*

Since 1995 Council members have met twice a year,[10] usually at the 'seat of the Secretariat' (that is, the World Bank headquarters in Washington DC). For three days the members and their advisors discuss and approve projects, policies, work programmes, budgets and annual reports mostly prepared by their Secretariat. They also listen to reports from the Conventions, the STAP and the three agencies (the World Bank, UNDP and UNEP) that plan and implement the GEF's actual spending.

Council members include officials mostly from ministries of foreign affairs, environment and finance: sometimes with opposite views even if they come from the same part of the world (interview, UNDP, 1997). For some, this diversity is a bonus, contributing to the GEF's mission to straddle the worlds of environment and finance, for others, it is a hindrance to effective communication and therefore to progress.

Each member of the Council has an 'alternate' who can attend the meeting in their place, and each can be accompanied by two advisors – although as we shall see below, certain countries seem to have been allowed to flout such rules. Large donors, notably the G7 governments, each have their own Council member, while smaller donors like the Nordic and most recipient governments have grouped themselves into constituencies, each represented with one seat on the Council.[11] Constituency representatives are expected to bring the views of all member countries to bear in their contributions to Council meetings:

10. In 1995 there was so much for the Council to do – preparing the Operational Strategy, sorting out its relations with the Conventions and of course approving projects – that it met four times.
11. A deadline of May 1994 was set for the negotiation of these groups, but with new countries coming on board the GEF all the time, the process still continues.

Each Member of the Council shall cast the votes of the Participant or Participants he/she represents. A Member of the Council appointed by a group of Participants may cast separately the votes of each Participant in the constituency he/she represents.

A few years after this arrangement was agreed, governments with active ministries and strong regional links – for example, South East Asia, East Africa and a Central European group of countries that included both donor and recipient nations – generally found their constituencies working well together (interviews, 1997). Other constituencies, however, lacked sufficient resources or interest in the GEF to consult effectively. In these circumstances, particularly smaller and poorer governments would leave GEF business in the hands of the one government with a representative funded to attend Council meetings.[12] Some constituencies did not even meet at all until the 1998 Participants' Assembly in Delhi, and the Iranian representative, (one of the most environmentally passionate people I interviewed in the GEF system in 1997) remained alone in his constituency.

As part of the deal with Southern governments, GEF Council meetings are co-chaired by Mohamed El-Ashry[13] and an 'elected chairperson': a Council member elected for one meeting, alternately from amongst recipient and donor members, by the Council membership.[14] Decisions are taken by consensus, avoiding the divisiveness of holding a vote,[15] but

if, in the consideration of any matter of substance ... no consensus appears attainable, any member of the Council may require a formal vote ... taken by a double weighted majority, that is, an affirmative vote representing both a 60 percent majority of the total number of Participants and a 60 percent majority of the total contributions.

12. Although representatives of other participant countries were allowed to observe the meetings, the GEF paid the fares only of Council members.
13. Mohamed El-Ashry was appointed CEO of the GEF Secretariat as well as chairman of the GEF at the first Council meeting in Washington DC, July 1994.
14. It was not clear where former communist states come in the alternating Council co-chairs arrangement; by 1998 no chair had yet been selected from this region.
15. El-Ashry's Opening Remarks on Decision-Making in the Restructured GEF, Beijing, 1993.

GEF Council seating arrangements are officially 'non-political', with members seated alphabetically by name around a long table headed by the co-chairs and senior members of the GEF Secretariat. Advisors in their delegations sit behind Council members. Behind them, staff of the Implementing Agencies sit along one wall, and along the other are a video crew, representatives from the Conventions' secretariats, the chairman of the STAP and, in the corner furthest from the chairs, up to five NGO people. Anyone wishing to speak can attract the chairs' attention by upending the folded name card on the desk in front of them.

The Council depends on the CEO and Secretariat to handle arrangements and manage the agenda for meetings, making sure that 'politics' raises its ugly head as little as possible. The Council is thus able to spend most of its time on approving the Secretariat's technical work, though as one Southern Council member observed, 'technical people must understand that politicians make decisions, and there it is' (interview, 1997).

With the help of the Secretariat, during the mid 1990s the operations of the Council became gradually more 'business-like'. According to some (Northern) participants it became more 'boring' as a result, yet for others

> The Council's consensus practice is strange. Perception counts for a lot. You can see that there is a lot going on under the table, voices that drive things in a way that's not transparent so not good. It's possible to feel an undertow when information is couched in vagueness. (interview, World Bank, 1997)

Inevitably, consensus had to be based around what is politically acceptable to important governments, and discussions in Council were often dominated by donor members – not least the UK and German representatives who often cooperated (and were for many years seated next to each other due to the alphabetical proximity of their names). As one observer noted,

> the balance of power on the Council is similar to that in the World Bank, but personalities are the most important thing. For example the German, Mauritanian and Caribbean representatives use their strong personalities to have impact way out of proportion to their power bases, which for the latter two are tiny. (interview, CBD secretariat, 1997)

By contrast, the US delegation's influence was less personal. Council rules stated that only members or their alternates had authority to represent a government; but the US was often represented by a shifting population of civil servants, mostly from the State Department and Treasury, several of whom spoke for the US in the course of a single GEF Council meeting.[16]

The Power of the Chair

No vote took place in the GEF Council during the 1990s, despite the trouble taken to negotiate a hybrid of the UN's 'one country, one vote' and the Bretton Woods institutions' 'one dollar, one vote' arrangements. This reliance on consensus implied a *de facto* veto for any member confident enough to step out of line and break the spell of North–South 'cooperation' in the GEF – unlikely since El-Ashry has been an expert manager of the GEF Council's trickiest moments,[17] always seeking the lowest common denominator (interview, NGO, 1997). As a Southern Council member observed in 1999, 'He is a very powerful person, who directs and guides the work

16. The US delegation's selective exemption from GEF rules became clear when a US representative persuaded the GEF Secretariat's secretarial staff to pass around a text which the US had prepared in the style of Secretariat drafts for Council decision. As a US proposal, it did not have the status of an official Council document. When Southern members protested the impropriety, El-Ashry took responsibility and claimed that it was a 'Secretariat mistake' – even though his staff had only passed the document around under pressure.
17. The elected Chair conducts deliberations on the following matters:

- *ensure* [regular monitoring and evaluation];
- *relations with the Conferences of the Parties to the Conventions ... including ... receipt of guidance and recommendations ... and ... reporting to them;*
- *appoint the CEO ... oversee the work of the Secretariat, and assign specific tasks and responsibilities to the Secretariat;*
- *review and approve the administrative budget of the GEF and arrange for periodic ... audits;*
- *approve an annual report and keep the UN Commission on Sustainable Development apprised of its activities.*

Meanwhile El-Ashry was to chair sessions where the Council would:

- *keep under review* [GEF's] *purposes, scope and objectives;*
- *review and approve the work program ... monitor and evaluate progress in implementation ... and provide related guidance to the Secretariat, the Implementing Agencies and other bodies;*

of GEF' (quoted in Howitt and Young, 2000). And in El-Ashry's own words:

> I have worked in the field for 30 years and know all about the realities of working with existing agencies ... [With the GEF] I learned how to get things done under very difficult circumstances, how to get people to set politics aside and get things done ... I have been presenting and delivering answers, becoming a negotiator with no experience. For example in the restructuring I learned the importance of ... factoring in the various views. Efficiency is not just about taking the smallest amount of time to decide; there is the need to get governments and all other interested parties in to ensure their ownership. (interview, El-Ashry, 1997)

El-Ashry's 'smooth operations' in the Council (interview, CBD secretariat, 1997) have been of great value to donors needing a body able to inspire support, move fast, and not be held to ransom by hours of the political speeches common in the UN system. The Rules of Procedure for the GEF Council (produced in late 1994) made clear how important his chairing role was to be. Besides having responsibility for calling Council meetings 'after consultation with Council members', it was up to the CEO (or four Council members) to request private 'executive sessions' – of only Council members, alternates and the CEO (or his representative). The Rules also stated that 'debate shall be confined to the question before the Council, and the Chair may call a speaker to order if his/her remarks are not relevant to the subject under discussion', but omit the phrase (present in a previous draft): 'the chair shall call upon speakers in the order in which they signify their desire to speak'. This may seem like a small point, but as anyone knows who has sat in a meeting with a vital point to make and a chair who seems to studiously

---

- *direct the utilization of GEF funds* ... [and] *cooperate with the Trustee to mobilize financial resources;*
- *approve and periodically review* ... *project selection* ... *project preparation and execution* ... *additional eligibility and other financing criteria* ... *the project cycle, and the mandate, composition and role of STAP;*
- *ensure that GEF-financed activities* ... *conform with the policies, program priorities and eligibility criteria decided by the COPs.*

The elected Chairperson and the CEO were jointly to:

- *keep under review* [GEF's] *purposes, scope and objectives.*

ignore them or decides that their point is irrelevant, it can effectively shape the outcome of a meeting.[18]

The restructured GEF is formally committed by its Instrument to transparency and democracy as well as efficiency and effectiveness in its operations, but in practice El-Ashry has preferred to work with 'elites', whom he can 'more easily control' away from prying eyes (interview, GEF Secretariat, 1998).[19] The Earth Negotiations Bulletin was, for instance, not allowed in to cover the meetings of the GEF Council. No official minutes have been kept – though Secretariat staff compile their own for 'internal use' (interview, GEF Secretariat, 1997). The chairman and the temporary co-chair together produce a two-to-three page Joint Summary of the Chairs at the end of each meeting, but this could hardly cover all the agreements reached, let alone the reservations expressed and discussions resulting. The Secretariat keeps video and sound recordings (of patchy quality) for use only in their offices, but 'who has time to sit through three days worth of videos?' as one World Bank economist asked. This interviewee continued:

> The Council makes decisions, one human sums them up, and a minuscule proportion of what is said in the Council reaches the Joint Summary of the Chairs. The GEF Council is so slender in its recording, I've had terrible experiences trying to keep tabs on what's happened. Transparent reporting would suit a lot of people. By contrast, transcripts of World Bank Board meetings are available within the Bank, setting out individual statements by Board members, which is useful for people working under their instructions. (interview, World Bank, 1997)

But then El-Ashry was appointed to run a more fragile organisation than the Bank, so avoided close and independent scrutiny where

18. For example, during a tricky session at the November 1997 Council meeting, donor members were having difficulty holding off a barrage of Southern concern about the incremental costs criterion not being 'in line with national priorities'. An NGO intervention on the issue held the risk of complicating matters further, and despite their clear and continuous requests, El-Ashry did not call the NGOs to speak.
19. While shooting in 1998 for a documentary about the GEF, *Suits and Savages*, El-Ashry told us that we could not film a Council meeting because the members had decided not to allow observers to record their deliberations (pers. comm., 1998). Yet three Council members independently told me that, on the contrary, they wanted their meetings to be as open as possible (see Appendix IV).

possible. He has, however, allowed a selection of environmental NGOs to observe and comment on much of what was said and done in the Council.

NGOs Creating Political Space

We saw in earlier chapters how the GEF's political support base lay not only in its establishing governments and administering agencies, but also in the myriad of organisations able or hoping to access the GEF's agenda and largesse. For many NGOs, the role of the World Bank, the complexity of GEF requirements and the potential for its cash to be used to co-opt them was sufficient reason to leave well alone; but others, especially those with the ear of the US Congress, pushed hard for greater NGO involvement in GEF meetings, policy and projects.

The logic of these NGOs' position is that the GEF remained malleable to some extent, and to be useful it simply needed more good people with access to the levers of finance and policy. Through their attention to the pilot phase and restructuring, NGOs developed links with donor governments and the World Bank and carved out political space for their own 'civil society' inputs that was unprecedented in a Bretton Woods' institution. As one Northern Council member put it, 'NGOs are in the family now, not on the streets as they were three years ago' (interview, 1997).

The process through which this integration took place was initially long and drawn out, involving sustained pressure for greater openness and access through private meetings backed up by public critiques and campaigns. Yet when change did come, the concomitant shift in advertised NGO perspectives could be sudden. In 1995, when the 50 Years is Enough alliance for the abolition of the World Bank was at its peak, a coalition of green groups including Friends of the Earth and Greenpeace condemned the GEF as 'dysfunctional, undemocratic and unaccountable'; a few months later, after grants had been pledged to several of the signatory groups, a new coalition acknowledged that the GEF was 'essential to solving critical environmental problems' (Sheehan, 1998).

Since the restructured GEF got underway in 1995, the GEF's unique openness to NGOs has allowed interested parties (including academic institutions and business interests – if the GEF Secretariat 'accredits' them as legitimately interested in the global environment) to observe and comment in Council meetings as well as to apply to run certain types of projects.[20] A 'voluntary fund' raised from donor governments and adminstered by the World Bank as GEF Trustee,[21] has covered the costs of regional NGO consultations and for six Southern NGO representatives to travel to attend Council meetings alongside their better-resourced Northern colleagues.[22] It is not clear how individuals or organisations have been selected for this support, but at least one of those invited was emphatic that they 'would not want to be rude' to their hosts by arguing with the GEF's terms or bringing along extra uninvited colleagues (interview, NGO, 1997).

Every Council meeting is also now preceded by an NGO consultation, co-ordinated by the active members of the network of NGOs interested in the GEF but chaired as a rule by someone from the Secretariat.[23] About 60–90 people came along from the start, including Secretariat and Implementing Agency staff, a few Council members and representatives of 40–50 NGOs (interview, NGO, 1997). Most of those regularly involved have been big Washington DC-based environmental groups like the World Resources Institute, the World Conservation Union, The Nature Conservancy and the World Wide Fund for Nature – as well as the Southern groups brought along with their help or that channelled through the GEF Secretariat.

NGOs Collaborating

Initially these NGOs mounted a sustained critique of the World Bank's role, the GEF's opaque and complex procedures, and particularly the lack of participation by local people and NGOs in project preparation and implementation. Latterly the critique has become more constructive, for example focused more on adding insights to

---

20. Five NGOs may sit in the meeting room at any one time and five observe via closed circuit TV from a nearby room. Though usually collaborative, the distribution of the requisite badges for each session of the Council among NGOs from around the world and across political spectra can become a source of tension.
21. Guidelines for Management of the GEF Voluntary Fund, GEF/C.5/11, 18–20 July 1995.
22. Visiting NGOs had their air fares and (smart) hotel bills paid, and received *per diem* expenses for their time in Washington DC of a sum way above what most of them were used to.
23. Initially NGO consultations were chaired by Ian Johnson, GEF administrator, and later by the Secretariat's head of external relations, Hutton Archer.

policy drafts and suggesting areas deserving of GEF funding. Never-theless one Eastern European NGO attended the Council consultations simply to ensure that the GEF did not 'make anything worse' (interview, NGO, 1997), and others declared that they still had to have low hopes for the GEF so as not to conclude that it 'stinks' (interview, NGO, 1997).

With the access thus won, some joked that they might use the GEF as a 'global Che Guevara pork barrel fund' (interview, NGO, 1997), channelling funds for 'globally' valuable projects to support grass-roots environmental needs in the South – including groups too politically challenging for GEF Implementing Agencies to finance directly. Focal points in the emerging network of NGOs interested in the GEF aimed to function to some extent as nodes, pointing GEF resources to deserving local initiatives and grass-roots groups while transmitting ideas and concerns from these levels back to the GEF. In Fox and Brown's (1998) terms, they adopted a 'sandwich strategy': gaining information and a degree of legitimacy from their partners in the South, and creating pressure for institutional reform through the Northern government representatives effectively controlling the GEF.

Meanwhile, from the point of view of the GEF Secretariat,

> NGOs are used as a sounding board for the GEF: if they say that nothing's wrong then they are not doing their job. They are like opposition parties, and can have a positive role ... however this is not always the case, and they are going to lose their advantages if they squabble. (interview, 1997)

Squabbling was not unlikely, not least since in many Southern com-munities, hostile to the World Bank and IMF, some suspected that while the Bank 'deals the cards and calls the shots', the GEF 'has no ear to hear' serious critique of the way it works: 'if David ever did tame Goliath, it was by using a sling shot ... not by sitting with him to discuss reform at workshops whose content was first cleared at 1818 H Street, Washington'.[24] In this context a degree of consensus seems to have emerged in the 'complex, multi-faceted and often divided community' (Conca, 1996) of NGOs that were represented in GEF consultations: that those unwilling to 'play the game' con-

24. E-mail message from Bittu Sahgal, 1998. 1818 H Street is the address of the World Bank's headquarters.

structively and be as 'businesslike' as GEF processes demand should leave the field clear for more reform-minded activists to engage.

So NGOs generally made every effort to maintain a united front when pushing home their key messages to the GEF Council. Yet still they could not always agree:

> The main fights in the GEF–NGO consultations have been North vs South over climate change (what particular energy forms should be promoted and how fast fossil fuels should be phased out), ozone, 'sustainable use' of biodiversity vs the Northern animal rights contingent, who will not accept that animals should be exploited at all; also the role of the private sector. (interview, NGO, 1997)

There was also some resentment on the part of smaller, more radical and especially Southern-based NGOs of better-resourced groups 'in the loop' with the World Bank – not least the IUCN, a central focal point to the GEF–NGO network and in places so closely tied to governmental institutions as to hardly even be an NGO.

Achim Steiner of the IUCN, who has been credited with getting the GEF–NGO network organised, described it as the 'prototype of self-organised networks of NGOs on no money' (interview, 1997). The network developed around up to 13 regional focal points (RFPs) who mostly 'fell into' the job or were 'in the right place at the right time' (pers. comm., 1998). Some members of this adhocracy were more dynamic than others; all were supposed to feed and propagate a GEF–NGO newsletter and official policy documents, to spread information regarding GEF job vacancies, and to feed back news and views from other NGOs and community groups in their region.

One RFP was keen to stress that they were 'not GEF's representatives on Earth' (interview, NGO, 1997). Indeed, using their own resources to publicise and help the GEF deal with challenging issues, many Southern NGOs found the work involved quite hard to justify for the amount of interest and/or funding they received in return. Some therefore felt that the network needed funding from donor governments – though ideally not through the GEF itself. A proposal for official aid funding for the network, in development for several years, seems to have foundered in the late 1990s on the question of what exactly any money should be for, after network members ended up calling on the GEF Secretariat and wider family for advice.

After their initial push for political space, many seem to have ended up following the GEF's agenda, in pursuit of funds and favours, as much as they set it, as a result of which the critical edge that a more independent strategy might have sustained was largely lost. One occasion where NGOs sought to be credible and collaborative, perhaps at the expense of their distinctive voice, was the GEF's first full Participants' Assembly held in 1998.

The Participants' Assembly

The Assembly shall ... elect its Chairperson from among the Representatives; review the general policies of the Facility; review and evaluate the operation of the Facility on the basis of reports submitted by the Council; keep under review the membership of the Facility; and consider, for approval by consensus, amendments to the present Instrument on the basis of recommendations by the Council.

The Participants' Assembly brings together all the GEF's member governments with the Implementing Agencies running its projects and representatives of the various Conventions supposed to guide them, as well as numerous other experts and official representatives. The first Participants' Assembly was hosted by the Indian government in 1998, partly as a showcase for both the GEF and the Indians' environmental achievements. However, due to various other international meetings being held at the same time, other than Indians only one government minister (Danish) attended. When it came to the speeches (of which there were many), any interventions needed to be arranged in advance, so there was little opportunity for feedback or responses to contributions. The Algerian delegate was apparently alone in raising a question (in French) about the authority of the Assembly to make changes in the Instrument, ostensibly receiving no official response.

The Assembly produced a 'New Delhi Statement' reiterating the importance of the GEF and of making it more flexible, transparent, consistent with national priorities and catalytic of other funds. In reality however, as one World Bank lawyer observed, there seemed little purpose to the Assembly beyond fulfilling the Instrument, with 'all these official delegations milling around not really knowing why they are here or what to do' while key actors held workshops and cut deals informally. Providing 'bureaucratic tourism' for national delegations, others called it a 'bureaucratic jamboree' (interview, NGO, 1998), and there was a general feeling among attendees that the

Assembly was a waste of time and money: 'fiddling while Rome burns' was said more than once, and with massive forest fires linked to El Nino then underway, some substituted 'the Amazon' for 'Rome'.

Perhaps the event could be compared to a 'ritual dance' – a public performance promoting a tribe's spirit (Page, 1972) – or a 'potlatch' – an indigenous American tradition where hard-earned resources are used up in pursuit of prestige.

Initially NGOs critical of the GEF planned a Civil Society Conference parallel to the Assembly, on the model of counter-summits held parallel to World Bank meetings from the late 1980s, the Other Economic Summits held in parallel with G7 economic summits and the NGO presence in Rio, 1992. But Mohamed El-Ashry told the NGOs' co-ordinator in Delhi that since 'NGOs have a full seat at the table now', represented in many government delegations[25] and speaking in official meetings, there was no need for them to sit apart. In the end there was a room set aside for NGOs within the Assembly compound, but it was hidden round the back of the building and only a few meetings held there attracted much of an audience.

Prior to the first Participants' Assembly one NGO wondered what formal role there would be in the Assembly for government officials involved in the Conventions but not in the GEF (unlike, for example, the UK and German and a few Southern representatives who had been involved in both). A member of Secretariat staff noted that there had been 'quite some discussion' on this issue but they were 'constrained by guidelines' which said that these officials, mostly from environment departments, would have to go through their national focal points to engage with their governments' representatives to the GEF. While this approach might conceivably encourage valuable co-ordination at a national level, it also meant that the Conventions had few outspoken official advocates to argue their case at the Assembly. In mitigation, the Secretariat representative told the NGO that 'a lot can be done through informal channels'.

However, it was not just the Conventions who felt shut out – the GEF's three Implementing Agencies found themselves 'banished' to running institutional stands in a long tent (known as the shed) outside the main building. An interviewee from the World Bank said the Implementing Agencies were 'not happy with the minor role we've been allotted. GEF is not meant to be its own institution and

25. For example, the Swiss Coalition of Development Organisations was represented in the Swiss delegation.

yet we are out in the shed, not running anything in particular beyond a few workshops' (pers. comm., 1998). On occasion, the GEF Secretariat's arrangements for these meetings, where policies were reviewed and priorities elaborated, seem to have kept weaker countries' interests from being dealt with effectively: for example, ensuring that the issue of land degradation was not allowed to rise up the Assembly's agenda.

Governments involved in the emerging Convention to Combat Desertification had suggested the GEF as financial mechanism, and primarily African representatives led a strong campaign at the Assembly (also through the STAP) for the GEF to formally take on land degradation as a new focal area. However, this environmental issue was not a priority for donor governments nor even most of the G77 bloc, because it affected mostly a few, poorer countries, many in Africa, whose governments were less influential than the key G77 players of Brazil, Colombia, Argentina, India, Malaysia etc. Having already agreed to finance land degradation issues as they 'relate' to climate change, biodiversity and so on, donors felt the GEF had enough to do as it was, and emphasised the importance of sticking to the existing four focal areas.

Can it be coincidence that a workshop on land degradation at the Assembly was largely taken up with a film on the issues, with the result that the speeches were only just finished when Secretariat staff moved everyone out for the next meeting – leaving no time for discussion, let alone conclusions to be reached? By contrast, discussions in workshops of more interest to donor ministries (for example 'Mainstreaming in World Bank Operations') featured no films but discussions went over time and produced action proposals – many of them preprepared, it seemed, largely on the basis of suggestions from the donor agencies. Overall, the 1998 Participants' Assembly seems to have been effectively stage-managed by the Secretariat, which decamped *en masse* to India for the duration. For all its limitations, the Secretariat was emerging as a highly influential institution and key member of the GEF 'family'.

THE NEW OPERATIONAL STRUCTURE

The Secretariat

[The Secretariat shall] *service and report to the Assembly and the Council ... headed by the CEO/Chairperson of the Facility ... Supported administratively by the World Bank* [it] *shall operate in a functionally independent and effective manner ... [and shall] coordinate the formulation and oversee the implementation of ... the joint work program, ensuring liaison with other bodies as required ... [It shall] ensure the implementation of ... operational policies ... including ... consultation with and participation of local communities and other interested parties, monitoring ... implementation and evaluation of ... results ... [and] ensure the effective execution of the Council's decisions and ... facilitate coordination and collaboration among the Implementing Agencies.*

Overseen by El-Ashry, the Secretariat serves the Council, preparing policies and liaising with the Implementing Agencies, Convention secretariats, NGOs and other interested parties. 'At the centre of a wheel with many spokes' (interview, GEF Secretariat, 1998), its central task is balancing the political needs of the major interests in the GEF. It could be said that the GEF Secretariat has many masters: not just the Council and the Participants' Assembly but the World Bank, the governing bodies of the Conventions for which the GEF is financial mechanism, the UN Implementing Agencies and also, to a lesser extent, the NGOs and others whose support helps secure GEF replenishments from donor governments.

Despite its formal independence, the GEF Secretariat remains hosted by the Bank – they share addresses, both physical and electronic.[26] The World Bank personnel office deals with GEF staff contracts and GEF salaries are paid by the Bank. Staff also move regularly from one side of the road to the other. At international meetings, Secretariat staff have tended to be seen and treated as World Bank people – not least because since the GEF lacks legal institutional status, the World Bank's name appeared on their badges.[27]

26. The Secretariat is based in World Bank offices in a building across the road from the main Bank headquarters at 1818 H Street. Its e-mail addresses are all at <www.worldbank.org>.

27. One senior participant in inter-institutional politics pointed to the messages transmitted by institutional logos: symbols to reflect the roots and values of an organisation. He mentioned how the CBD secretariat established its independence from the UNEP when it moved to Montreal with a new logo that bore no relation to the UNEP's. In the GEF's early years, documents bore no logo at all or were identified as outputs of the World Bank – whose logo is a circle representing the globe, divided up by a grid. After the GEF gained notional independence from the Bank, it ran a competition for a distinctive icon to establish its new identity. The logo chosen was another 'globe', stylised similarly to that of the World Bank, but 'spun' with a faintly organic swirl.

Although in the euphoria of the UNCED, governments' calls had been for 'no new institutions', the GEF Secretariat was soon 30 strong. It is staffed by lawyers, technical experts, economists and civil servants, as well as public relations and secretarial staff. Observers have therefore concluded that the Secretariat is 'in fact a new institution, whatever the rhetoric' (interview, CBD secretariat and UNDP, 1997). One member of its staff observed: 'By comparison with the World Bank, the Secretariat has a very flat hierarchy and informal working arrangements. It is young and will have to institutionalise, but it would be great if it can keep this adaptable structure' (interview, GEF Secretariat, 1997).

From the perspective of the parts of the World Bank expected to work with the Secretariat however,

> The problems with the Secretariat are that it is too big, has no clear management, they don't seem to talk to each other, they always tell the Implementing Agencies when they do things wrong but never when they do things right, and they have public explosions. (interview, World Bank, 1997)

Explosions were likely given the tension between the divergent goals and limited powers given to the GEF. A Council member suggested the Secretariat had grown larger than staff of the Implementing Agencies might like because 'It is essential that the GEF Secretariat be strong to put GEF on an even keel with regard to the Implementing Agencies; to the World Bank especially' (interview, 1997). And a member of the CBD secretariat staff concurred: 'The GEF Secretariat needs to be larger to enable it to cope with the Implementing Agencies and the pre-eminence of their own procedures in their GEF operations' (interview, 1997). Mohamed El-Ashry almost certainly agreed, but was afraid of seeming to be 'empire building', not least since some in the World Bank, which pays his wages, felt that the Secretariat's 'power tends to breed over enthusiasm to control and direct' (interview, World Bank, 1997). The Secretariat was therefore expanded quietly and on the cheap through secondments of staff from donor governments – part of a 'sophisticated bureaucratic game' (interview, GEF Secretariat, 1997) that put about ten extra professionals in the Secretariat by 1997 without tapping GEF budgets to pay for them.

The Secretariat's staff soon represented every continent, if not region, of the world. Besides people who had formerly worked directly for the World Bank, many were civil servants from national governments or less well-paid UN institutions. For them GEF work could be a step up: globetrotting from Washington DC with World Bank remuneration levels was more appealing for some than the bureaucracies of Delhi, Beijing or Nairobi. Some of these staff provided practical points of contact for governments from their home region, reflecting a pattern common throughout the Bretton Woods and especially UN systems. One (South East Asian) Council member told a colleague in 1997 that 'sadly, we don't have anybody in the Secretariat', but that it was not so bad since they could at least liaise with someone from a neighbouring (friendly) country.[28]

One Secretariat staff member came directly from the interim CBD secretariat before its move to Montreal under Calestous Juma with an almost entirely new staff.[29] Others brought skills, contacts and perhaps some prejudices from earlier work with research institutes, NGOs and elsewhere. One of these said 'I wanted to be closer to the implementation rather than just pontificating in an ideal world. I wanted to try working in the "real world" once in my career' (interview, GEF Secretariat, 1997). For another, work in the Secretariat was a shock:

> I was used to the politics of conservation from a scientific point of view in a big conservation NGO, now I have to get used to it from a political point of view, which is very different, with lawyers telling people what to do ... This is a new way of doing business ... unfortunately [scientists] can't dictate to people what to do in democracies. (interview, GEF Secretariat, 1997)

Secretariat staff had first of all to respond to their legal and political obligations. As an employee of the World Bank, one GEF Secretariat member said he was a 'minor functionary', a mere servant of governments; another felt like 'a soldier in a very large army'. From the UNDP's point of view meanwhile the Secretariat's public pronouncements seemed sometimes to stray so far from reality that 'the Secretariat is a propaganda machine'. Certainly their communication with the outside world took the form mostly of either

28. Overheard during a GEF Council lunch, 1997.
29. Everybody I asked was unwilling to speak about this abrupt change of location and staff. It clearly caused a lot of resentment and may have been bound up in the CBD's efforts to distance itself from the UNEP at a time when the latter was not in favour with donors.

insubstantial publications and corporate videos[30] or complex legalistic reports and targetted information dissemination. Much of the practical publicity work to raise awareness of and interest in actual GEF projects meanwhile was left up to the Implementing Agencies in whose hands the GEF's actual spending lay.

Implementing Agencies – the World Bank, UNDP and UNEP

The GEF shall operate, on the basis of collaboration and partnership among the Implementing Agencies … The Implementing Agencies of the GEF shall be UNDP, UNEP, and the World Bank. The Implementing Agencies shall be accountable to the Council for their GEF-financed activities.

Since the restructuring in 1994, there have been about 20 people administering GEF projects in both the World Bank and the UNDP, and ten or so in the UNEP.[31] Some suggested that it could have been more efficient to bring all three specialised units into the Secretariat, unashamedly creating a new institution, but there were 'conflicting objectives: efficiency is wanted, the responsibility for creating it is not wanted' according to a member of the GEF Secretariat (interview, 1997). From the UNEP, meanwhile, people wondered whether anyone had 'ever calculated the price of working with existing institutions' (interview, 1998).

As Maurice Strong put it in 2000, 'in principle the partners are equal, but the World Bank obviously carries the most weight'. Spending well over half of GEF funds, the World Bank remained the central player in the GEF even after the restructuring ostensibly reduced its influence. The Bank's status was also enhanced by being Trustee of the GEF's money, for which task it

shall serve in a fiduciary and administrative capacity, and shall be bound by its Articles of Agreement, By-Laws, rules and decisions.

---

30. For example, *Keeping the Promise* (GEF and TVE, 1998), featuring Harrison Ford, looking wooden in front of the (biodiverse) rainforest featured in the *Star Wars* movie.
31. The UNEP had only one representative in Washington DC whose job was 'exciting but difficult', with his boss 10,000 miles away. (He later went to work for the World Bank.)

The Trustee receives and holds governments' GEF contributions in a special account. 'Fiduciary' duty means that while in the Bank's care, GEF money is invested on the international money markets to maximise its value – with no special environmental restrictions – until it is time to release it 'in accordance' with requirements of the GEF Council and Instrument. As a lawyer in the Secretariat put it,

> Together with the governance structure of the Council and Assembly … the core legal structure is that of a trust fund. Naming the Bank as Trustee meant that the Bank is the institution legally responsible for the funds and as such the Bank governing board is legally the body with the authority to approve the trust fund. (pers. comm., 1999)

The Bank's Board is responsible for initiating and authorising GEF replenishments at the Council's request, and also for certifying that disbursements are used in accordance with overall objectives of the GEF as set out in its founding agreements. Translated, all this seems to mean that no payment can be made by the GEF, even for a project planned and run through one of the UN agencies from start to finish, unless the World Bank approves it. People working for the World Bank also wield power due to their experience and credentials as experts – even executive directors on the Bank's governing board found it hard to challenge those working 'in the field' (interview, World Bank, 1997).

The World Bank's role as Trustee of GEF funds was managed by a Financial Management Unit in a different department of the Bank from the Global Environment Co-ordination Unit running GEF projects, with a 'Chinese wall' between them. From the GEF Secretariat we heard that the World Bank has been 'very careful to keep these two roles separate' (pers. comm., 1999). Yet with the Bank's precedence in GEF project activities complemented by its potential veto on other agencies' GEF spending, it was certainly the dominant institution in the GEF 'family'.

Responsible for promoting sustainable development through capacity-building, the UNDP was probably brought into the GEF largely to make it more acceptable to the Southern governments mistrustful of the World Bank (interview, NGO, 1997). Donors stressed this 'development' aspect of the GEF because of the South's aversion to purely 'global' environmental goals – to the chagrin of UNEP people who were officially charged with connecting the GEF to international environmental science and scientists.

Overall, the UNEP's dedication to promoting global science does not gel well with the World Bank's economistic, or even the UNDP's more country-level, developmental perspectives. With their country offices worldwide and interests in regional development, the agendas of these dominant Implementing Agencies have 'blurred' the UNEP's scientific priorities for the GEF. Geographically and politically isolated, even 'a sinking ship' (interview, UNDP, 1997), the UNEP did not initially invest a great deal of attention in the GEF, and was further marginalised by other institutions' growing interest in environmental funds. The GEF Secretariat, despite being 'cut off from' global science networks, has sought to keep control of strategic processes itself (interview, UNEP, 1998). The main means by which the UNEP had hoped to connect GEF operations to the needs of global science was through its Scientific and Technical Advisory Panel (STAP).

Scientific, Technical and Strategic Advice

> UNEP shall establish, in consultation with UNDP and the World Bank and on the basis of guidelines and criteria established by the Council, the STAP as an advisory body to the Facility. UNEP shall provide the STAP's Secretariat and shall operate as the liaison between the Facility and the STAP.

The STAP is a panel of twelve respected scientists from around the world,[32] through which the UNEP aimed to translate the insights of global science into policy proposals for the strategic guidance of GEF resources. Meeting a few times a year, the STAP has helped to develop operational programmes, and, where requested by the GEF Secretariat, to translate the Conventions' guidance into something comprehensible and usable by project managers.

Yet some felt that the GEF Council and especially the Secretariat 'select where to listen' to the STAP (interview, scientist, 1997), and as a donor Council member put it, 'the STAP is not crucial to the GEF' (interview, Northern Council member, 1997). Projects were

---

32. Among them Britishers like John Woods, professor at Imperial College with expertise in international waters, David Pearce, professor of environmental economics from CSERGE, and Bob Watson, chairman of the IPCC and later head of the environment department in the World Bank.

designed with assistance from the World Bank or UNDP's own technical experts, and not only was the STAP not always given the resources to do the job asked of it by the Council,[33] but it lacked the authority to make demands. Both the pilot phase STAP and GEF-1's panel were slow in setting up and getting underway, so their policy work was often too late, even if it was relevant. By their own admission, the STAP was sometimes slow to respond to Council requests, and by the time their input arrived, the Council or Secretariat could have forgotten what they had asked for in the first place (interview, STAP, 1997). Finally, even where their comments were relevant and timely, the Implementing Agencies' revised project proposals rarely indicated how, where or even whether STAP advice had been integrated.

A place on the STAP may not offer much influence in shaping the GEF nor bring funding directly to an institution, but can provide international travel and a feather in a scientist's cap, as well as the chance to promote specific fields as targets for GEF funding. One member said they chose to review projects that were not in their exact field of expertise so as to learn about something new (interview, 1996). In more recent years the STAP's status has improved somewhat, partly perhaps since it is fairly technical by comparison with the more politicised advisory body of the CBD – where members represent countries as much as particular forms of expertise.

While Southern governments and NGOs wanted more use of experts with local knowledge (see Chapter 5), some Council members stressed the need for the STAP to know about 'social and cultural issues'. The US in particular requested that STAP membership should comprise more diverse expertise, notably from 'business', to help the GEF work more effectively with the private sector. In the early days of the STAP, some felt that an environmental lawyer and an environmental economist provided more valuable inputs than the natural scientists represented.[34]

More strategic than the STAP has been the GEF's private and strategic Senior Advisory Panel. Where the advice offered by STAP was

33. Report of the fourth meeting of STAP, Nairobi, February 1996.
34. Ken Piddington, a former vice president of the environment in the World Bank, told an Aberdeen conference in 1992 that the STAP was of value primarily because of the presence of an environmental lawyer and David Pearce, the influential UK environmental economist from CSERGE (internal memo, CSERGE, 1992).

'technical', the 13-strong SAP has provided 'policy' advice to the GEF – according to Mostafa Tolba, former head of the UNEP and 'senior' panelist.[35] The SAP is not mentioned in the GEF Instrument nor, apparently, anywhere in its official documentation. When questioned about a file on a shelf labelled 'Senior Advisory Panel', one member of GEF Secretariat staff would say only that they met annually inside the Watergate complex in Washington, coincident with the spring Council meeting, and that members were available 'privately' to provide advice by phone to the CEO, Mohamed El-Ashry.

A look at the list of individuals on the SAP shows they were mostly members of the international 'great and good' active in global resource management. A few were senior scientists (or scientific administrators), others politicians, financiers, and a couple from NGOs. They received no payment beyond expenses for their work on the Panel, which they were invited to join by the CEO.[36] They represented the major regions of the world; almost all were educated in the US if not Europe.

The Operational Strategy

Despite all the new arrangements put in place in 1994, the GEF's functions were not formalised until its new Council approved an Operational Strategy in 1995. The document was to be a

> road map to guide [the GEF's] actions and to ensure that its resources would be utilised cost-effectively to maximise global environmental benefits ... [and] to provide a framework for programmatic cohesiveness and integration among the many entities that participate in the GEF. (El-Ashry's introduction to the Operational Strategy, 1996)

The Operational Strategy was developed by the GEF Secretariat and Implementing Agencies with contributions from the STAP and in consultation with the secretariats of the Conventions to ensure it 'fully integrates the guidance' of the Conventions' governing bodies.

35. See Appendix I for biographical information on SAP members – in the absence of information about the strategic advice they offered.
36. Despite the GEF Secretariat's wariness of talking about the panel, several members freely admitted their status and responded to a brief questionnaire about their work.

Five regional consultations were held with 'thinkers and practitioners in the environment and development fields' in Europe, Africa,
Asia, North and South America. Around 50 NGOs commented on a
draft, many through the GEF's website (<www.gefweb.org>).

The publication of the Operational Strategy meant clearer priori-
tisation for spending in the focal areas, which began to reduce some
suspicion of the GEF and facilitate inter-institutional implementation. The Strategy added requirements to the promises of GEF's pilot
phase (which included additionality, incrementality, national
priorities, cost-effectiveness, flexibility, innovation etc.); newly
stressed issues were transparency or 'full disclosure of all nonconfidential material', 'consultation with, and participation as
appropriate of, the beneficiaries and affected groups of people',
performing a 'catalytic role ... leveraging additional financing from
other sources', and also to have 'programmes and projects monitored
and evaluated on a regular basis', because

> the GEF's unique mission in the global environment requires it to
> develop programs and projects whose design, although scientifi-
> cally based, may be more innovative and experimental than that
> of regular development projects, making it particularly important
> that activities be continuously tracked and results disseminated.[37]

Within ten basic Operational Principles,[38] a stream of Operational
Programs began to emerge for the four focal areas,[39] guiding
investment in freshwater ecosystems, forest conservation and so on.

37. El-Ashry's introduction to the Operational Strategy.
38. Ten Operational Principles for Development and Implementation of the
     GEF's Work Program:

     • For purposes of the financial mechanisms for the implementation of
       the Convention on Biological Diversity and the United Nations
       Framework Convention on Climate Change, the GEF will function
       under the guidance of, and be accountable to, the Conference of the
       Parties (COPs) [the governing bodies of the Conventions: made up of
       governments which have agreed to be 'Party' to their restrictions].
       For the purposes of financing activities in the focal area of ozone layer
       depletion, GEF operational policies will be consistent with those of
       the Montreal Protocol on Substances that Deplete the Ozone Layer
       and its amendments.
     • The GEF will provide new, and additional, grant and concessional
       funding to meet the agreed incremental costs of measures to achieve
       agreed global environmental benefits.

Some Southern governments represented on the Council felt that the Operational Programs were over-restrictive and needed replacing with rules allowing more of their own national priorities to be promoted, but people in the three Implementing Agencies generally found the Operational Programs useful, and one UNDP employee commented that they should have been put together earlier so that

---

- The GEF will ensure the cost-effectiveness of its activities to maximize global environmental benefits.
- The GEF will fund projects that are country-driven and based on national priorities designed to support sustainable development, as identified within the context of national programs.
- The GEF will maintain sufficient flexibility to respond to changing circumstances, including evolving guidance of the Conference of the Parties and experience gained from monitoring and evaluation activities.
- GEF projects will provide for full disclosure of all nonconfidential information.
- GEF projects will provide for consultation with, and participation as appropriate of, the beneficiaries and affected groups of people.
- GEF projects will conform to the eligibility requirements set forth in paragraph 9 of the GEF Instrument.
- In seeking to maximize global environmental benefits, the GEF will emphasize its catalytic role and leverage additional financing from other sources.
- The GEF will ensure that its programs and projects are monitored and evaluated on a regular basis.

Source: GEF Operational Strategy, 1996.

39. Initial Operational Programs
- Biodiversity: Arid and semi-arid ecosystems
- Biodiversity: Coastal, marine, and freshwater ecosystems (including wetlands)
- Biodiversity: Forest ecosystems
- Biodiversity: Mountain ecosystems
- Climate change: Removing barriers to energy conservation and energy efficiency
- Climate change: Promoting the adoption of renewable energy by removing barriers and reducing implementation costs
- Climate change: Reducing the long-term costs of low greenhouse gas-emitting energy technologies
- International waters: Waterbody-based program
- International waters: Integrated land and water Multiple Focal Area
- International waters: Contaminant-based program

Source: GEF Operational Strategy, 1996.

the GEF could have been more clearly and cooperatively run from the beginning (interview, 1997; see Chapter 6). However, another noted that as a negotiated document, the Operational Strategy 'makes no sense in English' so it is difficult to know how to use it practically (interview, UNDP, 1997).

Snapshot in the development of an Operational Program
Here follow my impressions of an informal consultation during the November 1997 Council meeting, at which discussions were held on the development of a GEF policy for investments in transport under the climate label.

Secretariat staff presented a fairly detailed proposal focused on pollution reduction through new technologies for private motorised transport – private because mass transit projects were 'too expensive', and the capital necessary to develop them unavailable. When representatives of the US Environmental Protection Agency and an NGO pointed out that large amounts of capital was in fact available for road building, and that environmentally informed land use planning would be a lot cheaper and probably more effective than buying new technologies, the Secretariat responded that cost-effectiveness was 'only one component' of the GEF's Operational Programs. Clearly put on the spot by this line of questioning, the presenters were ostensibly rescued by the chairman (the Secretariat's external relations officer) who interrupted an NGO who was asking more about the apparent preference for private motorised transport, in favour of a donor Council member (who it turned out wanted to know what an internal combustion engine was). The discussion was ended with a call for any further comments to be added to a draft posted on the internet.

Afterwards, a Southern Council member who had listened to the discussion observed that in Bangkok, for example, despite perfectly good laws, the transport situation remains terrible because of 'vested interests'. The GEF, with so little money relative to other investors and also operating at such a great distance from the ground 'can't touch' such obstacles to developing sustainable transport. A World Bank consultant later said

the Bank can never challenge the dominance of the motor car because of the fact that it is run in the service of the oil companies, and they cannot countenance change in the dominance of road transport. As a result, in the World Bank, new roads enjoy 'investments', while railways only receive 'subsidies'. (interview, 1997)[40]

THE NEW ISSUES EMERGING

Additionality and Incremental Costs

The GEF was set up to subsidise a limited range of investments with the 'additional' aid promised to Southern governments at Rio. According to the website:

> GEF funds the 'incremental' or additional costs associated with transforming a project with national benefits into one with global environmental benefits. For example, choosing solar energy technology over coal or diesel fuel meets the same national development goal (power generation), but is more costly. GEF grants cover the difference or 'increment' between a less costly, more polluting option and a costlier, more environmentally friendly option.[41]

GEF finance was therefore not intended to benefit just the countries where projects are sited. 'Baseline' costs were to be met from other sources: whether private investors, donor agencies or the recipient governments' own funds.

While the formal notion of 'global environmental benefits' originated in the GEF, the concept of 'incrementality' was taken directly from the Multilateral Fund for the Montreal Protocol. There it had been a fairly straightforward and effective method for ensuring that the Fund paid only for specific technical fixes: essentially the extra costs of replacing CFCs with ozone friendly chemicals in new manufactures. For some GEF projects under the Climate and Biodiversity Conventions (notably 'enabling activities', see Chapter 5), the entire project cost comprised incremental costs, because no action would have needed to be taken in the absence of the relevant Convention. Incremental costs have hardly been straightforward for

---

40. As evidence of the dominance of the big oil companies, he pointed to the fact that the World Bank usually insists on being the first creditor paid off by indebted countries, but had made an exception in Russia where the oil companies were paid back first.
41. <http://www.gefweb.org/Operational_Policies/Eligibility_Criteria/ Incremental_Costs/incremental_costs.html>

the GEF, not least when applied to the very complex scientific and political issues involved in conserving biodiversity and international waters. Indeed 'it is extremely difficult, many feel impossible, to distinguish in any measurable or otherwise credible way, between the global environmental benefits and domestic benefits of a biodiversity project' (RESOLVE, 1998).[42]

For climate change projects, the concept has been more readily adapted: estimating the amount of greenhouse gases (all six of those listed by the IPCC were to be treated as equivalent to carbon dioxide) not emitted as a result of the proposed activity, comparing it with a similarly hypothetical level of emissions likely to arise without GEF assistance,[43] then equating the cost of the activity with the 'amount' of climate protected. This may have resulted in farcical calculations from a scientific perspective, but, for GEF purposes, 'global environmental benefits' could thus be measured and allotted a price with which to calculate their incremental costs.

There are many arguments against the marketisation of natural value (see Chapter 5 and, for example, Shiva, 1993, McAfee, 1999). But even if commodity is accepted as a valid measure of all nature's value, the GEF's restrictions based on incremental costs calculations struck some observers as mean, perhaps disingenuous, even positively Machiavellian. McAfee (1999) noted that the

> policy is resented by Southern states and NGOs, particularly in light of the reduction in Northern development assistance since 1992 and the meager amounts of green aid offered. Many interpret the [incremental costs] policy as confirmation of the Southern suspicion that the real purposes of Northern-sponsored environmental aid and institutions are to restrict potentially-competing industrialization in the South and to assert Northern control over valuable Southern natural resources.

Desite recognising the practical as well as political difficulties that incremental costs were creating, donor Council members answerable

---

42. The GEF's twelfth Council meeting, held in October 1998, considered a report on incremental costs produced by 'RESOLVE', a Washington DC-based mediation consultancy.
43. A formal incremental costs estimation required the prior calculation of a 'baseline' – the investments which would have been made anyway – to provide a reference point for GEF financial decision-making.

to their home treasuries could not abolish this 'cornerstone of GEF financing' (intervention in November 1997 Council meeting). The GEF's pilot phase administrators had claimed the incremental cost concept 'allows for a structured dialogue between recipients and the Implementing Agencies', but with the former unconvinced, donors approved resources for consultants to 'finesse the concept forward' (pers. comm., 2001), hoping that environmental economists might come up with a paper solution to defuse building hostility to the GEF's cornerstone.

The Program for Measuring Incremental Costs for the Environment was launched in 1993 as a function of the GEF Secretariat,[44] and USAid agreed to provide another $450,000 to apply the concept specifically to the GEF's four focal areas. During 1994 the GEF Secretariat began producing a series of working papers dealing largely with the theoretical economic calculation of incremental costs, particularly for climate projects. While this process did contribute to tentative guidelines, as McAfee (1999) observed, they were useful largely insofar as

> Enforcement of the [incremental costs requirement] has brought about greater dependence by national governments and local NGOs on the GEF Implementing Agencies (mainly the World Bank and UNDP), which in turn depend on specialist consultants to calculate the 'global' and 'local' proportion of GEF project benefits. The process is giving rise to a new minor industry of [incremental costs] experts.

Meanwhile, for administrators trying to implement GEF projects with the help of this new industry, 'we could talk forever about these issues, the more you dig, the more complex the issues become' (interview, UNDP, 1997).

Chapter 5 will explore how GEF money was kept from falling too far into this indefinitely complex hole. First we turn to the conflicting agendas that remained to be resolved within the GEF family of institutions, with NGOs, and especially between the treasuries of major donors acting through the World Bank and the environ-

---

44. PRINCE employed many environmental economists with international ambitions, notably from the UK's CSERGE, whose director, David Pearce, had been environmental consultant to the World Bank and sat on the first GEF STAP.

mental interests gathered in the Conventions on Climate Change and Biodiversity.[45]

The GEF's Relationship with the Conventions

Mohamed El-Ashry called the relationship with the two big Conventions 'the axis around which the GEF must turn' (interview, 1997). However, this axis was skewed from the start, essentially because the GEF (and thus its powerful parent the World Bank) effectively holds the Conventions' purse strings, and as David Pearce (a member of the pilot GEF's STAP) noted early on, the Conventions 'are "bottom up" and focus on national benefits whereas GEF to date has been "top down" and focuses on global benefits'.[46]

Clearly anticipating a problematic relationship, in November 1992 Ian Johnson described the link with the Conventions as a 'cornerstone of the governance issues to be addressed over the next year', and promised that his administration would 'work closely' with the Conventions' secretariats. Yet within a year, the FCCC[47] Conference of the Parties was calling for more cooperation, and the UNEP requested the GEF to 'accelerate the implementation of the global Conventions ... [C]ountry studies, national strategies, and development of methodologies, identified by the Conventions' text and considered of great urgency ... could and should be financed from any remaining funds of the Pilot Phase' (UNEP statement to GEF participants' meeting, 1993).

Another part of the problem stemmed from the fact that donor governments had pacified NGOs and Southern governments at Rio in 1992 with promises of lots of new funding through a GEF restructured to be more responsive to environmental needs – which led signatories to the Conventions to expect the GEF 'to pay for everything'. As a result they all chimed in to complain when the GEF could not live up to all their expectations (interview, GEF Secretariat, 1997).

The text of the FCCC states that its 'financial mechanism' 'shall function under the guidance of and be accountable to the

---

45. The focus in this book is on the CBD, the more complex of the two major Conventions GEF served, and less well known and discussed than the FCCC of Kyoto fame.
46. Internal memo, CSERGE, January 1993.
47. Voiced by Ambassador Raul Estrada, chair of the intergovernmental negotiating committee for the FCCC.

Conference of the Parties, which shall decide on its policies, programme priorities and eligibility criteria related to this Convention'. And the CBD states:

> The mechanism shall function under the authority and guidance of, and be accountable to, the COP for the purposes of this Convention ... the COP shall determine the policy, strategy, programme priorities and eligibility criteria relating to the access to and utilization of such resources.

The language used by each body sheds an interesting light on the real relationships behind the legalese: for the Conventions, the GEF was a financial 'mechanism', while, for the GEF, the Conventions were members of an institutional 'family'. It seems that the Conventions' drafters had presumed to treat the GEF as inanimate, 'mechanically' following their guidance. By contrast, the GEF was presented as the new baby in a complex institutional 'family': in need of cherishing as it battles on behalf of the Conventions for the attention and resources of various parental authorities facing more pressing demands on their time.

Like the Climate Convention, the Convention on Biological Diversity instructed the GEF Council to promptly approve funding for their Parties to develop national surveys, plans and reports to the COPs on their conservation status and progress. But the GEF's complex internal procedures (see Chapter 5) meant funds moved slowly, and a lack of transparency about what was going on did not help endear them to the Conventions. When it came to GEF funding larger investment projects, the CBD wanted to target biodiversity 'hotspots' (in, for example, Brazil, Indonesia and Colombia) for efficient species and ecosystem conservation worldwide, regardless of who would benefit as a result (Myers, 1990). The United States Agency for International Development and most of the smaller recipient governments represented in the GEF Council preferred for all countries to receive a share of the money, regardless of how much rare biodiversity they had in their territory, because they saw conservation and capacity-building as potentially contributory to economic development. Thus wider implementation of the CBD could win broader political support than the more purely 'global' approach favoured by international environmental scientists like Myers and many of the big green NGOs like Conservation International.

Again, as so often in GEF's supposedly 'non-political' global conservation funding, 'The Facility's effort to implement a policy for prioritizing "global quality" biodiversity has run up against the political reality that the GEF and the CBD are organizations of states, not of scientists' (McAfee, 1999). In this context, most observers blamed ongoing inter-institutional tensions on the GEF Council's failure – or inability – to implement the Conventions' instructions in their entirety.

Operationalising Guidance

Faced with a fund they had not chosen guided by an agenda not all governments supported, the Conferences of the Parties[48] to both the Conventions produced ever more guidance for the GEF in a bid to make it serve them effectively. Yet most often they found that the GEF Secretariat translated (or indeed 'totally destroyed' (interview, scientist, 1997)) guidance from the COPs to render it into something that made sense in economic terms. The GEF Secretariat view was that the essence of COP guidance – 'inexplicit' by political necessity – was hard to translate into operational policies and practical projects, and they had to move ahead rather than waiting for clarifications. In the end, it seems 'it's a question of a political text vs good investment opportunities' (interview, NGO, 1997), or, as Steinberg (1998) put it, the GEF ends up making 'policy by default' when translating the CBD's 'vague mandate into specific projects'.

GEF Secretariat people seem to have done their best in a difficult situation; when they tried to report to the COPs about how their guidance had been integrated into GEF policies, problems were compounded by institutional timetables. When a COP session produced guidance for its financial mechanism, the following meeting of the Council noted it and asked the Secretariat for clarification and/or to prepare a draft response. By the time the next Council meeting considered their Secretariat's response – in terms, for example, of new draft Operational Programs – the COP had come round again to lament the lack of practical action taken in response

---

48. Governments are 'Party' to an international Convention once they sign it and ratify its text domestically.

to their earlier instructions, and issued more guidance for the GEF. In 1998, El-Ashry argued that,

> it has become increasingly clear that the provision of such guidance on an annual basis, thereby regularly increasing the number of priorities to such an extent that the idea of priority activities is severely diluted, seriously hinders the ability of the GEF to assist recipient countries in achieving measurable impacts in achieving the objectives of the Conventions.[49]

But while the GEF's CEO was frustrated by the number of demands placed on his staff, the Convention bodies were even more frustrated that they could do no more than request 'reconsideration' of GEF projects that they did not deem the best use of scarce environmental funds.[50]

GEF projects have been designed and put forward mostly by large development institutions with powerful pre-existing mandates. Neither Convention has the power to determine the level or uses made of the funds spent in their name. With its 'incremental' finance essentially 'added on' to development 'business as usual' in the World Bank and UNDP, the GEF could hardly produce the necessary subtle shift in values and far reaching reforms needed for the conservation and sustainable use promulgated in the CBD (interview, CBD secretariat, 1997).

The World Bank's backseat role in managing the only finance then available for the Conventions left many to conclude that 'the GEF is a big front for the World Bank' (interview, UN, 1998) and to attack it as such. From the point of view of the GEF Secretariat,

> The World Bank role in GEF is partly reason, partly excuse for hostility to GEF in the CBD. Perhaps certain countries didn't want the CBD to be strong, so they kept troublesome issues on the boil. The problem basically is a lot of agendas being played out, hence the endless working groups on 'reviewing the financial mechanism' which are really just slanging matches in which GEF is a political ping-pong ball. (interview, GEF Secretariat, 1997)

49. GEF/C.11/5
50. Meanwhile, with ever more guidance piling up, it was easy for agencies to find justifications for favoured projects – and by the same token a reason not to fund any proposed project could also be found.

The arguments that degenerated into 'slanging matches' on occasion reflected a very real struggle for authority over the GEF – between the environmental and Southern interests better represented in the UN Conventions and the rich governments largely controlling the GEF.

Whose Accountability?

In 1993 Jake Werksman[51] prepared a legal commentary on the accountability of the GEF to the Conventions. He noted that although the Conventions are legally binding on governments that have ratified them, as long as the GEF remains 'legally subordinate to the Bank's system of governance', its Implementing Agencies report to the Council rather than directly to the COPs. As a result there is no direct accountability between the Conventions and the Agencies implementing projects with GEF funds raised in the their names. Left out of 'the accountability loop', the World Bank and UNDP can neglect or directly contradict the Conventions' principles, continuing, for example, to invest in extractive mining, forestry and bioprospecting for global markets without ensuring 'equitable benefit sharing' (one of the CBD's three 'legs', see Chapter 2), as well as fossil fuels. In 1994 the GEF approved $60 million for climate change projects, while the same year the World Bank put $6 billion into mostly 'carbon-intensive' non-renewable energy developments (Caufield, 1996).

As we saw above, the Conventions can 'request' that the GEF Council 'review' its project decisions, but the Council is under no obligation to force Agencies to comply with the Conventions' expectations – even if it could legally challenge institutions with pre-existing responsibilities (interviews, GEF Secretariat, 1997, and World Bank, 1998). Managing the resulting resentful relationships has required detailed diplomatic and public relations work by the GEF's supporters, not least in and around the working groups of the third CBD Conference of the Parties, held in Buenos Aires in 1996. 'The point [of public relations] is getting people to behave the way you hope they will behave by persuading them that it is ultimately in their interest to do so' (Mobil Oil public relations executive Alfred Geduldig, quoted in Richter, 1998).

---

51. A lawyer at the Foundation for International Environmental Law and Development in London.

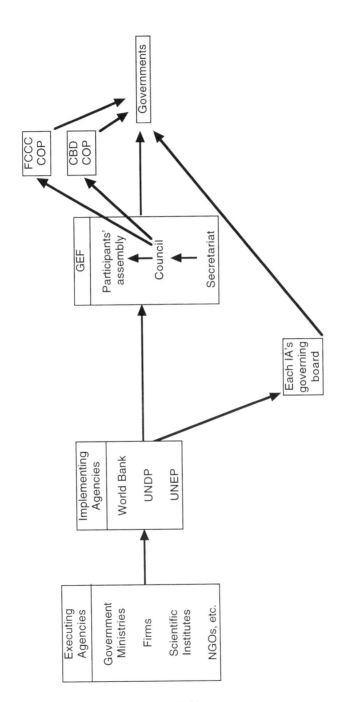

Figure 1 Accountability for funds and guidance offered

Persuading the CBD to Accept its Financial Mechanism

By 1996 the GEF was still the 'interim' financial mechanism for both Conventions.[52] Despite its restructuring, the governing body of neither Convention was yet satisfied enough with the GEF's performance to adopt it wholeheartedly, and both were still hoping for better funding arrangements. But at COP-3 in Buenos Aires, the Parties to the CBD 'decided to become more co-operative', and soon afterwards a Memorandum of Understanding (MoU) was agreed between the GEF and the CBD. Some attribute this overcoming of mistrust simply to the CBD secretariat gaining confidence once a full professional staff was in place in Montreal and a more mature institutional relationship could develop; others tell a more complex story.

The German civil servant who sat on the GEF Council throughout the 1990s, Han Peter Schipulle, also represented his government at the third conference of governments Party to the CBD. Working with other Europeans including the British, he aimed to persuade the CBD to give the GEF permanent status as its funding mechanism – since the donor treasuries would not look kindly on a fund that was not able to pacify the Conventions. At this meeting therefore Schipulle is said to have 'behaved as if he was executive secretary' of the Convention (interview, CBD secretariat, 1997). Whether or not this verdict is fair, the Europeans seem to have achieved their mission to the extent that by the end of the two-week meeting, 'the real executive secretary ended up kow-towing' (interview, CBD secretariat, 1997). Schipulle himself said he was merely engaged in 'damage limitation': making clear to the Southern governments the risks of their losing any chance of environmental finance if they did not support the GEF in the run up to new replenishment negotiations, due to start in 1997 (interview, Northern government, 1996).

To make sure the donors' favoured fund got at least a Memorandum of Understanding with the CBD to clarify their relationship, arrangements were made for registered COP-3 participants to spend the weekend visiting GEF-assisted projects to conserve whales off Patagonia and a wetland in Uruguay.[53] It seems that 40

52. In fact the GEF was the 'operating entity of the interim financial mechanism' to the CBD.
53. Beth Burrows, TWN Biodiversity Convention briefing (no. 6).

of the 60 weekenders from recipient country parties went for free, and the rest were subsidised[54] – many were members of the working group on the financial mechanism. With a large workload remaining to get through, a reduced working group continued to meet over the weekend drafting acceptable texts for the financial mechanism.

Officially there were to be no observers allowed into working groups, but senior members of the GEF Secretariat were present when it came to finalising the draft MoU. They were so frequently consulted by the British and German representatives that one Southern representative wondered 'Why not agree the whole MoU now, the GEF Council is here ...?' Normal rules were also flouted when the US representative gained access to the working group – despite the US not being Party to the CBD – by threatening to block biodiversity funding at the GEF Council if they were kept out.[55]

After the COP, private meetings continued between the key staff from the Facility's Secretariat and the head of the CBD secretariat, Calestous Juma. A private retreat hosted by the Germans in Frankfurt in July 1997 contributed further to mutual understanding, and a GEF–CBD Memorandum of Understanding was finalised in 1997 – to the great relief of the European donor governments, and surprise of many who had doubted that the CBD's Conference of Parties would ever really be willing to accept the GEF. Issues of accountability certainly remain because 'development business as usual will not fulfill CBD needs' however development business is modified because, as this CBD secretariat lawyer observed, 'the GEF can only finance conservation, not the sustainable development' that the CBD demands. Yet still, as another CBD lawyer concluded, 'the history of relations between the GEF and the CBD has been a history of improvement, because if GEF fell apart, there would be nothing: what would replace it?' (interviews, 1997).

The donors' message was clear: only by working with the GEF and its European and US-led backers could the CBD ensure funding for its global environmental purposes. By 1997 it seemed as if the same principle which sustained the GEF through Cartagena had also sustained it with the CBD: when some governments are much richer

54. The trips were subsidised by the GEF and the governments of Argentina and Switzerland. Beth Burrows, TWN Biodiversity Convention briefing (no. 6).
55. It was also rumoured that people from Europe who were supportive of the GEF were flown in for the meetings, possibly at Swiss expense (interview, CBD secretariat, 1997).

than others, a flawed aid fund is better than no aid funds, and when the ecology is institutionally devalued by economy, attention to a distorted 'global' environment is better than no attention to the environment. Even the people working in the GEF Secretariat who might have wanted to work differently faced regular replenishments, and any institutional steps out of line would not play well with the major donors. In this context, opposition faded into opportunism, with people at the COPs privately accepting that 'The GEF would eventually be made permanent financial mechanism. But saying so would only encourage World Bank/IMF-style arrogance. By not giving the GEF a permanent designation, the developing countries in the CBD COP were keeping GEF on its toes' (interview, CBD secretariat, 1997).

Once this relationship was established, cooperation between the GEF and CBD secretariats increased. GEF people started to go to COP meetings loaded with policy documents and project information translated into lots of languages in order to present their case and defuse hostility, and CBD people accepted that their guidance had not always been as clear as the GEF might have needed.[56] The GEF Council also put a new emphasis on 'expediting procedures' for 'enabling activities', projects directly supportive of the Conventions (see above and Chapter 5).

CONCLUSIONS

There may have been sufficient political accommodation to let the GEF survive another replenishment, but in the end '"there are no answers" to the incompatible goals of GEF and CBD' (interview, CBD secretariat, 1997). It was not going to be possible for the GEF to 'jointly determine' the Conventions' funding requirements or submit to their authority, nor for the World Bank to loosen its control of GEF funds. Strenuous efforts were made to suppress hostility to this situation in the Council as well as the Conventions, and also to attract support for the GEF's unique mission more widely in the 'global' community. In this context, how did the GEF's central actors go about allocating and spending the money they were given to administer, and were they able over time to overcome their political limitations and build meaningful partnerships for the Earth?

56. In fact even El-Ashry found time to attend the CBD COP-3 meeting in its entirety – 'For the first time in my life I stayed the full length of a conference', wanting to better understand the CBD (interview, 1997).

5   Putting Plans Into Practice

Summary of GEF Project Work; Raising the Money; Sources of
'GEFable' Projects; Allocating the Money; Distributing the Money;
Devolving Finance; Risks in the GEF Portfolio; Conclusions

This chapter departs from the narrative of the GEF's negotiation and
establishment to delve inside its functions, and see how some of its
many promises and compromises were translated into the 'Monday
morning world'[1] of raising, allocating and spending it's billions in
the mid to late 1990s. The expectation of 'innovation' and the
Implementing Agencies' enthusiasm for spending new money sent
GEF funds through an ever more diverse and complex set of
channels: testing new environmental instruments like trust funds
and the Medium Grants Programme, subsidising the entry of experimental low-carbon emitting or genetic diversity-based technologies
and investments into the South's new 'green' markets.

The GEF's Secretariat and Implementing Agencies often struggled
to make sense of the Council's multiple and often conflicting
objectives: cost-efficiency and widespread participation, mainstreaming and leverage, environmental and economic values. Yet
when it came to any particular project, 'incremental costs' and
'global environmental benefits' had only to be 'agreed' by a small
number of people, negotiating case by case in private; in meetings,

1. Norman Myers, speaking at a World Bank sustainable development
   conference, October 1997.

task forces, and the GEF Operations Committee. A favoured project could be provided with an 'incremental costs' rationale, then presented for signing off in the marginally more public forum of the GEF Council (interviews, World Bank and NGO, 1997).

Successful projects sometimes involved real-world plans and needs being contorted to fit the GEF's agenda, and accountability meant their managers had to deal with reams of paperwork, submitting detailed quarterly reports, etc. But how else would GEF's professional staff be able to keep the tight control over spending demanded by donors needing to see efficiency, transparency, accountability, and so on, in return for keeping the money flowing? Distrust of the GEF in the US drove the GEF Secretariat to produce figures indicating the flow of funds back to the US and other nations through procurement contracts for GEF projects (the fact that there were no additional environmental criteria for procurement under GEF projects did not seem to be an issue). NGOs too helped the GEF's case at the replenishment, and were allegedly rewarded by El-Ashry with better access to the GEF's money though a new Medium-Sized Grants (MSG) programme.

Meanwhile the tight budgets demanded for 'cost-effectiveness' and 'efficiency' drove GEF project people to seek economies of scale and work with well-resourced organisations where possible. They also sought to leverage other investments by sweetening the terms of other institutions' investments with free green money – facilitating new debt. A fund that takes responsibility for limiting the environmental impacts of World Bank investments out of its hands could find it difficult to simultaneously contribute to the 'mainstreaming' of environmental values in the Bank. Without a full assessment of both environmental and economic costs and benefits of proposed development projects, the GEF could not be used effectively to internalise economic development's environmental externalities – even if its funds were raised on the polluter pays principle in the first place. To keep a good image therefore and keep running projects despite serious political unease about the direction of the whole initiative, GEF governance required considerable stage management. This led one observer to conclude that, like its incremental costs analyses, GEF meetings are 'cooked ahead of time' (interview, NGO, 1998).

SUMMARY OF GEF PROJECT WORK

Apart from the inevitable 'overheads', the GEF's Business Plan of 1998 stated it would support projects in three categories: operational programmes,[2] enabling activities, and short-term response measures. The last category was basically intended to mop up ozone projects in Eastern European 'countries in transition' not covered by the Montreal Protocol fund; it received little in the way of either funds or attention. The second category was supposed to be promptly funded in full by the GEF, since the whole cost of supporting the Conventions theoretically creates global environmental benefits. Yet, as we will see below, even enabling activities projects were subject to severe delays. The first category of GEF activities – Operational Programs – made up most of GEF finance, and contained the diverse types of project summarised below.

To take a snapshot of one year of GEF financing: in 1997, six projects were global, two regional and 60 national. Between July 1994 and March 1998, the average cost of a GEF project was $5.5 million, and the Council approved $1.2 billion for projects under the four focal areas, around 34 per cent of which went to biodiversity, 40 per cent to climate change, 9 per cent to international waters, 10 per cent to ozone and 7 per cent was 'multi-focal'.[3]

In terms of distribution between geographical areas (which is officially not a factor in approval processes focused on project 'quality') the major recipients of climate change funds were big countries in Asia: Indonesia got three projects totalling $30.5 million; India a single project at $49 million and China three projects totalling $39.1 million; however Brazil, a similarly large country, received only $3.75 million.[4] The level of funding under

2. According to the GEF's 1996 Annual Report, 'an operational program is a conceptual and planning framework for the design, implementation and co-ordination of a set of projects geared to achieve a global environmental objective in a particular focal area'.
3. Draft CEO Report on Policies, Operations and Future Developments of the GEF, GEF/C. 11/5
4. Climate Change Project Distribution:

Stated Aim of Projects	Number
Country studies	4
Adaptation measures	2
Renewables	11
Energy Efficiency	5
Capacity Building	6
Enabling Activities	32
Emission Reduction	2
Capacity Building and Energy Efficiency	3
Sustainable and Participatory Management	1

Source: GEF Quarterly Operational Report, March 1997.

the biodiversity label in GEF-1 was less than in the pilot phase. This reflected inevitable fluctuations in the proportion of good projects in each focal area presented to the Council – according to the GEF Secretariat – and/or the ongoing difficulties experienced between the GEF and the CBD during this period – hinted at by the CBD secretariat.

RAISING THE MONEY

Replenishment

Closed intergovernmental negotiations to replenish GEF finances were completed along with the Operational Strategy in 1995 for GEF-1, and for GEF-2 in time for the New Delhi Participants' Assembly in 1998. Negotiations for a possible further phase are due for completion in mid 2002. This chapter mostly looks at the finances of GEF-1, which was offered $2 billion for 3 years mostly from Northern governments.[5] The US government was the largest donor on paper, closely followed by other European and G7 governments, though by the end of October 1997, the US government was in arrears by $132.5 million, or 41 per cent of their commitment. The other donors made their contributions to GEF-2 conditional on the US paying up as well as on evidence of the GEF's response to the findings of the 1998 Overall Performance Study.[6]

It was not always easy for GEF advocates in donor governments to argue their case with tight-budgeting treasuries. The GEF's lack of permanent status as financial mechanism to the Conventions did not help,[7] and with a Republican-controlled US Congress uneasy about financing international institutions in general, and environmental issues in particular, the Secretariat in 1997 provided the US government with data indicating the size and number of GEF procurement contracts won by US firms so far. With elements in the US administration 'determined to zero-budget us' (interview, GEF Secretariat, 1997), evidence that the GEF could benefit the US economy was evidently deemed to help the case for a second replenishment.

5. In the interests of 'equality' of membership, however, all participating governments had to subscribe to the GEF club with at least $1 million.
6. Other countries were also in arrears, for example Italy by 67 per cent, Ireland by 31 per cent, Egypt by 50 per cent, Argentina by 87 per cent and Brazil by 100 per cent (GEF/R.2/Inf.9).
7. German member's intervention at GEF Council, November 1997.

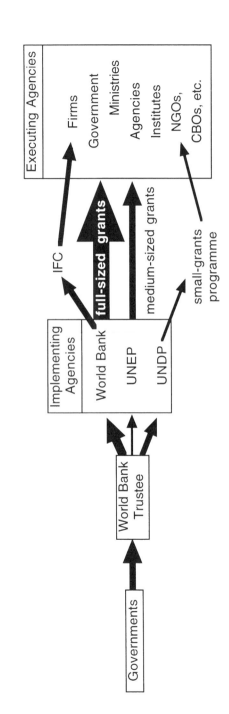

Figure 2   Simplified model of money flow through the GEF system

Eventually, with over half the money promised to the first replenishment carried over (unspent due also to delays in designing, approving and getting projects off the ground – see below), GEF-2 was promised a total of $2.75 billion for 1998 to 2002 – about $687,500,000 per year.[8] Given an assumption of 3 per cent inflation year on year and the four-year replenishment period from 1998 to 2002 (compared to the three years of GEF-1, 1995–7), as some observers noted, this was no increase in 'real terms'. As a result the growth in GEF financing advertised at the 1998 Assembly was deemed to be 'a con' (interview, UN, 1998).

NGOs were collectively of 'tremendous help' in the replenishment processes – according to El-Ashry, who often stressed his appreciation for their continued efforts. Birdlife International, for example, pointed out to donor governments that demand for GEF funds was growing, so it was important they to pay up on time and also genuinely increase their contributions. Some are said to have been later rewarded for their lobbying efforts on Capitol Hill and in Whitehall with funding (particularly with MSGs, see below): thanks for their 'busting a gut' and 'really coming through for GEF' (pers. comm., 1998). More of the time, however, NGOs focused on reforming GEF and particularly World Bank policies, and opening up their processes to NGO participation.

'Mainstreaming' or Marginalisation?

Donor governments under pressure from green NGOs were keen to see better environmental performance from the World Bank, so experience with the GEF was intended partly to help the Bank (also the UNDP) to understand and integrate global environmental issues into development 'business as usual'. Yet NGOs were soon complaining that the GEF's incremental costs limitation seemed to keep global environmental activities separate from the 'mainstream' of

8. Contributions to GEF-1, both promised and actual, laid the basis for scenarios of a new 'burden-sharing formula' prepared by the Secretariat for the 1997 replenishment meetings. Negotiators agreed in September 1997 that burden-sharing should be based on transparency, equity and ability to pay (GEF/R.2/10), starting from historical level of contributions. Countries eligible to receive GEF finance were not part of the burden-sharing arrangement; for the most part they promised a contribution of $4 million each.

the Implementing Agencies' development and policy work. As a result, 'mainstreaming' (the environment) became a popular buzzword during GEF-1.[9]

But as we saw in Chapter 2, the World Bank doesn't like having to meet new goals imposed from outside (Wade, 1997; Rich, 1994). Despite some World Bank staff being happy that their children know their work involves conserving wild animals (interview, 1997), 'organisational learning that threatens the dominant paradigms – such as the hegemony of neo-classical economics at the World Bank – is likely to provoke resistance' (Fox and Brown, 1998). A World Bank technical expert who tried to get biodiversity issues included in structural adjustment policy was told, for example, that 'biodiversity isn't a sector'. More generally, a lack of internal incentives and processes for institutional learning limited the internal impacts of the GEF, as with other of the Bank's environmental initiatives (Wade, 1997).

The GEF's Overall Performance Study (OPS) of 1998 found that mainstreaming was not effectively achieved in the Bank, to the extent that management gave economic staff no mandate to integrate the global environment into their influential Country Assistance Strategies for client governments. Even National Environmental Action Plans assisted by the Bank 'seldom identify and examine the shortcomings of government sector policies and their impact on biodiversity loss and climate change' (OPS, 1998) with the result that 'the global environment is weak or absent' where it might really count. As McAfee (1999) put it, 'Environmental policies remain segregated from the serious business of lending and neoliberal policy adjustment.' In fact, Caufield (1996) reports that some World Bank staff privately criticised the GEF for taking away the Bank's own responsibility for environmental protection: 'After a long battle, we finally agreed to allocate from 1 to 5 percent of each loan for environmental work, but now countries are saying, why should we borrow money for the environment when we can get GEF grants?'.

---

9. By 1998 not only the Implementing Agencies, but donor and recipient governments, the private sector, and everyone down to Southern farmers and fisherfolk were supposed to be taking global environmental issues into account in every aspect of their work (head of World Bank's GEF unit, in a presentation to the GEF Participants' Assembly, 1998).

'Leverage' or Development Subsidy?

We saw in Chapter 3 that the GEF was intended to 'leverage' other investment capital into environmental projects by using its concessional funds to 'sweeten' development projects that might otherwise have seemed uneconomic for either borrower or lender. By linking with other North–South resource transfers, the GEF's limited funds were thus to be made to go further. Certainly the World Bank was enthusiastic about the prospect of leveraging some of their less concessional loans to reluctant Southern governments, and the 1998 OPS found the GEF paying an average of 9 per cent of World Bank project costs, with the Bank mobilising nearly 70 per cent from other – often private sector – sources. The 1998 OPS observed that, in the pilot phase, GEF mobilised an extra $2.24 billion in other international loans with $733 million expenditure. Between the start of GEF-1 in 1995 and June 1997, GEF had leveraged $2.2 billion: around two and a half times the $861 million it gave as aid.

Yet behind these figures hides the fact that it has proved difficult to measure the true nature and extent of leverage. No clear definition was provided by the GEF Secretariat or Council, and the three Implementing Agencies have used the term inconsistently. The UNDP, for example, wanted to include all investments in health, education, and so on, that it deemed necessary for GEF activities to succeed, while the World Bank counted only directly linked project funds. Meanwhile for the UNEP the term was fairly meaningless since all their work was 'environmental'.

The 1998 OPS notes that to achieve leverage, the Implementing Agencies had by definition to fund 'baseline' projects from elsewhere – from sources not already creating global environmental benefits. This raises the question of whether, if the Implementing Agencies were effectively mainstreaming the global environment in pursuit of sustainable development, they should be providing any such funding in the first place. For example, in the GEF's archetypal case – an energy project transformed from fossil fuel to renewables technology by the addition of GEF funds – the baseline investment could be said to have been leveraged into greener technology. But if the Climate Convention's principles were mainstream in development institutions (and their client governments), low carbon-emitting technologies would presumably have been favoured for investment anyway, without the need for GEF assistance. By a similar token, a forestry project with an additional forest conservation component paid for by the GEF could be presented as development funds being channelled to support GEF goals – even if the 'baseline' activity involves logging an old-growth forest and replacing it with monoculture trees, and GEF funds are used to conserve only an additional area of forest or preservation of local biodiversity *in vitro*.[10] As Caufield (1996) commenting on the Facility's early days concluded, the GEF

> encourages the Bank to externalise the cost of the environmental damage done by its projects. The cost of avoiding or mitigating the damage done by large Bank projects is shuffled off to the GEF instead of being considered as a cost of the project itself. This violates the widely accepted principle that the polluter should pay for the damage he or she causes. It also makes the project seem to have a higher rate of return. And when a GEF project is attached to a privately funded project, the environmental cost is not only externalised, it is transferred from the private sector to the state.

In addition, sweetening more less-concessional finance into otherwise uneconomic projects would be likely to increase Southern governments' international debt, without directly generating the foreign currency needed to repay it (interview, NGO, 1996).

Sideshow or Insurance for Other Development Finance?

The GEF Council has regularly stressed the importance of engaging with the private sector – which, potentially, can offer not only funds for leverage but also skills, contacts and scope of action perhaps lacking in governmental or non-profit organisations. However, since public and private sectors usually have divergent priorities, ways of working and ethos, with one free-ranging in the deregulated quest for private profit and the other bound about with requirements of transparency and accountability for the public good, the problems besetting so many other 'public–private partnerships' afflict the GEF's efforts. As a result collaborations between the GEF and the private sector never took off as ostensibly planned.

One of the GEF's occasional documents setting out a Strategy for Engaging the Private Sector suggests removing market barriers to

---

10. Such situations were the basis of sustained NGO critique of pilot phase GEF biodiversity projects in Poland/Belarus and the Congo, see Chapter 3, Rich, 1994 and Caufield, 1996.

environmental investments and compensating for regulatory changes, as well as direct assistance of firms moving into untested markets. This kind of assistance to private investors was meant to be 'not permanent like a subsidy, but reducing transaction costs, facilitating private sector involvement in environmental finance' (interview, UNDP, 1997). According to its private sector strategy, the GEF was not to risk 'causing a significant distortion of competitive market conditions locally or internationally', but it is unclear how such principles were to be checked or enforced. Meanwhile, like others in the World Bank, GEF staff generally found it more convenient to deal with the transnational private sector than with smaller, less highly-capitalised companies and investors.

Nevertheless, while there was lots of procurement of goods and services from private firms (see below), large private financial institutions hardly became involved in running GEF projects at all. According to the OPS (1998),

> In nearly all cases, the private sector party being leveraged is the beneficiary or sponsor of the project, such as the developer that is converting to non-ozone-producing equipment or the developer of wind energy projects. There are very few instances, for example, where GEF projects seek to leverage institutions in the private financial sector, such as commercial banks, insurance companies, pension funds and other institutional pension funds.

The only instances identified in the 1998 evaluation of private finance involvement in the GEF were the Renewable Energy and Energy Efficiency and Terra Capital Biodiversity funds run by the IFC, the World Bank's semi-independent 'private sector wing' (see below), and the World Bank's *Solar Home System* project, in which local commercial banks provided credit lines to buyers of solar power installations – similar to the Zimbabwe PV case study project in Appendix III.

Part of the reason for this dearth of private interest must be that many people in international investment regard the GEF as an irrelevance or 'sideshow' (pers. comm., 1996), with little or nothing to do with their day-to-day work. Another possible reason was a fear on the GEF's part of being seen by its critics to give public money as a subsidy to profit-seeking enterprises. The private sector was hardly represented at the GEF Participants' Assembly in New Delhi because Council members did not know who to invite – which body devoted purely to its own economic interests could be asked to represent all its fellows equally? This is a fundamental problem with any public–private partnership – what relationship is likely between institutions with a duty to the public and those whose raison d'être is to centralise benefits into private hands?

A solution promoted in the IFC was a kind of insurance for investors, using GEF funds to back up loan guarantees for private investments in risky new environmental technology markets – thus allowing funds to be used again if the investment was successful. This approach was piloted in Hungary, in an initiative IFC staff described as 'third-generation thinking': potentially a more efficient use of the money than applying incremental costs principles directly and simply giving the cash away (interview, IFC, 1997). But as some IFC staff accepted, this initiative still involved interference in 'free markets' (interview, 1999), and for their part the private sector mostly found less demanding ways to express any environmental urges. Overall it seems the GEF offered assistance to infrastructure that they might find useful, rather than making payments directly to private institutions.

Other publicly financed development agencies also found the GEF's requirements too demanding for the limited funds it made available. The Regional Development Banks – the Asian, African, European and Inter-American Development Banks[11] – were initially enthusiastic about the GEF's potential to help them to engage with 'the technology of tomorrow', subsidising experimentation with renewables and so forth (interview, FCCC secretariat, 1996). The Inter-American Development Bank did participate in a Costa Rican wind power project, of which the GEF paid $3 million out of $30 million raised (De Senarclens, 1996), but early hopes of collaboration receded when it turned out that staff of the RDBs disliked having to work under a GEF Implementing Agency (interview, World Bank, 1996) as much as the private sector did. The RDBs found GEF processes too slow and its procedures for transparency and accountability, especially the incremental costs criterion, obstructive:

In the Asia Pacific region, [the RDBs] were not really happy with the idea of working under other institutions, and they had no

11. The RDBs are comparable to the World Bank insofar as they make loans to governments guaranteed by governments multi-laterally – but they do so on a regional rather than global basis.

real incentive to do so. The Asian Development Bank did get involved in a GEF climate change project, but the RDBs have not come to the table with new proposals. Accountability procedures were arranged, but they have not proved workable. (interview, UNDP, 1997)

New efforts to bring the RDBs on board with the GEF were made in the late 1990s, and they requested to be made official Implementing Agencies on their own behalf (interview, World Bank, 1998). When this was refused the RDBs again seem to have turned away from the GEF to deal with their own initiatives, for example the Asian Development Bank contributed to the Asia Sustainable Growth Fund, which in 1996 hoped to raise $150 million for eco-efficient and long-term profitable companies in the Pacific Rim (Schmidheiny et al., 1996).

SOURCES OF 'GEFABLE' PROJECTS

National Priorities and the Focal Point System

The GEF ... shall fund programs and projects which are country-driven and based on national priorities designed to support sustainable development.

The GEF's 'global' environmental agenda fed Southern governments' fears of loss of sovereignty, and led to doubts about its relevance to their own sustainable development. To meet such concerns the restructured GEF promised that all its investments would be 'country-driven'. But given the Council's need to ensure the 'global' value of a project, what did this term mean in practice?

Essentially, a project is deemed to be country-driven if it has been approved by the host government's focal point (FP):[12] an official whose task it is to formally approve projects on behalf of their country. Ideally the FP's office 'conducts the orchestra' of other departments with a related remit: national ministries involved in the GEF and the multilateral environmental agreements. Yet each Imple-

12. Eventually the task was split into operational and political focal points for recipient countries, with the latter dealing with GEF's political negotiations while the former got on with co-ordinating project approval and spending in the country.

menting Agency has its own entry point to national governments: the World Bank usually to finance or foreign affairs, the UNEP to environment and the UNDP to planning or similar (interview, UNDP, 1997). In this context it is up to the FP to decide what 'country-driven' means when ministries disagree.[13] As we saw in Chapter 3, such disagreement is not unusual. Often based in relatively new and/or weak environment ministries, FPs have hardly been able to manage the claims of stronger foreign, finance and other ministries: 'Brazil and Argentina for example had good infrastructure, but others did not. It did not help when ministries were restructured or personnel changed' (interview, UNDP, 1997).

Official evaluations of the GEF also suggested that overloaded national FPs had difficulty accessing and responding to GEF policy directives – even assuming that they understood enough about the GEF's complexities to engage with it in the first place. Besides facing varying capacity in different countries, it could be difficult for GEF people to keep track of who the FP was – at one point the Secretariat's list of FPs was said to be four years out of date (intervention in Council meeting, November 1997).

For some people promoting GEF projects in the World Bank,

GEF FPs have been almost irrelevant ... countries don't show much interest in being proactive on GEF. This could be because of the lack of familiarity with GEF Operational Programs and criteria – I can't think of any FPs that do understand them – and because development is higher up the agenda than the environment in most countries. (interview, World Bank, 1997)

Some Southern representatives to GEF Council felt that donors could have provided more support for national co-ordination and capacity-building for GEF work, especially in light of the numerous other Northern-inspired environmental policy initiatives, among them National Environmental Action Plans, National Strategies for Sustainable Development, and Agenda 21, cluttering up development assistance (interviews, 1997). From the GEF Secretariat's point of view, however, this was not a priority since

13. In 1996, a project was due to start in Kenya and staff began investing in arrangements. Yet the promised money wasn't coming through, because the UNDP was not able to release the funds with different ministries still battling for control (interviews, Southern government, 1996, and GEF Secretariat, 1997).

The FPs basically serve to 'provide cover'; governments can't complain that they weren't notified or consulted once the FP's letter of approval of a project arrives at the Secretariat. In Bolivia one FP was only in the post for two weeks, and prioritised something which the government later didn't like, but that's not the Secretariat's fault and we were covered by having the FP's letter. (interview, GEF Secretariat, 1997)

Early on, the UNEP proposed a project to strengthen the national FP system (many GEF FPs were also points of contact for the UNEP's Infoterra initiative) with no success. When the GEF Secretariat developed something similar in response to problems with the FP system in the lead up to the Participants' Assembly, they countered the UNEP's annoyance by saying that only then was it 'the right time' for such an initiative (pers. comm., GEF Secretariat, 1998). As part of this process, the tasks of the FP were divided between a 'political FP' – who would deal with GEF information and correspondence and provide a point of contact for the constituency of a Council member – and an 'operational FP' who would provide a point of contact for the Implementing Agencies on project-related matters, and organise in-country consultation with stakeholders. In the meantime, it seems that 'country-driven' remained a box for the Secretariat to have ticked by a country's operational FP, allowing projects to go ahead while disagreements remained at the national, let alone local or global, level. As a result the coherence and integration of GEF projects with existing policies and initiatives was often limited.

Advice for Projects

Among the official targets for GEF support are 'programs that advance the scientific and technical capacities in recipient countries to reduce global environmental threats' (Operational Strategy, 1996). But as we saw in Chapter 4, the relative sidelining in GEF operations of the UNEP – and by extension its STAP[14] – meant that projects

14. In a paper entitled *Promoting Coherence*, produced as a pamphlet through IUCN-NL, Sheila Aggarwal-Khan of the UNEP challenged the World Bank's dominance of the GEF, and proposed a more science-based strategy. Yet, as one of her colleagues noted, this report was 'not promoted' within the GEF family: 'it may have been too challenging for some' (interview, 1998).

would rarely be designed with much meaningful input from scientists. This meant excluding people with experience of the relevant locale in the project's host country, experience which is particularly important for biodiversity conservation, where social, cultural and other issues can be as important as the findings of natural scientific and economic analyses.[15] In this context Southern representatives on the GEF Council, especially from countries like India with their own strong research base, made repeated requests for more Southern experts to be employed in the development and review of GEF projects.

Despite the appointment of eminent Indian scientist Mahdav Gadgil as STAP's chairman in 1998, many of its members were still UK-educated and the strongest institutional links were to international bodies like the IUCN and UNESCO, as well as to London's Imperial College which had also provided a couple of members of the first STAP.[16] In this context Southern Council members continued to suggest replacing the STAP with several regional panels made up of people with more local scientific expertise.[17] This would, it was said, give GEF projects a sounder basis in ground-level realities and to some extent move the whole fund away from the dominance of Northern ideas about how to manage global environments. But even after the STAP developed a roster of 200-odd international environmental scientists from which the Implementing Agencies could select appropriate experts to help develop projects,[18] US and UK influence was 'absolutely' disproportionate in the GEF (interview, UNDP, 1997) – particularly through the graduate education of con-

15. Usually this marginalisation of grounded science was implicit rather than explicit, because of the need for projects to have scientific legitimation. But according to Goldman (2001b), sometimes project investors directly 'wagged the scientific tail'. The Nakai Plateau in Vietnam, for example, was designated as a global biodiversity protection site in preparation for GEF funded conservation. However, the same plateau was also the site of the World Bank's Nam Theun 2 hydroelectric project, so the World Bank somehow had the designation rescinded because their plans would directly conflict with the conservation goals of the GEF.

16. Note on the Reconstitution of STAP for the Second Phase of the GEF, GEF/C.11/Inf.4, 6 March 1998.

17. Intervention in GEF Council meeting, March 1998.

18. Another purpose of the roster is to assist GEF outreach in the 'scientific community' (Annual Review of the STAP Roster of Experts, FY98, GEF/C.12/Inf.15, 2 October 1998).

sultants. In private some GEF people were very definite that 'In terms of consultancy there was a bias. Local knowledge was not always used where appropriate, and top experts would be flown in to make comments instead' (interview, UNDP, 1997). For example, in the 1997 financial year, of all those experts selected to review GEF projects, 14 came from the US, seven from the UK and three from Africa. Overall, 79 per cent came from 'developed countries'. Even when the level of 6 per cent of reviewers from the South in 1997 was increased in 1998 to 18 per cent, 55 per cent still came from the US and UK.[19] When challenged on this tendency in a GEF Council meeting, a World Bank representative said it simply reflected a preference for using their own 'local' expertise – that is, familiar people situated close to agency headquarters in North America from where projects were largely developed.

There was a feeling in the World Bank especially that they had their own experts 'in house', or could find them through existing contacts who understood their priorities and ways of working. Clearly GEF processes were difficult enough for them to manage without dealing with scientists trained and experienced in foreign lands whose priorities, analyses and input could not be guaranteed to be compatible with their own needs.

Project Initiation

The staff of each Implementing Agency see their task largely in terms of developing fundable project ideas, to the extent that their jobs depend on there always being more projects to work on. As one noted, their job is 'projects, projects, projects', and if the GEF did not fund projects, they 'would get a new job' (interview, UNDP, 1997). Nevertheless vast amounts of paper begins to move when they seek potential projects for funding, because it is important to ensure that proposers are suitable for and capable of GEF tasks:

> Any eligible individual or group may propose a project ... GEF project ideas may be proposed directly to UNDP, UNEP, or the World Bank ... Developing countries that have ratified the relevant treaty are eligible to propose biodiversity and climate change projects. Other countries ... are eligible if ... party to the

19. Annual Review of the STAP Roster of Experts, FY98, GEF/C.12/Inf.15, 2 October 1998.

appropriate treaty and ... eligible to borrow from the World Bank or receive technical assistance grants from UNDP.[20]

Full-size GEF projects with FP approval and apparent potential to benefit the global environment are formally initiated as a 'project concept' in the office of an Implementing Agency (IA).[21] For organisations seeking GEF funds, project briefs and especially applications proving their worth and trustiness took a huge amount of time and effort to produce, and many were rejected before they came to the Council.

While the World Bank largely designs and makes arrangements to run GEF projects itself with government contacts, as we have seen in earlier chapters it increasingly works with Washington-based NGOs (especially WWF, IUCN, etc.) and selected Southern NGOs, for example the Argentine Fundacion Ecologica Universal (FEU).[22] Yet it took a visit by an FEU representative to the Bank's Washington headquarters for contact on the project proposal to be established, thereafter continued by e-mail because the Bank's Buenos Aires office literally would not let enquirers through the door – dealing with them only through a narrow slit (interview, 1997).

The FEU had turned to the World Bank however because the UNDP 'did not respond' to letters at all. From Kenya too, the feeling was that, for all its flaws, the World Bank was easier than the UNDP for NGOs to deal with: 'The World Bank is getting better with letting in civil society, but there's a real problem with UNDP ... People in UNDP offices may want to help, but they are really tied by bureaucracy' (interview, NGO, 1997). Perhaps this reflects the fact that World Bank staff dealing with GEF work have learnt to keep the bits of paper away to get anything done because 'the paper flow is enormous due to the number of players, it's staggering, mindboggling the amount of paper produced' (interview, World Bank, 1997). Within the US meanwhile, NGOs found the Facility's staff in the UNDP headquarters mostly constructive, and they worked together to develop projects including the small and medium-sized grants

20. <www.gefweb.org/Operational_Policies/Eligibility_Criteria/eligibility_criteria.html>
21. See below for the procedure for smaller GEF projects – SGP and MSG – and trust funds.
22. The World Bank and FEU developed a project for briefing recipient country NGOs about applying for MSGs (see below).

programmes and to move their relationship from one of procuring services to 'partnership' (see below):

> in the Asia Pacific regional bureau of UNDP more than a quarter of projects are implemented by NGOs. UNDP is now taking technical inputs from previous adversaries. For example Southern NGOs who had been highly skeptical of the GEF ... are now working together with UNDP. This is a measure of the success of the GEF: that groups who once were strong critics are now involved. (interview, UNDP, 1997)

The fact that the GEF held the prospect of improvement to development practice in hands that also offered money to resource-starved groups meant that, for all its flaws, it was sometimes given chances by NGOs who otherwise might not want to work with US-based 'development' institutions. However, as stressed by a UNDP communications officer, people had to realise that 'GEF is not traditional development assistance, it is not supposed to be easy to access' (interview, 1997). In this context few national-level organisations had the wherewithal to initiate a 'GEFable' project without direct support from an Implementing Agency. As an interviewee from the World Bank noted (1997), 'I give quite a lot of technical help to national consortia preparing ideas into projects ... I steer the process.' And, as a fairly recent WWF report concluded, 'there is no question that a personal contact/ally is the best way to get a successful proposal on paper and to have it approved quickly' (WWF, 1999). It has been possible for some NGOs to make those contacts fairly easily, not least where the World Bank and UNDP have been seeking new partners, ideas and skills to justify their respective claims on GEF funds.

With perhaps more friends in the environmental field than the other Implementing Agencies, the UNEP was initially a popular target for project proposals. With its budgets falling fast, the UNEP was 'desperately trying to do projects' (interview, scientist, 1997), but it was relatively rare for proposals coming through the UNEP to be favoured with GEF funding. By contrast the World Bank, with numerous country offices (though not as many as the UNDP) in the South and more resources than the other Implementing Agencies, was well prepared to develop projects. And while the Bank was not desperate like the UNEP, it was persistent, and, according to one observer, wouldn't abandon projects once it started. The UNDP meanwhile seemed to launch 'as many projects as possible in the hope that at least some will get through' (interview, UNEP, 1998). A member of the Secretariat seemed to concur: 'The World Bank says it has more money than good projects, while UNDP says it has more good projects than money' (interview, GEF Secretariat, 1997).

When it came to the type of projects chosen, the costs of transparency and accountability (preparing, translating, duplicating and distributing documents, consulting widely and evaluating constantly) meant that the Implementing Agencies needed to seek economies of scale if they were to keep within the tight requirements of efficiency and cost-effectiveness also expected of them by the Secretariat and Council. Despite criticism in the evaluations that GEF projects were often too big, some in the GEF Secretariat would have liked to see fewer, bigger projects coming through: 'Allowing larger projects would need less staff for the same amount of money [and] allow catch-up with existing funds. It's administratively intensive finding enough good projects for the money' (interview, GEF Secretariat, 1997).

Project Preparation

The Implementing Agencies may make arrangements for GEF project preparation ... by multilateral development banks, specialized agencies and programs of the UN, other international organizations, bilateral development agencies, national institutions, non-governmental organizations, private sector entities and academic institutions.

Having given operational instructions and set out the potential range of project partners, the GEF Council did not really want to have to 'micro-manage' GEF processes. Instead they generally left the GEF Secretariat and Implementing Agencies to find partners and thrash out projects, then report back with a proposed Work Programme prepared for Council approval. Though the Operational Strategy was the first of many publications setting out GEF policy and experience,[23] initially at least there was little guidance available

23. <www.gefweb.org/Outreach/outreach-PUblications/
     outreach-publications.html>

on how to actually prepare successful proposals for GEF projects and guide them through the complex procedures. NGOs like the Climate Network Europe and the IUCN filled the gap to some extent with publications like *An NGO Guide to the Global Environment Facility (Letters to Nani G. Oruga)* (CNE and IUCN, 1996) and *Biodiversity, International Waters and the GEF* (Griffen, 1997).

However, even where GEF publicity was effective in bringing people and ideas in, the conditions on its funding were so prohibitive that on occasion experts employed specifically to develop 'GEFable' projects had difficulty. In response to this, the Implementing Agencies (especially the 'capacity-building' UNDP) have themselves helped governments to run project development workshops across the world, with consultants providing training in GEF priorities and procedures mostly to national civil servants, as well as some NGOs and staff of other international organisations. These deal, for example, with incremental costs and the detailed technical 'logframe' (logical framework) for GEF project preparation. Some NGOs meanwhile run their own programmes for 'partner' Southern NGOs to learn sufficient 'GEFese' to work with it effectively. The Nature Conservancy, for example, brought people they knew from NGOs in South America to Washington DC to gain the necessary personal experience and rapport with GEF project managers (interview, NGO, 1997).

In response to COP complaints (echoed by many GEF participants) about the expense and length of project preparation processes, the Secretariat promised to produce clear guidelines for applicants, and in November 1994 the Council approved a stream of funds known as Project Development Finance (PDF). Provided initially with $15 million, the PDF offered funding in three blocks for project proposals likely to meet GEF requirements. PDF-A was in the gift of the Implementing Agencies. On the basis of a very simple project brief, they offered funds of up to $25,000 for initial project identification and 'pre-project activities at the national level'. Proposals for PDF-B – up to $350,000 for documentation including 'information necessary to complete project proposals' – and PDF-C – up to $1 million to complete the necessary 'technical design and feasibility work' for larger projects – were submitted to the GEF Operations Committee (GEFOP, see below) before approval by the CEO. The CEO was authorised to approve Block C funding of up to $750,000 himself; for larger sums – the upper limit being $1 million – he had to consult with the Council before giving his approval.

Through the PDF fund, Implementing Agencies and the CEO were presumably able to shape the GEF's work programme strategically by enabling selected organisations to make approved plans into reality. However, it is hard to be sure, since the Secretariat would not provide tabular information on the entry and movement of proposals through the PDF system, which might have allowed analysis of what kind of project, proposed by whom, fell at what stage in the process.[24] When it comes to potentially sensitive information, it seems that GEF's transparency does not go all the way.

Meanwhile, as we saw in Chapter 4, the COPs of the Conventions on Climate Change and Biodiversity provided the GEF with 'guidance', which they wanted to see implemented in the design and preparation of projects. The Conventions' secretariats had no mandate to clarify or elaborate on their COPs' sometimes vague guidance for the GEF. When they found themselves forced by circumstance to do so, they tried to be very conservative, 'coding what we want to say very carefully, and always thinking in terms of what the GEF will think' (interview, CBD secretariat, 1997). With no formal access, 'time or mandate to go over each project with the Implementing Agencies' (interview, CBD secretariat, 1997), the Conventions rely on the GEF Secretariat and Council to transmit their guidance to the Implementing Agencies.[25] This is presumably why CBD people felt the GEF Secretariat should be larger to have more clout with the Agencies in charge of actual project preparation and implementation, who in turn felt the Secretariat should be smaller and stop interfering with 'their' projects.

ALLOCATING THE MONEY

The Incremental Costs Criterion

The GEF has frequently made rhetorical commitments to local 'partnerships' and to 'stakeholder participation' in project design and implementation ... but the cumbersome [incremental costs] requirement has frequently meant that such communities are

24. In November 1997 a database of PDF grants was said to be under development, viewable once complete, however access was never actually granted.
25. The CBD eventually drew up an MoU with the World Bank in an attempt to achieve more direct influence over its operations than they could through the GEF.

totally unable to take part in 'negotiations' over incremental costs, which many of those interviewed regard as a sham exercise in any case. (McAfee, 1999)

Most people working closely with the GEF understood that donor treasuries demanded a strict restriction of GEF funds to paying incremental costs for global environmental benefits. Yet, as hinted in the last chapter, there were very divergent reactions to this. While the Dutch Council member described the incremental costs requirement as 'a beacon in a potential sea of financing modalities', the German member noted 'The Council can't discuss the usefulness of the incremental costs requirement, it is not acceptable to question their usefulness because incremental costs are fundamental to the GEF' (intervention in November 1997 GEF Council by German member). For his part, the UK member of the GEF Council often stressed that incremental costs were not merely a GEF imposition but came from the Conventions whose requirements the GEF had a legal duty to observe.[26]

Meanwhile it was not clear to Southern governments that GEF funds were, as prescribed at Rio, 'new and additional', and they wondered why this fundamental principle had been abandoned while incrementality was given so much stress – and proved so troublesome.[27] From the perspective of many Southern representatives in the GEF, 'incremental costs are not difficult, they are impossible to apply' (Brazilian intervention in November 1997 Council). A civil servant from a tropical island state complained that calculating the incremental costs of a proposed biodiversity conservation project had proved endlessly contentious, to the extent that a stream of consultants had made the trip to assess the tropical island's biodiversity – each taking the opportunity to explore the hotels and beaches at the same time (interview, 1996).

From the point of view of the World Bank, incremental costs analysis – for all its Bank-style economic calculations – was 'a new beast both in the Bank and in country', and while they were 'learning fast', the 'incremental costs of effectiveness' slow down the

26. Others suggested that he *would* be the one to stress this fact, because 'he put them there' through his department's participation in CBD negotiations (interview, CBD secretariat, 1997).
27. A 1997 analysis of reported OECD aid found that GEF funding had at least partially *replaced*, rather than supplemented, other international aid from the OECD countries (Lake, 1997).

integration of such innovations (interviews, World Bank, 1997). An environmental economist retained by the GEF Secretariat as a consultant to deal with incremental costs analyses stated that there are 'margins of uncertainty, but the work could be done', and while donors would regularly acknowledge the difficulties and promise to review the incremental costs criterion, when it came down to it,

> GEF's own review of the problem has a call for *more* paperwork: preparation of an 'Incremental Cost Kit' and training of a team of experts for hire – i.e., *more* 'technification' and greater dependence on outside, 'globally'-informed environmental–economic expertise. (McAfee, 1999)

In response to sustained complaints not least from frustrated recipient governments, the Secretariat placed the following text on the GEF's website:

> The process of determining incremental costs can be complicated. In response to the GEF Council's request to 'clarify and simplify' this concept, simplified guidelines for calculating incremental costs are being developed by the Secretariat to accelerate this step in the project approval process. Until the simplified guidelines are available, the following [nine] documents represent GEF efforts to develop and demonstrate the concept of incremental costs.[28]

By 1997 the GEF Secretariat was directing GEF funds to types of project for which incremental costs analyses were relatively easily

---

28. The documents listed are:
  • Incremental Cost Policy Paper (GEF/C.7/inf.5)
  • Report on Incremental Costs (GEF/C.14/5)
  • Note on Incremental Costs (GEF/C.13/7)
  • Progress on Incremental Costs (GEF/C.12/Inf.4)
  • Program for Measuring Incremental Costs for the Environment (PRINCE)
  • Standard Reporting Format for Incremental Cost
  • Streamlined Procedures on Incremental Cost Assessment
  • Paradigm Case Illustrations of Incremental Cost Analysis
  • Designing Projects within the GEF Focal Areas to Address Land Degradation: with Special Reference to Incremental Cost Estimation

  Source: <www.gefweb.org/Operational_Policies/Eligibility_Criteria/ Incremental_Costs/incremental_costs.html>

produced (McAfee, 1999), presumably because the environmental economics consultants who produce incremental costs analyses are expensive. Furthermore some people in the GEF Implementing Agencies did not favour 'multi-focal' projects[29] because their preparation confuses incremental costs calculations (interview, World Bank, 1997). GEF work was complex enough for them without mixing up the few simplifications – in this case focal areas – that made their jobs a little easier.

Despite numerous issues papers, guides and formulae, the GEF Council eventually resorted to a mediation service. As it turned out, they hardly helped the donors' case:

> experience to date has shown that incremental costs determinations – as they are currently implemented – are highly vulnerable to manipulation, artificiality and arbitrariness. This is not diminished by the use of highly sophisticated technical expertise and economic analyses ... It was suggested that no two individuals or teams would arrive at the same incremental costs estimate for the same project, and further, that an elaborate process is sometimes used to arrive at a pre-determined number. (RESOLVE, 1998)

With incremental costs a 'hoop to jump through,' and accountability for their determination unclear, RESOLVE found that figures emerged from 'magic at best, back room politics at worst'.

In practice, incremental costs were agreed on a 'flexible' and 'case by case' basis (interviews, World Bank and UNDP, 1997). In the words of the German Council member: 'ICs [incremental costs] are not in the hands of scientists, but are negotiated between governments. So governments have to have the capacity to escape the consultants and do it between themselves' (intervention in November 1997 Council meeting). However, not all governments have that capacity, especially those in poorer Southern states perhaps most in need of assistance to make sense of incremental costs. As one former member of the UNDP GEF unit stressed,

> It is important to make incremental costs work for governments. It can't look as if the costs are imposed upon them. The test is one of 'reasonableness': Northern taxpayers [sic] have to be reasonably

---

29. That is, projects falling under more than one of GEF's four 'focal areas'.

happy, and recipient governments have to be reasonably happy. This 'reasonableness' is negotiated between Implementing Agencies and governments, and between Implementing Agencies and the GEF Secretariat. The Implementing Agencies are thus in the middle, having to negotiate with each side and sell them the other side's picture. (interview, UNDP, 1998)

This interviewee stressed the importance of representing Southern governments' interests at the meetings where GEF projects are decided upon – that is, primarily in New York and Washington. For not only were the economic measurements of natural value used for incremental costs analysis next to meaningless in any real sense, but decisions were generally made in languages, places and cultures that can only be called exclusive (see Chapter 6).

GEF Operations Committee

Before successful project proposals (complete with convincing incremental costs analysis) came to Council for formal approval into a 'work programme', in the early years of GEF-1 they had to pass through an opaque inter-agency Operations Committee. Known as the GEFOP, it met every three months or so to check that the Implementing Agencies' project proposals met GEF criteria and fulfilled operational guidance. The GEFOP consisted of staff from the Secretariat, the three Implementing Agencies (often the head of each GEF unit) and the chair of the STAP. Representatives of the CBD and FCCC secretariats could be invited to 'relevant' meetings 'as appropriate', and the chair was free to invite others as needed 'for GEFOP to conduct its business effectively' (GEF Instrument, 1994).

The GEFOP was initially chaired by the assistant CEO of the Facility's Secretariat, Ian Johnson, and with all three Implementing Agencies exchanging views, the meetings were to be a key site of promised 'inter-agency synergy'. However, it was hard to find out what actually happened inside the GEFOP, where initially up to 50 individuals could be 'present' in some form or other (see below), at meetings lasting up to seven or eight hours.[30] It is not always clear from the minutes on what basis some decisions were made.

30. Some GEF Secretariat staff were not sure if minutes were available, others claimed that none were kept. Meanwhile the CBD secretariat held a file of GEFOP minutes clearly prepared by the GEF Secretariat.

Convention representatives rarely saw their guidance reflected clearly, and after the first GEFOP meeting the chairman was moved to note that participants should examine only the 'quality, relevance and timeliness' of projects, and not discuss 'thematic, geographic or institutional balance', nor 'political considerations with regard to country choice etc.' He also made clear that the GEFOP would not approve proposals for

> [funding] staffing and administrative costs for the functions that the Implementing Agencies would be expected to perform in the normal course ... under their own institutional mandates ...

– a probable response to UNEP's keen interest in GEF as a possible solution to their own chronic underfunding. Minutes show that the GEFOP discussions were mainly technical, but also the favour with which World Bank proposals were treated (generally having their projects approved,[31] even sometimes gaining access to other agencies' projects[32]), and the marginal status of the UNEP. The intensity of criticism directed at UNEP project proposals led one observer from the CBD secretariat (not institutionally disposed to be friendly to the UNEP)[33] to note that even if some were of poor quality, the UNEP 'maybe has a point' when complaining that 'GEFOP was abused'.

The UNEP's problems in GEFOP meetings were compounded by logistical difficulties. Sometimes the later pages of UNEP proposals would be lost in the faxing process, and the project dismissed for being incomplete. At a cost of about $5,000 per four-hour GEFOP session, electronic conferencing was used to enable those who could not easily fly to Washington regularly – notably the UNEP in faraway

31. Questionnaire respondent, 1997, although in the early days of GEF many World Bank projects were rejected (GEF Annual Report, 1996) – ostensibly because they were inappropriate old proposals that had failed to get funding when renewables and energy efficiency were last fashionable in the 1970s (pers. comm., 1996).
32. For example, the UNDP's PDF Block B for the Black Sea was to be redesigned in consultation with the World Bank since it involved the design of a 'sustainable financial mechanism', 29 June 1995 GEFOP.
33. The CBD secretariat was not disposed to be sympathetic to the UNEP because it was involved in institutional battles with the UNEP – ostensibly rooted in a dispute about funds and staffing when the CBD moved from Geneva to Montreal.

Nairobi – to talk with a roomful of people in the US. This technology was supposed to create 'considerable travel savings over time' for the Implementing Agencies involved.[34] Yet from the UNEP's perspective 'Teleconferencing never worked due to time differences and technical problems. Connections in Africa are not always good and a piece of paper for example, crackling in Washington, would cut off the voices from Africa' (interview, 1998). This cost-saving innovation seemed to have only compounded inequitable participation by the Implementing Agencies in the GEF.

In 1996 the GEFOP was replaced with 'inter-agency task forces' – shorter bilateral meetings between the GEF Secretariat and each of the three Implementing Agencies to go over their proposed projects, followed by an 'executive GEFOP' where GEF Secretariat staff talk to their counterparts in the Conventions' secretariats.[35] One observer from the GEF called the change 'a formalisation of the upstream discussions that had always taken place', but even for the UNEP this further exclusion from the supposed site of 'inter-agency synergy' made little difference because 'there never was any comparative advantage' gained by having all three Implementing Agencies 'present' in the GEFOP (interview, UNEP, 1998). But by reducing opportunity for inter-institutional arguments, this change in the project approval process may have sped up the rate at which project proposals reach the Council for signing off.

Approaching Approval

Governments hoping for prompt funding of their responsibilities under the new conventions were frustrated at not only the investment of time, energy and expertise required to prepare a project proposal, but also the slow pace of progress once a proposal entered the GEF 'pipeline'. The GEF project cycle has been notoriously long and complicated – initially taking two years on average from proposal to final approval, irrespective of the size of the

34. GEF Secretariat office memo, El-Ashry to Ian Johnson, 22 December 1994, GEFOP Minutes.
35. Despite their willingness to share GEFOP minutes, even the CBD secretariat would not open their files of minutes from the biodiversity task force meetings.

project.[36] According to the 1998 OPS, hold ups occurred because projects had to pass through the Implementing Agencies' screening and project cycles as well as the GEF Secretariat, STAP and Council reviews.[37] In the late 1990s there were more moves to 'expedite' certain project categories (see below), but still 'Every Council meeting adds more layers of difficulty, more conditions for GEF funding – an average of three per meeting' (interview, Council member, 1997) and 'Every request from Council for more information on a proposed project adds anything from three weeks to several months to the project approval process' (interview, UNDP, 1997).

As with decisions proposed by the World Bank's governing Board (Caufield, 1996), being close to the Secretariat allowed US government officials to look over GEF draft decisions a few days before other Council members. In fact, Council meetings were merely the crowning event to a long process of 'subtle' development of consensus positions by El-Ashry, culminating in a private lunch the day before a Council started – the same day that NGOs held their formal consultation with the GEF: 'Pre-Council negotiations facilitate the exchange of views, not trying to neutralise exchange but to smooth it. It is very informal ... if observers were allowed in, it would become an official meeting and would be called bureaucracy' (interview, El-Ashry, 1997).

Thus working in his favoured private mode, El-Ashry used his dual position to smooth the way to Council consensus. Some saw this as a benefit, since

> Clearly, reaching consensus among 32 constituency representatives on the Council, is a very tall order. And I think that's what bringing the CEO and chairman together in the body of one person really does facilitate. It allows him to work with individual Council members, in the corridors, to get issues out on the table

36. In 1996–7, proposals for projects of $750,000 or under – medium-sized grants (MSGs) – were given an 'expedited' approval procedure, without the Council becoming involved. If they were small enough to fall under the auspices of the SGP, projects could go ahead with only national level approval.
37. The Secretariat was required to meet the Council's demands as closely as possible, with the result that they became almost 'another review body' (interview, World Bank, 1997) delaying project approvals. Additional reviews by any of the Conventions' bodies would have added even more delay.

in a more private and constructive environment to address them. (interview, World Bank, in Howitt and Young, 2000)

Yet some observers felt that El-Ashry had more power than was perhaps necessary – echoing Southern governments calls for more independence for GEF bodies in the run up to Cartagena (see Chapter 4): 'There is no need for the GEF CEO to be Chair of Council as well' (interview, UNDP, 1997).

Sometimes the temporary co-chair too seems to have been selected for political reasons. For example, at the Council meeting in spring 1998, a Southern member known to have reservations about the new monitoring and evaluation report was selected as co-chair – meaning that he could not speak out from the floor as he chose. While he was being elected as co-chair, the microphones transmitting Council proceedings to the observers' room and recording for the official record went down, so it was not clear to those out of earshot how exactly he was chosen.[38]

On another occasion, El-Ashry told his co-chair in November 1997 that he was 'a great artist' for his work to finalise the wording of the Joint Summary of the Chairs. In GEF Council meetings, careful diplomacy seems to have been a useful art, since 'GEF governance requires considerable stage management' (interview, GEF Secretariat, 1997). As chief 'stage manager', with consummate charm El-Ashry would help to smoothe ruffled feathers whenever they risked derailing 'consensus'. One observer noted that

At face value, North–South tensions on GEF Council have decreased, but then Council members are treated like kings by El-Ashry, and they wouldn't want to respond rudely. [One prominent Southern Council member] might say that the rest of the South has been 'bought'; but then he hasn't sold his soul ... he's one of the few on the Council who has not. (interview, CBD secretariat, 1997)

This interviewee compared the GEF Council's silver service meals[39] with the paper cups in which the CBD COP participants drank

38. This was not the only occasion on which technical difficulties masked apparent political intricacies, but it would be wrong to impute a pattern from so few cases observed.

39. For all the silver service presentation, the food provided by the World Bank for lunch during GEF Council meetings was somewhat

coffee from a machine. Perhaps he saw in GEF meetings something of a Solomon Islands *Mumi*: the use of hospitality as a form of aggression – as described in Page's (1972) study of corporate tribes. Either way, it certainly struck newcomers that when it comes to GEF Council decision-making, 'things are cooked ahead of time' (interview, NGO, 1998).

DISTRIBUTING THE MONEY

Administration Costs

With regard to the proportion of GEF funding spent on administering processes and projects in the GEF Secretariat and Implementing Agencies, from the perspective of implementing staff 'The Council wants ever more performance and information from the Implementing Agencies, but we can't expand our GEF work, we must stay within our administrative budgets and the limits of the portfolio as initially agreed by the Council' (interview, UNDP, 1997). And 'The Bank would love to minimise bureaucracy, but Council requirements do not allow that' (interview, World Bank, 1997).

When I visited in 1997, the full-time staff of the UNDP's GEF office seemed to be snowed under with work.[40] A former member of staff said that

UNDP's GEF unit is very hardworking and effective while totally understaffed. The situation in itself is probably unsustainable; although it is very cost-effective from a money point of view. The co-ordinators are among the most dedicated staff in the UNDP, they have a missionary zeal, and take great pleasure in their work. (interview, UNDP, 1997)

---

insubstantial, neither organic nor particularly local. The hospitality did stretch to NGOs attending Council meetings, but on the day of the pre-Council NGO consultation the fare was usually a soggy sandwich, fruit and crisps in a cardboard box. In November 1997 there was no drinking water available at the consultation – apart from ice melted in a paper cup with hot water from the tea machine. The next consultation, held in New Delhi, was provided with countless small plastic bottles of mineral water as well as, for once, the same class of food as fed to official delegates.

40. Consultants in the UNDP meanwhile seemed more laid back, and had more time to talk.

One of those still there wondered 'perhaps this is a sort of experiment, a test to show the rest of the agency's development-oriented staff how much work can be done with so little resources by committed environmental people' (pers. comm., UNDP, 1997). By contrast, World Bank offices seemed very quiet, and more of their staff made time for a visiting researcher than in the UNDP (I did not visit the UNEP so cannot compare), though as to be expected, Bank staff also complained of too much work.

Staff in the GEF Secretariat too felt overworked, and felt that their budgets were fairly tight for the travel and communications necessary to fulfil their research, liaison and monitoring duties. 'We did the shoestring thing' said one, regretting that the Secretariat was criticised for not reaching out widely enough when the Council was not willing to expand their budget. However, by not filling some staff positions and relying on secondments in an 'administrative game' (see Chapter 4), the Secretariat was able to be flexible with budgets to cover emerging expenses – such as translations into Japanese for the Kyoto climate change COP and the production of a book for the Participants' Assembly.[41]

Apparently, when the Council told the UNDP that their administrative overheads were too high, they brought them down from around 13 per cent of total project costs to between 6 and 8 per cent (interview, UNDP, 1997). However, a close NGO observer estimated that 'Currently about 30–40 per cent of GEF cash is lost in transaction costs before it hits the ground. Some of this is the necessary price of consultation and participation processes, but much is waste' (interview, 1997). Eventually the GEF introduced flat commission fees per project, which were not universally welcomed, largely since each Agency had different needs and resources.

Procurement

GEF spending is subject to the Implementing Agencies' rules on co-financing and Byzantine systems of procurement. A large proportion of it also flows back to the Northern countries from where it is raised. In response to donor enquiries, in 1997 the GEF Secretariat produced figures showing that 68 per cent of contracts to supply projects funded in GEF-1 were sourced from OECD countries, including 40 per cent from G7 and nearly 30 per cent from the US and UK. Under

41. *Keeping the Promise – Actions and Investments for a 21st Century*, 1998.

a third of procurement contracts were sourced from suppliers in 'recipient' countries.[42]

According to the World Bank's rules for procurement ('intended to inform the business community to the opportunities generated by Bank-supported projects'), 'contracts are awarded to the lowest evaluated responsive bidder ... [although] other factors may also be taken into account, such as quality, durability, availability of after sale service and spare parts, training and even maintenance and operating costs' (World Bank, 1995). Yet there were no specific environmental criteria for goods and services procured by the World Bank, even for those procured for GEF's 'global environmental' projects. It seems that this would be a check too far for Bank staff. When questioned about the potential implications for GEF's environmental goals, an economist in the GEF unit said

> While [environmental procurement] guidelines would be laudable, the practicality of their application in developing countries would have to be considered. In some [cases, seeing that GEF meetings are served] organically grown food, for instance, this might work against developing countries by forcing purchases in international markets at considerably higher prices ... How would one determine that organizations share GEF principles – through what they profess, or what they do in reality? Who would certify? Again, this is morally defensible, but may be extremely difficult to put into practice. (e-mail from economist at the World Bank, 1998)

Easier for the Bank to manage than environmental conditionality for their procurement contracts was price-based competitive tendering: 'World Bank project managers aim for the best effort to meet the price ... to instill money management in partners, earn interest for the Bank ... so they shop around. It's not rocket science' (interview, World Bank, 1997).

The Bank's rules for procurement conclude 'you have to compete in order to win'. Yet for many local conservationists, 'competing' globally is impossible – even were it desirable. Not only are most firms and grass-roots environmental groups totally under-resourced for the World Bank's complex bidding process, but with experience

---

42. GEF Procurement Report; GEF/R.2/Inf.2.

in their area they embody local expertise and commitment that can be neither found in other bodies nor generalised to other places. In the UNDP too, once projects developed through a partnership between the Implementing Agency and a local NGO were approved, they would generally be handed to the procurement department for competitive international bidding at the risk of losing all the delicate inter-agency arrangements agreed, and often cutting out local organisations who had worked for ages on the environmental issue and/or project proposal.

This situation began to change in the UNDP in 1996, by which time NGOs were participating in 145 out of 184 UNDP–GEF projects. *Partners or Hired Hands?* (Curtis et al., 1997) was the report of a GEF–NGO working group to discuss transforming the relations between UNDP and NGOs from purely commercial procurement for services within projects to more of a partnership. In the World Bank, experience with different partners made some relationships more conducive, although there remained limits on the kind of organisation which could engage with the international agencies constructively to provide services, let alone to try and execute their projects.

Executing Agencies

The Implementing Agencies may make arrangements for GEF project ... execution by multilateral development banks, specialized agencies and programs of the United Nations, other international organizations, bilateral development agencies, national institutions, non-governmental organizations, private sector entities and academic institutions, taking into account their comparative advantages in efficient and cost-effective project execution.

To become an executing agency, paid through one of the Implementing Agencies to implement a GEF project on the ground, an organisation had to be a formal entity with legal status, accounts and experience with the proposed level of funding. Many were therefore government agencies at the global or national level – especially environmental ministries on limited budgets seeking GEF funds to pay for pre-planned initiatives – while some were NGOs and research institutions.

Some NGOs were keen to execute GEF projects, yet, as we have seen, many others were either unaware, misinformed or hostile to the GEF, or found its requirements so demanding for the money promised compared to other aid funds that it was not worth exploring (interviews, NGOs, 1997–9). The NGOs who did engage, however, generally offered the GEF more help on biodiversity than on climate change. By bringing in selected NGOs for both advice and project implementation, the Implementing Agencies were able to take advantage of their environmental expertise and contacts – consultancy services which were often provided, initially at least, for free. An employee of the IUCN estimated that a project they ran with GEF assistance could have been done more quickly if they had done it alone, and the IUCN had probably put more resources into identifying, drafting and following up priorities (unpaid) than they eventually received from the GEF in funds (interview, NGO, 1997).

In this context mere execution was not enough for all NGOs, especially given the problems some have had trying to work with the Implementing Agencies. The US delegation to the Participants' Assembly in 1998 expressed the desire of some NGOs to function as a 'fourth Implementing Agency' dealing directly with the Secretariat. Yet the French[43] and other representatives were concerned that the international US-based NGOs were already an unannounced fourth Implementing Agency, and spoke out for more accountability from them instead.

Meanwhile, as we saw in Chapter 4, there was also resentment among some of the other NGOs interested in GEF of these well-resourced Northern groups relatively 'in the loop' with the World Bank (and often also based 'inside the beltway' of Washington DC). Southern groups especially questioned the role of the IUCN as not only central focal point of the GEF–NGO network, but also a privileged executing agency with strong links to governments at the national level and globally. With its quasi-governmental status, smaller Southern NGOs felt it unfair that the IUCN should compete with them to execute projects, especially where there was good capacity in local NGOs and community groups.

A similar relationship pertains to some extent with private sector interest in working with the GEF: where they are involved, the 'big boys' generally have it easier. For example, when a representative of the US solar technologies export council attended a GEF Council

---

43. Perceived by a UNDP interviewee as an ally of Southern governments, they wanted indigenous Southern NGOs to be more involved in the GEF – rather than being anti-NGO in general (interview, 1997).

meeting in the hope of learning through observation how the small-scale solar businesses they represent might work with the GEF, they left looking fairly baffled. Yet in an impromptu meeting at the Climate Change Convention COP in Argentina, 1998, an executive of the British oil and petrochemical corporation BP was able to meet with Mohamed El-Ashry, James Wolfensohn of the World Bank, a key player from the FCCC secretariat and consultants willing to put together a project helping BP convert its Pacific oil supply lines to solar technology distribution (interview, consultant, 1998).

Whether or not this proposal succeeded in spreading renewables technologies and creating environmental benefits, it is doubtful that BP needed publicly-funded assistance more than emerging renewables companies did – even those from the US. However, the BP representative clearly found it much easier to engage usefully with GEF actors than did people without the resources of a major organisation behind them.[44]

Recognising these limitations to some extent, the GEF decentralised some assistance to the smaller-scale private sector through a Small and Medium Enterprises (SME) Program, run as a single project by the World Bank's private sector arm – the IFC – with $5 million for the pilot phase. Examples of uses of the fund include opening lines of credit for energy conservation in industry, or for ecotourism, or non-timber forest products ventures undertaken by a local company, financial intermediary or NGO. The GEF notes that SMEs are 'where much of human activity happens', but the programme, which generally involves 'concentrating resources through an intermediary' is not very high profile within the GEF. This may be since, from the GEF perspective, 'The administrative costs of financing SMEs are proportionally large for an international organisation relative to larger projects and the impact of an individual SME is small.'[45]

Enabling Activities

As a first task for their 'financial mechanism', governments party to the multilateral Conventions on Climate Change and Biodiversity

44. When questioned about the GEF's relations with private sector bodies, people working inside the GEF and its Implementing Agencies seemed hardly to register the disparities between Northern and Southern, small and large firms within the private sector.
45. From a leaked 1993 draft GEF document on 'small and medium scale private sector participation in the GEF'.

wanted assistance with national reports and plans required by the Conventions.[46] As the GEF hinted in its operational policies, enabling activities could lay the ground for bigger GEF projects when they:

> help countries to prepare national inventories, strategies, and action plans in cooperation with the CBD and the UN FCCC. This assistance enables countries to assess biodiversity and climate change challenges from a national perspective, determine the most promising opportunities for project development, and subsequently pursue full-scale projects.[47]

Preparation of 'national communications' to the Conventions demanded a high level of scientific and technical expertise. Much of the information produced for the Conventions was also of socioeconomic value – less to Southern-based interests than to an international community of scientists and investors with ambitions to fill in gaps in 'global' data sets and to map the status of 'global' resources from rare genes to power utilities (Goldman, 1998; McAfee 1999).[48] Therefore Southern governments were generally unwilling to act for these 'global benefits' without GEF's additional 'global' money. Yet still it took a while for GEF's Implementing Agencies to get up much momentum on developing enabling activities projects.

46. When governments became Parties to the Convention on Climate Change, they agreed to conduct thorough national assessments of the distribution of sources and sinks of 'greenhouse gases' (GHGs) in their territory, and under the CBD they agreed to summarise their biodiversity. These assessments were in addition to the national Environmental Action Plans, National Sustainable Development Strategies, Local Agenda 21, etc., also underway in the 1990s.
47. <www.gefweb.org/Operational_Policies/Eligibility_Criteria/ Funding_Options/funding_options.html>
48. Vogler (2002) notes that environmental conventions have been operationally dependent upon a small transnational community of technical specialists. Under the FCCC, these were primarily the people compiling national GHG and carbon sink inventories, and under the CBD they range from systematic biologists compiling national biodiversity inventories to the lawyers advising on intellectual property rights, etc. These communities are composed of national civil servants and scientists; their status reflects their link to an interstate regime. Their tasks therefore involve promoting the interests of the states and agencies for which they work, and the field in which they work, as combined in the negotiated agreements of the conventions.

With the progress of the Conventions dependent on timely reporting by their Parties, the Conventions soon grew very impatient with GEF's complex requirements for project preparation and opaque, lengthy approval procedures.[49] By 1998, under pressure from the Conventions for an 'expedited procedure', the GEF's approval cycle for enabling activities was reduced to 4–6 months.

Partly because of 'not wanting to burn our fingers on a political hot potato',[50] the World Bank took a strategic decision fairly early on not to do enabling activities (interview, World Bank, 1997). The design and running of these projects therefore fell largely to the UNDP, who hired a consultant to devise a generalisable structure for enabling activities projects. Some of the work was farmed out to NGOs like the World Conservation Monitoring Centre in Cambridge, UK, which helped to develop biodiversity plans in ten Southern countries. By the start of 1998, 40 reports on the development of National Biodiversity Strategies, many of them 'interim', had been submitted to the CBD secretariat. Yet questions were raised about the relevance of these reports, most of which were produced by consultants with little time for engagement with the practicalities. Critics said that the plans may have reflected international scientific standards but were hardly designed to deal with local realities, needs or skills (interview, NGO, 1997), with the result that many governments now have another set of reports sitting on a shelf saying what should be done, while officials carry on doing what can be done.

Meanwhile others had an interest in the information aggregated for the Conventions. For example, the GEF provided some assistance to taxonomic training and database development through a biodiversity project in Costa Rica that involved training local people as 'para-taxonomists' to gather indigenous knowledge of local species and their properties. They would help to translate information into scientific language, adding it to computer databases complete with

49. Only seven countries (out of the 30-odd that should have done so) had reported by the Kyoto COP in December 1997. One member of GEF Secretariat staff endured a 'baptism of fire' on this issue when their first official visit for the Secretariat was to an FCCC COP in Geneva, 1996 (interview, GEF Secretariat, 1997).

50. Other reasons for the Bank's reluctance were that they had no comparative advantage for delivery in terms of programming procedures, for free-standing technical assistance, which is the UNDP's area of expertise, and because the Global Overlays Program, which was more allied with Bank strategies, was already planned.

bar codes ready for formalisation into the scientific canon – and for
the sale of rights to the genetic material on international markets.
According to some NGOs (interviews, 1996), while this may have
been scientifically valuable at the global level, it did less to conserve
nature than effectively to subsidise bioprospectors seeking new genes
for possible exploitation in the (then bubbling) biotech economy.

DEVOLVING FINANCE

Trust and Capital Investment Funds

While most GEF finance went to fund project activities directly, the
GEF's requirement of 'innovation' meant it could not fund the same
initiative twice. As a result, unsustainability of its investments was
often listed as a problem in GEF's evaluations, and it was partly in
response to this flow that GEF funds were increasingly devolved to
support, for example, conservation trust funds.[51] More easily
accessed and influenced locally than the GEF, national environmental funds were favoured by NGOs for providing long-term
support to environmental initiatives.

The governance structures of trust funds, as well as the national
committees of the SGP, reinforced country ownership in a way that
traditional project implementation arrangements could not. As a
result they initially created difficulties for a Council determined to
ensure that only 'global environmental benefits' were supported. For
GEF's dominant donor governments,

> The problem was control. The US government in particular would
> not release its control. They always wanted to micro-manage GEF
> spending, largely in response to the intensity of political advocacy
> in Washington DC, which meant that everybody's 'say' had to be
> codified. (interview, NGO, 1997)

According to some World Bank staff, there were few trust funds in
the GEF portfolio because at 8 per cent discount or more they

51. Interviewed (1997), an economist in the World Bank GEF unit noted the
Anglo Saxon origins of trust law. Crusaders (notably the Knights Templar)
with a 'chain' of castles along the route collected money for safekeeping
from individual crusaders as they were about to set off. The Knights then
invested the money in their order's activities and doled back it out to
their 'investors' at points along the way to and from the Holy Land.

provide very meagre returns after management and administrative costs are removed – and with little prospect of revenue generation, they are not sustained. The GEF's Implementing Agencies also did not emphasise trust funds because 'they could not make assumptions about what was coming' (interview, UNDP, 1997). Without having given their wholehearted commitment to trust funds, Agency staff felt the Council could at any minute produce new guidance for spending GEF resources, so they did not invest much time and money in devolutionary trust funds at the expense of developing other ideas and avenues for investing GEF money.

The few new funds proposed to the GEF were usually 'conceptually developed by the Implementing Agency based on market signals from private companies, NGOs, and government officials' (GEF/C.12/Inf.5). Examples of such funds include those run by the IFC,[52] which brought some more private sector involvement into the GEF by allocating $30 million each for the Renewable and Energy Efficiency Fund and the Photovoltaic Market Transformation Initiative (PVMTI). Another experiment was the regional TERRA Capital fund, intended to attract private finance into biodiversity conservation and sustainable use, including prospecting for genetic resources. Here the GEF funded not the capital invested but the 'incremental costs' incurred by the IFC in setting up and managing the fund.

When it came to seeking advance endorsement from the GEF Council for the IFC's non-country-specific market-driven fund proposals (also the expansion of the global SME Program), problems also arose with the 'country-driven' requirement for GEF finance. How could a 'globally' designed and driven fund meet the national priorities of a particular country, if it is designed to suit all countries equally? When the IFC came to implement the PVMTI, originally developed as a general global fund for photovoltaics (that is, without identifying the recipient countries), specific target countries had to be identified[53] so that their endorsements could be sought in advance.

The Small Grants Programme

In response to sustained demands not least from NGOs and scientists for more devolved, grass-roots conservation spending, the SGP was

---

52. The IFC could become involved in GEF projects only if there was at least 15 per cent private sector involvement.
53. Countries selected initially were Morocco, India and Kenya.

launched in 1992 in 35 pilot countries. It was approved as a single GEF project implemented by the UNDP and worth a total of $5 million – 0.5 per cent of total GEF funds.[54] Its purpose was 'to provide a supplementary opportunity for NGO involvement in the GEF... [and] to test and demonstrate small-scale projects, strategies and processes' (SGP project summary, UNDP, 1994).

In countries selected for an SGP by the UNDP and GEF, a 'broad-based national steering committee' (NSC)[55] was set up to provide guidance and strategic direction, establishing country-specific criteria to screen and select projects within the framework of overall GEF guidelines. Supported by the UNDP, the committee could approve funding to NGOs and 'community-based organisations' (CBOs) of up to $50,000 for national projects, and $250,000 for regional projects.

Members of NSCs serve on a voluntary basis and typically represent the government (which has to endorse the programme if not individual projects); CBOs and NGOs; national academic, scientific, and technical institutions; and the UNDP country office. A national co-ordinator is responsible for managing a country programme, helping small organisations to formulate proposals, visiting the sites of proposed activities,[56] and monitoring and evaluation. The NSCs, like the governance structures of national trust funds, reinforced country ownership. This was perhaps because the incremental costs criterion did not have to be applied to each individual SGP project, the Council having decided that the overall goals of the Programme would contribute to GEF goals.

SGP recipients have to be deemed able to address the GEF's global interests through actions taken at a local level, with community participation. The SGP would not, however, fund large NGOs, not because UNDP people 'don't love them' but because these NGOs themselves funded many of the same groups as the SGP, and could engage internationally with the rest of the GEF's operations (interview, UNDP, 1997).

'Giving good people the space to move' (interview, NGO, 1997), the SGP was to involve no international consultants. The very busy

54. The rest went on big projects, or 'GEF macro' as opposed to 'GEF micro', a popular name for the SGP in French-speaking parts of North Africa and West Asia (interview, UNDP, 1997).
55. Small island Caribbean nations, for example, were subsumed into bigger countries' committees.
56. In big countries like India the national co-ordinator was only able to visit project sites if they were within a localised area (interview, NGO, 1998).

people administering the SGP in the UNDP GEF office in New York described a 'really neat' and 'very sexy little programme'. Replenished in the operational phase of the GEF with $24 million in July 1996 for two years, 750 small grants altogether were expected to have been made by June 1998. In the event the figure was closer to 1,000, as the number of countries participating expanded fast – but still insufficiently to meet demand. In 1997, the CBD secretariat wrote to tell the UNDP that they preferred the SGP to much of the rest of the GEF's approach. The SGP generated a lot of goodwill towards GEF among non-governmental organisations and others interested in small-scale conservation funding (interviews, NGOs, UNDP, 1997), because it 'develops local capacity, laying the necessary foundation for larger projects, building up NGO communities. SGP may not have a lot of immediate global impact, but it has a catalytic effect – like rings in water' (interview, UNDP, 1997). Its popularity stemmed largely from the 'appropriate' scale of the funds involved and the devolution of decision-making and accountability to the national and local levels (interview, UNDP, 1997).

Some examples of SGP-assisted projects in the 1990s: In the biodiversity focal area, $38,361 went on a *Mass Manatee Education and Surveillance Campaign.* In Poland, $7,290 went to assist the reduction of the bird death rate on transmission lines. In Brazil, the Center of Agro-Ecological Technology for Small Farmers received $24,125 under the climate change label. To Chile went $50,000 to support *Recovery of the Native Shrub and Edible Flora of Easter Island.* The Union of Independent Non-Industrial Fishermen of the Juan Fernandez Archipelago received a similar amount to help raise local funds for conservation and sustainable use. The Bolivarian University in Chile received $8,500 for *Training and Application of a Systematization Methodology for the Development Process of SGP Projects.* In Barbados, for a project under the international waters focal area entitled *Promoting Organic Farming to Reduce Coastal Pollution from Pesticide Runoff,* $39,452 was granted to the Theocratic Government of His Majesty Selassie I Churchical Order of the Nyabinghi. The Permaculture Trust of Botswana received $42,900 for a community seed bank. Meanwhile, in Indian fishing communities, the UNDP and two NGOs ran *Popularising the Use of Turtle Excluder Devices in Coastal Orissa* – at the same time as the WTO ruled that fish caught in this way could not be favoured in international trade.[57]

Overall there has been strong demand for SGP grants in countries where programmes are in place, as well as from governments wanting SGP in their country: 'It is very, very wanted ... in places there is astounding enthusiasm' (interview, UNDP, 1997). Nonetheless the Programme has suffered from many of the same problems as the GEF in general – notably a lack of appropriate capacity at the grass roots, unsustainability of initiatives after the project grant has run out, lack of resources for recurrent costs and limited lessons generated. In addition, small community-based groups who raise GEF cash, have faced the multiple problems as well as potentials traditionally involved in 'scaling up' organisations which had thrived largely through being small, informal and close to the ground (Edwards and Hulme, 1992).

The SGP had support in the GEF Council not least from the French, who preferred to see small-scale, in-country NGOs supported than the bigger international groups. Many other members of the GEF Council were, however, wary, expecting problems with accounting and accountability for such decentralised funding. In fact, by late 1997 only one co-ordinator had been fired for malpractice, and out of nearly 900 projects, only ten or so had any real difficulties over accountability (interview, UNDP, 1997). The actual experience, this interviewee suggested, thus 'blows out of the water' any arguments that sufficient trust would not be forthcoming to make such an innovative programme work.

Meanwhile people running the Programme from the UNDP felt that

More resources are needed to fulfill the commitments made in reality, in particular more resources ... [for] the day-to-day running of the Programme. This includes all the costs associated

57. At the same time the possibility of limiting trade in fish caught with turtle-unfriendly nets came under question at the WTO, and a conservation-based ban was eventually deemed unlawful under WTO 'free trade' rules. The GEF–SGP project may have been effective on a small scale, but at the same time a bigger institution in the same system of global governance was undermining turtle conservation at the international level.

with developing and financing the projects that are not covered by the grants. (interview, UNDP, 1997)

They also felt that the GEF Secretariat needed to 'beat the drum' for the SGP if it was to reach its full catalytic potential. For despite the Programme's value as a 'showcase' of GEF's potential to assist grass-roots conservation, and its capacity to do more for 'outreach' than the rest of the GEF put together (interview, UNDP, 1997), the Secretariat was said to be 'not committed' to the SGP. Like the rest of the World Bank, the Secretariat is considered to have had a fairly dismissive attitude to projects with such little potential for capital investment.

Medium-Sized Grants Programme

Big NGOs denied access to the SGP and unhappy with the scope of their participation in larger GEF projects have used their political space in the GEF to push for an 'expedited pathway' for Medium-Sized Grants. In 1997 a GEF–NGO working group finalised a framework for a programme offering up to $1 million through 'expedited procedures that speed processing and implementation' of project proposals from 'a wider range of interested parties'.[58] Conservatism among World Bank and UNDP resident representatives in recipient countries tended to mean that only established and/or elite NGOs would be likely to benefit from MSGs. However, some such groups aimed to act as 'conveyor belts for ideas' developed by smaller groups on the ground (interview, NGOs, 1997), and staff in the World Bank GEF division feared being swamped by ideas from NGOs in need of Bank help to develop MSG proposals. Grants of up to $750,000 needed the approval only of the CEO, above that amount they needed the stamp of the Council. The MSG pathway thus provided El-Ashry with the opportunity to directly reward NGOs for their efforts to promote the GEF – for example arguing the GEF's case with donor governments when replenishment was coming up (see above).

More than three times as many applications were received from NGOs, research institutions and even government departments than were expected in the 1998 financial year, which somewhat over-

58. <www.gefweb.org/Operational_Policies/Eligibility_Criteria/
Funding_Options/funding_options.html>

whelmed planned resources.[59] In this context national GEF focal points tended to favour NGOs that they already knew. Projects submitted to the World Bank were ruled eligible in 85 per cent of cases, while 54 per cent of those submitted to the UNDP and 29 per cent of those submitted to the UNEP were approved. The GEF's review of experience with MSGs attributes this bias to the World Bank doing more 'upfront screening' before sending concepts through to the GEF Secretariat – presumably meaning that the World Bank's parental relationship to the Secretariat meant it knew what kind of projects and partners would suit it best.

By 1999 MSG concepts submitted to the GEF Secretariat were: 116 biodiversity, 30 climate change, 19 multi-focal and 5 international waters. However, for all its appeal as an instrument to 'break the terrible irrationality of having to have big projects to cover the overheads' (interview, NGO, 1997), like SGP, the MSG Programme was still of very limited scope, and was described by one actively involved NGO as 'a pimple on the arse of progress' (interview, 1997). Others complained about inconsistent rulings on the eligibility of MSG proposals, and bottlenecks remaining in the process. They therefore called for improved working groups, more transparency, better legal frameworks[60] and implementation procedures for NGO participation in the whole of the Implementing Agencies' portfolios – not just components associated with GEF, let alone the MSG.

RISKS IN THE GEF PORTFOLIO

The diversity of GEF's funding streams, the agencies channelling them and the bodies receiving them reflected the GEF's vague agenda and tendency – like the term 'sustainable development' – to try to be 'all things to all people'. Yet the GEF was widely criticised (not least by NGOs) for lack of originality in its project portfolio, and an apparent risk aversion that denied its avowed aim to be experimental in order to 'reduce the risk caused by uncertainty' in environmental investments. Given Mary Douglas' analysis of *Dominant Rationality and Risk Perception* (1994) it is interesting to note what is and is not classed as a risk to the GEF's portfolio in its Operational Strategy. Four types of risk are listed:

59. Review of Experience with Medium-Sized Project Procedures, GEF/C.12/Inf.7, 10 September 1998.
60. GEF–NGO Newsletter, June/July 1998.

- the normal commercial and technical risk associated with any development project
- additional project risk as a result of opting for a measure that also protects the global environment [for example, substituting a new renewable energy technology for a familiar fossil-fuel based technology]
- the expected global benefits may not arise or may not be incremental [for example when an ecosystem conserved through a GEF project is later destroyed]
- the measures ... adopted may not prove to be the best or most effective in meeting ... overall objectives [for example if most of the GEF's resources are invested in one or two technologies which] do not become financially self-sustaining as expected.

Unlisted is the risk that aspects of a GEF-assisted project may directly create negative environmental externalities. This risk is not negligible since there are no specific environmental criteria for the procurement of goods or services under GEF projects (see above), so GEF funds could be used to buy environmentally damaging technologies and support environmentally and/or socially irresponsible firms.

Under the biodiversity-focused *India Ecodevelopment* project in Nagarhole (see Appendix IV), for example, GEF money helped to build roads and buy jeeps for the government, even though indigenous forest-dwellers were adamant that timber and wildlife smugglers use the roads, and vehicles frighten the threatened animals – meanwhile emitting GHGs. The project also deprived forest-dwelling Adivasi[61] and local landless peasants of traditional rights to use forest products, driving them to seek a living from smuggling or other unsustainable practices when the compensatory trees and goats they were offered proved useless in the absence of irrigation and good land for them to grow. Forest dwellers claim their practices are missed in the forest's ecology when they are thrown out – little science has been done to prove or disprove this claim, and research is not a priority for GEF financing.

Another level of risk not listed in the Operational Strategy is that any of the focal areas might not be as much of a global environmental problem as feared; for example, if perceived climate change turns out to be not anthropogenic but due to solar flaring or another

61. 'Adivasi' refers to tribal communities in the Indian subcontinent. Its literal translation is 'original dweller'.

alternative hypothesis (Boehmer-Christiansen, 1997). Obviously, this line of thinking could be taken to extremes, but the fact remains that GEF investments inevitably face more risks than its administrators can effectively list, let alone manage. This makes the tasks of people operationalising GEF strategy all the harder – charged with innovation, but constrained by organisational, ideological, social, political and financial arrangements, they risk any number of experiments gone wrong.

As we shall explore further in Chapter 6, there are many practical, financial and political constraints on project managers and consultants. One result has been that the design, implementation and evaluation of GEF projects have generally been carried out with incomplete attention to wider contexts or to projects' potential impacts on interactions between economy and environment – and the consequent risks of unforeseen effects.

CONCLUSIONS

In response to Council demands for accountability, the Implementing Agencies required bodies channelling GEF funds to become bureaucratised, to talk 'GEFese' and produce reports (instead, perhaps, of doing conservation work), if they were not already civil servants with these duties to perform. This kind of accountability – 'upwards' to funders needing paper evidence of money spent efficiently, rather than 'downwards' to beneficiaries and others seeking fair as well as effective conservation – is hardly unique to the GEF. But as we shall see in the next chapter, it has telling implications for the scope of 'efficiency' that donor governments foresaw for GEF, a kind of efficiency that maintained the GEF as a more productive experiment for its supporters than the environment programme set up in the UN 20 years earlier.

6   Competition, Cooperation and Distorted Feedback

Inside GEF; Relations in the GEF Family; Participation and Feedback; Democracy, Science and Knowledge; Conclusions

Previous chapters have delved into GEF structure, process and spending; this chapter steps back to examine some of the patterns emerging so far – both within the GEF 'family' of institutions, and in their relations with the outside world. The focus here is on the political, practical and ideological constraints on professional people guiding and managing GEF finances.

The term 'global environment' can be seen as an intellectual convenience for globally active conservationists and global public servants coming together in the GEF. Some say that lacking scientific justification or connection to local ecologies, the global distinction also undermines the potential for popular understanding of and interest in the GEF (McAfee, 1999). It certainly leaves the definition as well as the pursuit of GEF's benefits – global environmental or otherwise – in the hands of a small group of unelected people active at the international level. For, as an insider to one of the governments funding the World Bank and GEF observed, 'The answer to the problem of World Bank staff getting too pally with the recipient governments is centralisation, ensuring leadership from the top.'[1]

1. Chatham House rules, 1997.

Political compromises on the shape and scope of the GEF are inevitable given the range of unsolved contradictions involved. These emerge from global geo-politics; and from incompatability between, on the one hand, expectations of transparent communications with the outside world and widespread participation of non-governmental interests and, on the other, effective intergovernmental diplomacy, political control, and bureaucratic efficiency. Meanwhile turf wars and jockeying for position between international institutions with different goals and loyalties only compounds the unevenness of accountability demanded by donor and recipient governments in the complex system emerging. In particular, the distance between decision-making fora and the sites of real-world impacts prevents the kind of feedback necessary for effective institutional learning. Unease in some quarters is inevitable given the people and environmental issues excluded by the GEF's need to find and work only with 'credible' partners, that is, organisations and individuals promising to help reconcile divergent objectives without challenging hegemonic ideologies or undermining the GEF's own institutional environment. For as one Northern member of GEF's governing Council observed: 'We are writing history, and must leave a well-oiled machine for those following' (intervention in Council meeting, 1998) and perspectives coming in at a tangent to 'businesslike' operations tend to put a spanner in the works.

If the GEF is to be more than simply a smooth-running system suiting existing financial and political power bases, perhaps the solution would be not to exclude or disarm potential spanner bearers, but to adopt machinery which copes with and even welcomes different environmental value systems, strategies and tools. This would involve a degree of inversion of current practices, starting from the real-world needs and ideas of people actually living in and creating threatened environments – as expressed through participatory social science and democracy. The concluding chapter, Chapter 6, explores further such idealised possibilities for reform.

INSIDE GEF

Evaluation Overload and Feedback Limits

When society's economic, political, and social structures become institutionalized, power tends to flow from people into institutions, but not back again. Power becomes concentrated. (Draffan, 2000)

Despite the centralisation of political power embodied in the GEF, insofar as the Facility was required to be participatory and build partnerships, it had to listen to the people executing its projects in Southern governments, national institutions and NGOs, as well as the people affected thereby. The Council was therefore firm that GEF should be regularly and comprehensively evaluated – so that criticism could be heard, issues arising dealt with and lessons learned. With the precedent of the Independent Evaluation of the Pilot Phase (1994, see Chapter 4) to live up to, the 1998 Overall Performance Study was wide-ranging in its search for inputs and in places highly critical.[2]

Yet the very breadth of remit of the OPS's reviewers – whose 'main mandate' was to establish whether the GEF was 'the best mechanism for providing funding for global environmental purposes' – meant that they could not realistically complete their task fully with the time and resources available.[3] Furthermore, reviews were underway by the Conventions and the Implementing Agencies at the same time, so people both in the international institutions and on the ground felt their work was at risk of being 'evaluated to death' (interview, World Bank, 1997). One member of the 1998 OPS team confided that 'big shot' evaluations with large teams of consultants attempting to cover every aspect of GEF's work were not the best use of scarce resources, and suggested instead a targeted study 'adding value' to the other evaluations (interview, consultant, 1997).[4]

A conclusion more publicly reached by the official team was that the amount of money the GEF was given was 'far short of adequate levels' (OPS, 1998) for its primary intended goal of meeting the needs of the Conventions (although no clear statement of the costs of actually doing so had been prepared from any official source).[5] As

2. In early 2002 another official evaluation was completed – with feedback on the effectiveness of early projects beginning to come through – see Chapter 7.
3. I am aware that a similar critique could with justification be levelled at the study on which this book is based.
4. Mittermeier and Bowles' (1993) suggestion that GEF projects should be reviewed by local experts rather than flown-in consultants seems not to have had a great deal of impact.
5. In the absence of official figures for the cost of biodiversity conservation, the GEF's Overall Performance Study, 1998, noted the World Conservation Monitoring Centre's extrapolation of the UNEP's figures to cost biodiversity conservation at $20 billion per year. The OPS also noted that for climate-related projects the GEF – like most other donor organisations –

in 1994, the evaluators were concerned that the money available had to be distributed across countries and sectors, rather than targeted to where it could have the most systemic impact on an ecological or political level (not that expert advisors always agreed on where this was). And with money following initiatives imposed largely 'from above', projects rarely attained institutional sustainability when GEF funding ceased (OPS, 1998). As a result it was difficult for consistent lessons to be generated, let alone learned.

Differentials in financial and technical capacity also affected the thoroughness of feedback and participation, even within the GEF Council. For example when the draft OPS was presented to the Council in autumn 1997, feedback was requested by e-mail. Those (Southern) governments lacking effective e-mail facilities were at a disadvantage given the tight time frame for comments. In the same context, one Council member requested to see the country-level reports making up the overall analysis of the OPS. He was told that pressure of time meant they had not been compiled for publication – since this would have taken another two months.[6] With the Council also expecting the Secretariat to stay within tight budgets, funds were not available to enable this kind of accountability and feedback to the GEF's central governing body.

The assessments of the GEF emerging from the OPS (combined with my own interviews and observations) seem to produce a verdict almost Zen Buddhist in its contradictions. The GEF was both too ambitious and not ambitious enough, and it had both too much money and not enough money to achieve its aims. By this I mean that lacking the courage or power to risk spending in innovatively adaptive ways, administrators pursuing pre-existing agendas were able neither to spend all the GEF's money nor to fulfil all its require-ments. At the same time, the money they did spend was 'too big', with too many administrative strings attached, to contribute to the more decentralised, less capital- and bureaucracy-intensive forms of aid that many environmentalists deem necessary for effective

---

put the greater part of its investment into wind, solar and geo-thermal projects. If the GEF was to be filling in gaps in investment and experi-menting in new areas it would, by contrast, be advised to focus more on bio-mass projects.

6. The Council member was advised to ask the report's author for more detail – thus Council members (let alone NGOs, COP secretariat representatives, etc.) were not offered the chance to compare and learn from the detail of GEF's impact in particular countries without extra work.

conservation (Pimbert and Pretty, 1995). And as a veteran World Bank staffer told Caufield (1996), 'the trouble is, GEF money can only be spent for four international issues, so everything else, everything local ... is suffering'.

Creating Global Benefits

In theory, the GEF was to transfer money efficiently from those who enjoy the benefits of global environmental protection (that is, the public worldwide) to those who bear the costs (that is, governments in poorer countries). Yet as Gill and Law (1988) observe, in the global capitalist system, 'references to efficiency tend to gloss over the question of "efficiency for whom?"' and according to McAfee (1999), when it comes to putting GEF promises into practice, '"Global" benefits really represent elite benefits, i.e., some combination of amenities imaginable by, affordable to, and valued by upper-income sectors of industrialized societies.'

Despite the burgeoning of economic models to meet the demands of environmental accounting, the GEF was not designed to be an effective conduit for internalising environmental costs to the equations of economic development. As a member of the CBD secretariat's staff noted (interview, 1997), for the GEF to be an effective tool for this task, it would need a full appraisal of all the actual and potential costs, and whoever meets those costs would have to be reimbursed with revenue raised from beneficiaries on an obligatory basis. Instead, GEF contributions are made on a voluntary basis and despite the incremental costs requirement, spending has not been directed specifically and proportionally to meet all costs incurred by all those involved in creating 'global' environmental benefits. Even with the most simplified of its analyses, by 1997 the GEF still lacked a methodology for internalising the costs of carbon dioxide emissions to the World Bank's preferred models of development, and tended to use traditional economic analyses as if all the relevant costs had already been accounted for in the model (interview, UNDP, 1997).

So not only did the GEF lack a mechanism for linking incremental costs with global environmental benefits, but any real effort to develop one would have been futile. The entire GEF budget would disappear into research to identify actual and potential costs and benefits to communities and ecologies worldwide. Full environmental accounting would require total knowledge – which exists only in theoretical free market economics and a few scientists' dreams – and without it, funding decisions cannot effectively be guided by the principle of internalising costs. One logical conclusion might be to use GEF funds to support regulatory processes forcing polluters to internalise and therefore minimise their environmental impacts at source. But it would probably not be seen as very professional for any member of GEF staff to demur from the accepted approach to pursuing 'global environmental benefits'. Especially since they are employed by a Bank which has, in the meantime,

> established itself as the world's leading expert in environmental impact assessments (EIAs), social assessments (SIAs), and green cost-benefit analyses (CBAs) [which] implicitly and explicitly assign values to groups of people and parcels of environment. (Goldman, 2001b)

Behind the Paper Walls

According to several interviewees, the GEF's guidelines on transparency began to break new ground in the Implementing Agencies – a positive impact of the GEF since 'eventually the other [international financial institutions] will go the same way – although by definition some things will need to remain confidential, for example loan agreements' (interview, GEF Secretariat, 1997). Yet despite numerous innovations and publications, it is not clear that GEF has been very much more participatory where it could make a difference. Like the rest of the World Bank's work, GEF operations are answerable in the final analysis to treasuries, and hardly at all to the people who mostly pay for them (mostly Northern citizens, through tax) nor the people who mostly experience them (mostly Southern citizens, affected by projects). They are also conducted in a language laden with acronyms and technicalities.

Staff of the Secretariat recognised this difficulty, but with the Council unwilling to expand their budgets, they had few solutions beyond producing a few simplified and glossy brochures, videos, etc., and relying on NGOs to reach out with information on their behalf.[7] Formal transparency has involved the publication of numerous

7. One Secretariat interviewee wondered if they could produce videos of people explaining the GEF for distribution where written words would not reach.

official documents: operational programmes, project plans, annual reports, work programmes, implementation reviews, legalistic analyses of the GEF's 'relations with the conventions' – in fact, a policy for almost any issue GEF has had to deal with, and often expert reviews as a result of earlier challenges to contested issues around incremental costs, mainstreaming and so forth.

Many of these documents have been translated into several languages and sent in fat packages to Council members and alternates, Implementing Agency offices and interested NGOs around the world.[8] There they have clarified certain issues for those with the time, language and experience to read them usefully, but still they have hardly reached people who do not speak official UN languages,[9] let alone the remote, illiterate and/or marginalised, and even many of those able and interested in the first place have little time to wade through all the texts.[10] Meanwhile the piles of official documents, drafted and stacked by the Secretariat around every GEF Council meeting can seem like walls of words and paper, doing more to obfuscate than to explain what was really going on in face-to-face meetings in the GEF family – let alone to assist anyone coming in from outside to engage in GEF's global funds and dialogues.[11]

It has been the job of GEF's CEO and chairman, Mohamed El-Ashry, to hold the GEF's processes, image and mission together with a mix of positive public pronouncements, sleek diplomacy and tight management, advised and guided by his colleagues in the GEF Secretariat, the World Bank, motivated members of the GEF governing

---

8. By the late 1990s this practice was replaced where possible with e-mail notifications of updates to the GEF website.
9. Even Council members complained that they needed help with translation to deal effectively with GEF – for example, very little was translated into Iranian (interview, Council member, 1997).
10. With 56 different local languages spoken in Mexico alone, GEF could hardly be expected to translate its documents into every one.
11. In 1997 I was assured by Mohamed El-Ashry, GEF Secretariat CEO and co-chair of the Council, that 'there are no secrets'. He gave his personal word that my research on the GEF would benefit from its famous 'transparency'. However, when told of this guarantee – and the implication that all facts, figures, views and analyses could be made freely available – one member of his staff in the Secretariat literally choked with astonishment. In the event this disbelief proved justified, as the flow of information from the Secretariat dried up after I wrote articles partially critical of the GEF (Boehmer-Christiansen and Young, 1998; Young, 1999).

Council and the 'private' Senior Advisory Panel (see Appendix I). We saw in Chapter 4 that he prefers to work in private, steering his 'tight ship' through discussions with elites whom he knows and understands. The Secretariat forms a protective layer around this beating heart of the GEF: serving central players on a practical level while mediating between El-Ashry's closest *confidantes* and the wider Council membership, the various international agencies also involved in GEF, and approved consultants and NGOs.

Gupta (1995) analyses the GEF in terms of an 'onion' model, made up of concentric layers of institutional and conceptual organisation. At the core, El-Ashry and the key players from the Council and Implementing Agencies make decisions, produce rules and norms, approve processes and projects. They are enclosed, guided and defended by their departments and institutions, which by producing documents and spending money – approved by the Council under El-Ashry's guidance – reach out from the core to impact on the wider world. These institutions meanwhile are conditioned by pervasive politics and ideologies in that wider world, which shape their overall actions and loyalties.

Gupta noted that in this model, features of the GEF seem to become less negotiable the further out of the 'onion' they are – for example, a particular draft Operational Program on say, agricultural biodiversity, can be challenged freely by NGO observers in a Council meeting, but the use of the World Bank to host these debates and administer resulting projects is not up for discussion. From outside, critics of the GEF tend to range wide with their comments on the whole system, while those with access to the middle of the 'onion' tend to stick to more technical 'agenda items'. Taking on the role of an 'official opposition' (interview, GEF Secretariat, 1997), 'constructive' NGO critiques thus serve to marginalise more fundamental criticisms of the whole system as irrelevant if not destructive.

Critical Southern governments too have to be wary of the political power blocs and ideologies involved in GEF processes. Active dissent on any issue (apart perhaps from incremental costs, see below and previous chapters) risks the fear of reprisals, isolation and rejection by other 'client' governments wary of the consequences for cash flows if any one of their number won't play along. Partly as a result, Gupta's interviews with people involved showed that while mention of the GEF elicited cynicism or dispassion in the North, in the South it aroused distrust, fear and anger. And as Gupta points out, emotions colour perspectives, and in diplomacy, perspectives are reality.

When it comes to the GEF's external relations, its defining terms – such as 'global environmental benefits', 'mainstreaming', 'guidance' (from the Conventions), 'accountability' (to the Council) and of course 'incremental costs' – give the impression of being technically definable and fairly straightforward to implement. But as previous chapters have suggested, implementation demands political–diplomatic and administrative deals to overcome conflictual priorities – often leading to people 'playing safe', sometimes extending to institutional 'war' (see below). Such operational and political realities have been obscured by professionals wary of stepping out of line, let alone drawing public attention to difficulties faced internally which would only feed resentments and make agreement even harder to reach.

Professionalism

In this institutional ecosystem, vague but agreeable-sounding concepts like 'global environmental benefits' can contribute to minimising democratic debate on how best to achieve the public good of improving environmental protection worldwide. Espousal of 'depoliticised' leadership – avoiding radical challenges to tasks presented as 'technical' – can strengthen the role of the GEF's CEO and the professionals he guides through the real-world political maze that such words disguise. Most of the accountability for GEF policy and funding decisions comes back in the end to the donor treasuries who pay the wages of the people putting the GEF into action – and therefore command their loyalty.

Individuals tend to find work with the GEF through what they call 'the network', a shifting community of transnationally active economists, consultants, civil servants and others with expertise in international environmental science, law and diplomacy. Often brought together through shared education, employment, social class and/or nationality, members of 'the network' exchange work opportunities and information privately. They do so probably less because they aim to be exclusive, than because it seems natural that their experienced fellow professionals should have the right know-how and be committed to working with organisations employing people in their field.

It is rare for professionals in the GEF to reflect in public on the conditions of their own employment, performance and experience.

When I prepared a draft questionnaire asking the following of international civil servants doing GEF work,

> Are there incentives for you to ensure that GEF money is spent as efficiently and effectively as possible?
> Are you given too much work to complete in normal working hours?
> Please list your main sources of job satisfaction.

I was told by a contact in the Secretariat that

> It seems that these questions are not of the same caliber or sophistication as other questions in the questionnaires. They should not be an issue for any of the professional staff members, including those of GEF. I do not think answers to those questions will add value to your study. I would prefer to see them removed from the questionnaires.

In the end I included the questions, and got next to no answers.

Within the GEF system 'professionalism' has meant different things to different people. For El-Ashry, it meant 'competence and the ability to work with others, to listen and adjust views, not to take the marbles and go home if you don't like the way the game is going' (interview, 1997). This echoes a World Bank task manager's perspective on NGO activists – who were seen as more or less incompetent if they did not engage constructively with his work. Similarly in the UNDP, professionalism meant 'do your work and do it well, don't indulge in diatribes' (interview, 1997), that is, do not repeatedly raise issues which can not be effectively dealt with within the GEF's existing structure and budget. Meanwhile, for another UNDP GEF staffer, 'the driving issue of professionalism is being an effective spokesperson for the [Southern] governments who are not present when decisions on GEF projects are taken in Washington DC and New York' (interview, 1997). In this usage, 'professionalism' is opened up to mean not just loyalty to key players but also some responsibility to those remaining on the margins of the game – in this case governments whose grudging support remains essential to the GEF's survival. Only a very few interviewees showed any sign of speaking for the needs of citizens – for example indigenous peoples, whose voices are not heard at the national level, let alone the global – presumably because it is not professional to raise the profile of problems about which governments tend to be embarrassed or in denial.

Political and Ideological Context

With the GEF legally and practically constrained in so many ways, its professional culture has been largely one of pragmatism in response to the overarching political and ideological climate: 'The narrow and special interests of the commercial sub-system of our society have been elevated to the status of society's basic values, and consumption is overwhelming conservation' (McNeely, 1996). Commodifying environmental value as just another consumable in money terms may make the work of professionals unchallenging to political masters, but it can also mask the inconsistent, unprecedented or contradictory – and thereby hinder the systemic adaptation needed for long-term institutional, let alone ecological, survival. Many people involved in the GEF understand this, and do try to work differently, but one new member of the Secretariat's staff observed: 'I'm not sure that World Bank people realise how much they are prisoners of intellectual ideology. They can't escape from their chains. They are struggling and making good faith efforts, but they are really trapped' (interview, GEF Secretariat, 1997).

A biodiversity expert in the Bank, asked about the importance of cultural differences in their work, said that cultural diversity is a 'side issue' to conservation. But in the World Bank the 'rational' means for dealing with environmental protection is putting a price on nature, whereas in the indigenous settlements in Nagarhole for example (see Appendix IV) the 'rational' approach is to take money out of the equation and leave nature in the hands of people who know, love and need it whole. It seems that in an economics-based culture, there is little critical self-awareness or space for awareness of, let alone ability to work respectfully with, the contrasting values of people 'living in a different world' (interview, NGO, 1999).

Ethics and learning tend to be constrained by the conceptual and social parameters of the system through which actions can be taken and feedback arises. Anthropologist Bourdieu (in Harker et al., 1990) and philosopher Foucault (1980) echo in the social sphere the conclusions of Gibson's (1979) ecology of learning: that both perception and learning are fundamentally conditioned by context, including history, society and culture. Like all good environmentalists, both World Bank economists and Nagarhole Adivasis therefore work within their culture to practise basic ecological care for the systems that sustain them and their friends and families in a known and valued social world. The difference is that the Adivasis as a group seem to bother nobody but a few unreconstructed forest officials and wildlife activists who would wish them away from their forests, whereas the World Bank and GEF spend vast amounts of public money and natural resources in their quest to manage our whole planet, and manage to alienate millions of ordinary people in the process. But staff of the GEF institutions have little time to extend their understanding to people on the outside of their bureaucratic world, because they also have to manage difficult relationships and culture clashes within it.

RELATIONS IN THE GEF FAMILY

Purposive Institutions

When the GEF came along, both the UN and the World Bank had already been under fairly constant pressure to reform for some years. The World Bank in the mid 1990s was going through another period of restructuring[12] and trying, like the UN agencies, to maintain public support and its financial position. As a result Bank staff were not well disposed to respond to the GEF Council's demand that it invest scarce resources in trying to work together with rival institutions on a new agenda. Staff in the GEF Secretariat found they were 'able to identify closely with corporate aims and goals, but in the Implementing Agencies the loyalty and future careers of the individuals are with the Agency' (interview, GEF Secretariat, 1997). Staff in each Implementing Agency are required first and foremost to follow their own procedures, accountably to their own board of governors. Meanwhile, when the GEF Secretariat sought to enforce compliance with Council instructions on, for example, mainstreaming, or working with new NGO partners, the GEF unit in the Bank was

by definition focussing on the expectations and obligations of external constituencies, passing them on to the operational

12. This restructuring involved creating and merging departments and moving a lot of managers out of the headquarters into country offices – which had a low status in the overall institution.

complex of the Bank, and at the same time dealing with internal demands for access to the resources available ... and dealing also with internal resistance from Bank staff because of the additional work, the extra elements of processing ... We are stuck between facilitation of GEF within the Bank and responding to the GEF's external governance structures. (interview, 1997)

World Bank staff were reliant on the Secretariat to be their main 'interlocutor' with those governance structures, and regretted their lack of a channel for direct communication with the GEF Council:

Our work with the GEF is heavily dependent on the way the CEO wants to do business ... almost all substantive discussions, also success and failure ride on interactions with the Secretariat, which, lacking operational experience, tends to be cautious and driven to excessive regulation in an untrusting process. (interview, World Bank, 1997)

Although the Secretariat had a duty to ensure Council directives were implemented, there was a feeling in the Implementing Agencies that the Secretariat should not interfere with their projects and processes:

Relations between the Implementing Agencies and Secretariat are now deteriorating ... perhaps this is related to the immaturity of the GEF as an institution ... all institutions pass through the same stages in their evolution: at first they are risk averse. This is why the Council has been in micro-management mode. It did seem to be getting better, but the Secretariat is now in the worst possible micro-management mode, and has been for the past 18 months. (interview, World Bank, 1997)

Recognising this problem, a member of Secretariat staff suggested that some

staff come to the Secretariat with a project mission and maybe they should be in the Implementing Agencies, and maybe some people in the Implementing Agencies have more of an interest in policy and should be in the Secretariat. I hope that this tension is creative and not destructive. (interview, GEF Secretariat, 1997)

But when it came to dealing with the priorities of other Imple menting Agencies each aiming to promote their own approach and expand their funding for new areas of work, they were already treading on each others' toes.

Every global institution has its own parentage, resource flow and goals. As such global institutions can be described as complex dissipative structures interacting and evolving in the global institutional ecosystem. If societies are systems through which information as well as energy flows (Acselrad, 1996), I might add that institutional 'organisms' also feed on favour, staff and legal authority like plants feed on water, air, soil and sun.[13] For the individuals – cells – comprising the body of the GEF and other institutions, the fight for livelihood, and the pursuit of personal goals – is tied up with those of the institution they work for. And when institutions and social groups behave at all like individuals, it raises the question of how to reconcile aspirations to managerial rationality with the social and psychological solidarities of groups of people working together on a common project. People working together for shared goals have by necessity to pay attention to each other's needs and desires, probably at the expense of values not represented inside the working group, while a 'rational' model of management suggests that such biases would not exist (Douglas, 1987).

Inter-Agency Synergy

One of the GEF's official tasks was to bring about rationalisation and reform in the institutions with which it was involved, persuading them to work together to their 'comparative advantage' and learn from each other's experience. Yet, as we saw in earlier chapters, tensions and fissures inside the GEF were primarily due to multiple actors at various levels with often incompatible missions competing for scarce resources. Conflicts resulted partly because political

13. Other essential inputs to GEF's institutional physiology include the outputs of science, publications and reports from other legal organisms, as well as all the material inputs needed to create an institution including office space and facilities, paper for print runs, visual identity, etc. Central are people: to provide labour, energy, experience and diplomatic skills for ongoing interactions with other organisms of various kinds. Metabolic functions are carried on by people – who reach out to and cross between the central layers of Gupta's kind of institutional 'onions' round and about.

debates over responsibility and strategy for environmental management had not been effectively resolved within donor governments, let alone between the governments of the North and South. Unsolved issues therefore spilled over to the global institutions, to be fought among the individuals and agencies allied to different governments, ministries and agendas.

The misunderstandings and culture clash between the GEF and the Conventions (see earlier chapters) are reflected in the political and ideological distances between UN agencies, especially the UNEP, and the World Bank. Some therefore concluded that 'The GEF needs more of a common culture for smoother interactions' (interview, GEF Secretariat, 1997). One task the donor governments gave the GEF was to help reform the UN to be more businesslike, where it was 'shocking that governments have let [management] get so bad', according to a representative of the US Treasury. This interviewee felt that the GEF to some extent enabled a 'backflow of positive benefits', including a World Bank style of financial management and personnel, into the UN. For example, the GEF Council requested that the Implementing Agencies move towards a standardised format for GEF project documents – based on the World Bank model.

Staff in the Bank's about 20-strong GEF Unit felt that

> Within the GEF, the biggest drumbeat for more efficiency is coming from the World Bank. It is not desperate for more resources like the UN system, but wants to do GEF work efficiently and see it done cost-effectively. We want to create a smooth-running machine. (interview, World Bank, 1998)

As part of this move towards efficiency and the sharing of experiences, the GEF Implementing Agencies began to share the results of their own monitoring and evaluation (M&E), and 'New M&E units in the Secretariat, World Bank and UNDP are working together very closely, using some common guidelines' (interview, UNDP, 1997). Yet this interviewee did not even know if the UNEP – supposedly an 'equal' GEF Implementing Agency – even had a M&E unit, let alone whether they were using the same guidelines; despite the fact that the UNEP was the Implementing Agency most widely deemed in particular need of help to learn to be 'businesslike'.

We saw in the last chapter that the UNEP's projects were generally not favoured in the approval process, and, seeing their institution as the poor relation in the system, its staff sometimes seemed stressed at GEF meetings.[14] In private, for some in the UNEP the World Bank seemed like 'the enemy' – and a World Bank economist felt the UNEP had a 'screw the guys in Washington DC attitude', not least because the World Bank's approach, hegemonic in the GEF (and increasingly in the UNDP)[15] did not effectively gel with their institutional and environmental priorities.

Furthermore both the UN agencies felt threatened by the World Bank's moves into their social and environmental fields of work. The World Bank may have been widely hated in the South but, for its funders, it mostly got the job done – compared to the UN which seemed inefficient and corrupt in the hands of 'elites' from Southern countries. For its part, the World Bank wanted to access GEF money to assist its own adaptation to the environmental agenda. It succeeded to the extent that a donor Council member was quoted as saying that 'rather than the World Bank being an Implementing Agency for the GEF, the GEF is a funding agency for the World Bank' (intervention, November 1997 Council).

Turf Wars

The Secretariat was supposed to mediate in any clash of interests between the Implementing Agencies, ensuring they worked together to meet GEF's goals.[16] However, as we saw above, the Secretariat was already involved in a power struggle with the Implementing Agencies for its own influence over the development of projects. A biologist observing the situation in 1997 told me 'All over the GEF system, conflicts are about personal agendas, power and especially big men with big egos. It could be called an egosystem.' When it came to inter-Agency disputes: 'The Secretariat won't police the Implementing Agencies, it won't be an arbiter so there is conflict.

14. At GEF receptions UNEP people sometimes seemed socially isolated as a group – sticking together at a slight distance from where other agencies' people networked.
15. By the late 1990s the UNDP was led by Mark Malloch-Brown, formerly head of external relations in the World Bank.
16. According to the GEF Instrument:

    In the event of disagreements among the Implementing Agencies or between an Implementing Agency and any entity concerning project preparation or execution, an Implementing Agency or any entity referred to in this paragraph may request the Secretariat to seek to resolve such disagreements.

The Implementing Agencies would like the Secretariat to intervene, but like with sibling spats, the current phase of parenting techniques say don't intervene' (interview, World Bank, 1997).

The Secretariat seems to have been unwilling to interfere partly because GEF had become a rope in the tug of war between UN agencies and the World Bank for the right to take the lead for 'sustainable development' and the global environment. This is part of a bigger international issue (see Chapter 2) than a 30-strong 'professional' Secretariat could begin to deal with, so for the most part they left the Agencies to fight it out for new income to aid and sustain their own institutions' operations at a time when overall aid levels were falling: 'I can't pretend to understand the pressures on the people in Implementing Agencies ... some individuals are aware that every dollar they bring in may mean the survival of a colleague' (interview, GEF Secretariat, 1997).

The UNEP's funding had been on the slide for a while, and the UNDP's allocation too was falling as more UN resources went into peace-keeping operations in the 1990s. As we saw above the World Bank has plenty of money, but sought GEF help to spend it. Yet, with GEF funds officially distributed on the basis of 'project quality', 'some bullets were never bitten from the beginning. Distribution issues were never clarified ... [The issue is] whether everyone is well resourced or battling for resources. The more battles, the less well people work together' (interview, World Bank, 1997). In practical terms, 'battles' often took the form of straightforward arguments for the right to implement GEF projects.[17] For example the World Bank came out 'on top' after a dispute with the UNDP over an initiative in Mauritius (interview, UNDP, 1997), and, in Georgia, the Bank apparently moved in on a Black Sea conservation project prepared with assistance from the UNEP (Chatwin, 1996). In the Caribbean, the UNDP and UNEP clashed over an information workshop organised by one and dominated by the other (NGO intervention in GEF Council, 1997).

Rivalries also took more subtle forms, for example over the kind of expertise which should be mobilised to support GEF goals – local and situated in a country's national development priorities or ecological complexities, or global and situated in the international

17. There was even competition for GEF funds within the agencies, with regional co-ordinators picking off each other's projects: 'like six year olds' spats among 45 year olds; it was weird' (interview, World Bank, 1997).

epistemic community of economic and environmental consultants. These tensions were reflected in the GEF Council where, as we saw in the last chapter, Indian and Chinese members among others often stressed the importance of the UNEP's STAP and its roster of experts featuring more national and regional expertise. Donor members and the World Bank, however, preferred to use 'business' expertise and consultants located in proximity to their own offices in the North.

Generally in the GEF, Northern governments favoured the World Bank. Southern governments favoured the UNDP as an Implementing Agency with more country offices and connection to their own national development priorities. Council members from some African and other governments, especially the Kenyan, stood up for the UNEP, and demanded the GEF's financial attention be paid to wider environmental issues than just the four core focal areas, in particular land degradation. They found occasional allies from NGOs and the ministries, especially Nordic, sharing the UNEP's more ground-level environment-driven agenda. When it came to the turf wars however, a UNEP staffer quoted the Kenyan saying: 'when the elephants fight, the grass gets trampled'.

Negotiating a Ceasefire

> Between the World Bank and the UNDP there was something akin to war for several years – until [new people came in to lead the UNDP GEF unit]. They are very nice, collaboratively minded people, good soldiers in their institution and they turned around the situation. (interview, World Bank, 1997)

Despite the inevitable importance of the personal factor, many interviewees attributed underlying misunderstandings between the Implementing Agencies to the fact that for years after the restructuring, they were operating without clear guidelines on their respective responsibilities within the GEF. With publication of the Operational Strategy in 1996, 'the Implementing Agencies began to move into business mode. The process of collaboration between the World Bank and UNDP thereafter has been an amazing rollercoaster of goodwill as cooperation is worked out' (interview, UNDP, 1997). Much of this cooperation came through 'upstream' discussions on 'project pipelines', teleconferencing and joint 'project missions' between the UNDP and World Bank staff (interview, UNDP, 1997).

Although spats continued, eventually it seems that more 'businesslike' relations between the Implementing Agencies came with a pecking order: the World Bank channels over half of the money, the UNDP tries to defend its 'technical assistance' and 'capacity-building' territory while the UNEP still struggles to be noticed. Despite it being officially the UNEP's responsibility, all the Implementing Agencies have been running research activities, and the World Bank has spent more than half the funds for some projects[18] on technical assistance – officially the UNDP's job (Aggarwal-Khan, 1997). This led one interviewee to observe that

> Cooperation between the Implementing Agencies has increased, but in the process the reason for their different roles has been blurred, undermining the efficacy of cooperation ... Now the World Bank is doing small-scale activities identical to UNDP's work; and given their record, this seems highly inappropriate. It's not that either the World Bank or UNDP are incapable of the work, but is this what was intended for the GEF? (interview, UNDP, 1997)

A World Bank task manager meanwhile felt that 'Most of the time the Implementing Agencies are working within their comparative advantage, but sometimes they step over the line in their clients' interest' (interview, World Bank, 1997).[19] With inter-institutional dynamics inside the GEF system evolving partly through the establishment of precedents, perhaps there is still some scope for evolution in GEF's relationship with outside interests.

PARTICIPATION AND FEEDBACK

NGOs Crossing Boundaries

For individuals without institutional or diplomatic status to access GEF's central processes, they have to work with an Implementing Agency, government delegation or formal environmental organisation that the GEF Secretariat has accredited. To get a voice at the

18. For example Ecuador Biodiversity protection, Romania/Ukraine Danube Delta Biodiversity and Egypt Red Sea Coastal and Marine Research Management Plan.
19. The World Bank's 'clients' are the governments taking on its loans.

GEF–NGO consultations, they have to cooperate and present their case first to the mostly big NGOs organising a day of discussions to plan what issues to raise with the GEF. Each one-day consultation seems to go very fast (I have attended three); especially when apparently insoluble issues like *Ecodevelopment* come up, there is no time for every issue to be raised. To interact effectively, NGO individuals have to be able to mix fairly comfortably in international circles, and participate in the technocratic–diplomatic discourse of the GEF's decision-makers and implementers. For the Council to listen to the NGOs' suggestions, they need to reflect an agenda that international civil servants can both understand and respond to constructively.

As we saw in Chapter 4, for the most part only those NGOs willing and able to work with a World Bank-hosted trust fund went to the twice-yearly GEF–NGO meetings. For others, the dominance of the World Bank was sufficient reason to leave well alone, not least because of a 'long history of failed consultation processes between the World Bank and NGOs' (Globalization Challenge Initiative, 2001).[20] As a result, those few NGOs willing and able to give the GEF a chance to prove itself different from the World Bank, ended up having to represent the 'NGO community' as a whole – while working and talking increasingly like the World Bank.

Those interested but not attuned to the GEF's internal arrangements, preferred terminology and technocratic, if not anti-democratic, thinking, have to rely on more experienced friends and contacts to get near. If they lack a personal contact inside the system, people are encouraged to take information from the GEF's website, because there is little time and few resources spare for dealing with enquiries, and little way for staff to know beforehand how informed and/or useful any particular petitioner is likely to be. Lobbies with the easier access to the inner workings of the GEF include English-speaking civil servants obviously, selected scientists, politicians, businessmen, and a few NGOs like the IUCN (represented in the SAP). Yet, for all the synergistic, participatory and 'country-driven' rhetoric, even officials from UN bodies and many recipient governments seem to have found that effective participation in the GEF can rely on personal connections with people with credibility closer to its heart.[21]

20. World Vision, US, Bank Information Center, Bread for the World.
21. As was found by the Argentine NGO FEU attempting to launch a project for MSG workshops in South America, see Chapter 5.

The World Bank's president, James Wolfenson, is reported as saying that when it comes to debating World Bank policies, 'no credible voices should be excluded from discussions'. But what is 'credible' to whom? Some of the NGOs attending the GEF's 1998 Participants' Assembly in New Delhi were deemed 'incredible' by GEF and World Bank staff (interviews, 1998), meanwhile for many of the victims and critics of World Bank policies, neither Wolfenson nor his institution are particularly credible either (interviews, 1999). Nonetheless, for some critics of the Bank, it seemed as if 'The GEF could be a good thing, so we have to sustain good will – while still maintaining battle lines or people will walk all over us' (interview, NGO, 1997). As part of this mission, the GEF–NGO network has tried regularly at Council meetings to get at least some relevant outsider voices heard and unmet needs expressed, and to influence it from within on behalf of those still left outside.

Centre to Periphery

But even the most constructive NGO efforts have hardly bridged the chasm between the crushing scale of GEF funds and the intricacies of real-world needs for conservation funding, and between decision-making and action on the ground. Project executing agencies implement GEF directives and deal with the consequences first hand, but have little or no say in policy. The Implementing Agencies and Secretariat report to the Council on the implementation of their decisions, but neither Council members nor most of their servants in the Secretariat and even the Implementing Agencies have meaningful connections to the sites of implementation.[22] Whatever feedback does make it in has to be translated to fit the language and concerns of busy professional people, losing values and substantive detail in the process.

Under NGO pressure channelled through the US Congress, the GEF Council made wider participation one of the means by which they would enable 'new partnerships for the global environment' through the GEF.[23] Participation was intended to occur at several

22. One member of UNDP staff lamented that very few Council members had any experience 'on the ground' with project management (interview, 1997).
23. See, for example, <www.gefweb.org/Operational_Policies/ Public_Involvement/public_involvement.html>.

levels: inter-institutional – that is, between the agencies and individuals involved in the decision-making fora of GEFOP and the GEF Council; intergovernmental – that is, between the participants variously represented in the Council and its members' constituencies; and finally with the diversity of 'civil society' interested in and/or affected by the GEF's remit.

But where GEF implementers reach out to invite outside affected communities to participate, it seems to be more often to present an expert-designed project and seek minor local inputs (as, for example, in *India Ecodevelopment*, see Appendix IV) than to find out what is hindering local conservation, which grass-roots initiatives could do with extra assistance, and so on. Presumably people on the ground in the South, untrained in the identification of global environmental benefits, could not be relied upon to fulfil GEF requirements like professionals. And if just anybody was able to access their funds and functions, an institution might not be able 'effectively' to pursue its prior strategic goals.

The GEF may be 'all about people, trying to cross institutional barriers' (interview, NGO, 1997), and had there been a budget for it, many of those involved would have liked to enable more exchanges between the mainly Northern worlds of GEF's decision-making and lobbying and the Southern worlds of its implementation and opposition. But there was little opportunity for the busy people there to reach out further than they had to, to get the job done. There is only space and money for a few to work on the GEF, and they could not be expected to understand, let alone deal with, every local issue arising – even if recipient governments were happy for foreign agency staff to attempt micro-management of projects in their countries.

This tendency reflects the wider problems of globalisation and of aid. Where decisions are made by distant officials for the greater good, even if elected national governments accept their authority, there is little reason for people at the local level to feel part of the process. With fewer people involved, agencies may find their own experimentation from above easier, but without widespread engagement and support from people in the actual environments impacted, it is likely that diverse experience will be integrated, that lessons will be learned or that more stable and effective strategies will be developed. It is quite possible too that, as in Nagarhole, the natural environment will suffer as a result of failures to build the trust of locals while supporting government officials who have already alienated local people.

Unable if not unwilling to engage directly with the complicated people and places where problems in ecological politics arise and may realistically be tackled, the GEF's key decision-makers have found themselves dealing with simplified issues without full responsibility for either context or consequence. Yet the results, if and when they become known, may exacerbate the political vulnerabilities of international bureaucracy, and expose the costs of pursing 'efficiency' to the GEF's other objectives – especially transparency and accountability, and quite possibly cost-effective conservation.

Periphery to Centre

For well-meaning people working inside the GEF system, there is a dilemma: how far can they realistically 'democratise' their work, opening up to diverse, often conflicting interests with a legitimate interest in the GEF's field of work, without threatening their own professional role? It seems the scope of participation in GEF processes has had to be restricted not just for political reasons, but also to prevent too many ideas, communications, objections and questions from divergent perspectives slowing down procedures and blurring their focus. In this context busy people in the UNDP, for example, felt that

> There's no point in hanging onto the fact that maybe one village was not consulted about a project when 15 others were. It's more important to look at the inputs from those 15 villages, and think about how much time the Implementing Agencies have to engage in these consultations. You have to work within the factors affecting the Implementing Agencies, and not expect the world. (interview, UNDP, 1997)

However much Mohamed El-Ashry stresses the importance of public participation for effective projects to the GEF's attendant community of mostly urban, English-speaking, constructive NGOs, not everyone has something to say of interest to the GEF. For example, when indigenous people from Nagarhole, South India, (see Appendix IV) attended the spring 1998 GEF–NGO consultations in New Delhi to demand an end to the *India Ecodevelopment* project and respect for their land and cultural rights, they were not allowed into the GEF's opening outdoor reception at the Habitat Centre,[24] because they had no shoes. When it came to the meeting there were no translation facilities for their language, so they did not hear El-Ashry speak about the value of participation. And when an allied NGO representative put their case to the meeting in English, World Bank representatives rejected their demands.[25]

One possible reason was that the Nagarhole Adivasi's claims had already raised negative press attention for *Ecodevelopment*, the Indian government, the World Bank and GEF.[26] With the Participants' Assembly hosted by the Indian government, a capitulation by the Bank might have been a breach of diplomatic etiquette if not a challenge to national sovereignty, while an admission of fault might have drawn attention to the GEF's flaws. So when every NGO speaking at the consultation seemed to be supporting the Adivasi's call for a halt to the *India Ecodevelopment* project, the chairman (the head of external relations for the GEF Secretariat), concluded the increasingly vehement debate:

> We have ventilated this issue, the views are clear. I think any attempt to reach any other conclusion of this discussion would be dreaming at this stage. May I therefore move on to the next agenda item ... we are two hours behind. (quoted in Howitt and Young, 2000)

The GEF system was not unused to deflecting indigenous perspectives which would only complicate matters. In 1996, a UNEP/GEF consultation with representatives of indigenous people worldwide was described by the latter as 'laboured and tense', featuring a 'paternalistic attitude' and 'autocratic style' on the part of GEF people – who had sent out the meeting agenda too late for indigenous representatives to consult with their own people (Indigenous People's Representatives, 1996). The Council meeting in autumn 1997 was addressed for the first time by a representative of the indigenous peoples' movement in North America. He questioned the level of respect in both GEF institutions and their attendant NGO

24. Habitat Centre is a smart compound housing many environmental organisations near the World Bank offices in New Delhi.
25. A subsequent private meeting with the Indian government officials working on the project also resulted in no further changes in the project.
26. For example, in the *Hindu*, 1 April 1998.

community for the ability and rights of indigenous cultures to manage sustainably resources found within their traditional territories. He left having received no real reply from either the GEF or the NGOs. The latter said they aimed to represent all different interests in their approaches to the GEF – which did not satisfy the native American who felt that, in the light of a history of racist and paternalistic attitudes towards peoples with traditional cultures, they needed to represent themselves.

Commenting on Nagarhole and similar cases, one member of the GEF Secretariat observed that

> The GEF is not pro-active for indigenous communities, it only deals with them if they are affected by a project. It should instead target them as beneficiaries. GEF needs to do a lot more work on gender, indigenous people, displaced people ... for example what to do about indigenous people who don't use monetary measures of value? Everybody here in the Bank thinks they know it all about issues like indigenous people and gender, but they rarely even take social scientists in project mission teams. (interview, GEF Secretariat, 1997)

In 1999–2000, the World Bank began moves to rewrite its directive[27] on indigenous people – ostensibly to be less demanding because it was being breached so often (interview, NGO, 2001). Seeing little real commitment even in the 'innovative participatory' GEF to the concerns of indigenous people around the world, by 2001 another indigenous representative was 'making themselves unpopular' with the attendant NGOs at GEF consultations by demanding separate status and a permanent pass for an indigenous representative to sit in Council meetings (pers. comm., NGO, 2001).[28] With situations like that at Nagarhole far from unique in indigenous peoples' experience of the GEF and, more so, of the World Bank, most remained too worried about their human and land rights, and indeed their cultural survival, to participate passively as the GEF's 'official opposition'.

27. World Bank directive 4.30.
28. All 'outsiders' wanting to attend GEF Council meetings were classed as NGOs and had to share passes between them – whether they were environmental groups, representatives of indigenous people, trade bodies or academic researchers.

Where their resulting radical critiques could not easily be internalised and dealt with, they were deemed an attention-seeking hindrance, taking time and attention away from work which had to – and could more easily – be done. As one World Bank economist put it,

> There are the more extreme and self-serving critics, who are generally biased in their use of information, and more damaging than constructive. For example the *India Ecodevelopment* project was subject to wildly inaccurate allegations, especially of its social aspect. It is the GEF's most progressive effort ... but NGOs seeking the spotlight have been calling it a mechanism for perpetuating authoritarian conservation. (interview, 1997)

Learning from Boundaries Redrawn?

One measure of progress used by people working with the GEF was the number of critical groups who could be persuaded to give up 'the spotlight' and come in 'off the streets' to cooperate – and the placation of critical local NGOs, possibly with funds to help implement the project themselves, was a goal for the planned second phase of *India Ecodevelopment* (interview, NGO, 1999). Yet the Indian authorities were not willing or able to put into practice the demands for local participation made by the GEF, and the World Bank/GEF were not willing or able to ensure that they did always respect local realities. When World Bank staff visited the area they stayed in smart hotels and saw the area and its population as much as their government hosts arranged. Consultations were limited by time, translation and a diplomatic reluctance to pay too much attention to problems raised by discontented locals (interviews, 1999); the GEF was not set up to protect tribal or indeed any poorer peoples – especially those defined or defining themselves as separate from 'mainstream' society – against their own governments' interest in their territory.[29]

Indian culture and politics therefore shaped the reality of *Ecodevelopment* at the local level, and even the last option for meaningful feedback from this reality to the global level – the World

29. However, as we shall see in the following chapter, some might conclude that the GEF defends richer peoples worldwide against the risk of governments imposing effective environmental regulation and democratic planning for their terrains of interest.

Bank's independent inspection panel – was not permitted to complete a full investigation, ostensibly by the hand of the Indian representative on the World Bank's board (interview, NGO, 2000). Whatever their sympathies, there is little that the GEF Council or Secretariat can realistically do for relatively powerless groups at the local level if a sovereign government is unwilling to give up any authority to communities.

People working in secretariats generally understand their place in these dynamics and in inter-institutional disputes at the global level, though they tend not to be empowered to do much about them. As central participants in the GEF, they gain many insights into how things really work, but official evaluations have hardly featured real inputs from this coalface.[30] The 1998 OPS had much to say on what the GEF Secretariat had done and should do, but said hardly anything about the Secretariat's experience of trying to fulfil earlier instructions.[31] But busy professionals dedicated to institutional survival have little time or desire to talk about the underlying difficulties of their work (see above), even were evaluations really designed to explore this area. As a result, in institutions like the World Bank, incremental 'adaptive behaviour is common, whereas true learning is rare' (E.B. Haas, 1990). In this context particularly, 'we need to rethink the power we give to global institutions to whom we have endowed, symbolically at least, the future of the Earth' (Goldman, 1998).

DEMOCRACY, SCIENCE AND KNOWLEDGE

Bottom-up Participation as Imposition

With its official dedication to using the latest science and an experimental, participatory approach to saving nature, the GEF's initial

30. More than one international civil servant interviewed queried why anyone would be interested in people like them when it is governments that make decisions. One referred to his role as 'menial'.
31. Similarly, the terms of reference for the CBD's 1998 evaluation of its financial mechanism seemed to preclude seeking the views of those best placed to judge the GEF's day-to-day work: the staff of the CBD secretariat – this despite the fact that they were the people with the closest daily dealings with the Secretariat of the GEF. They had also been at the rough end of disagreements between GEF and CBD governing bodies about priorities for biodiversity spending, and therefore had a fairly critical understanding of where the conflict lay.

promise captured some of an emerging 'bottom up' spirit in development thinking (Gan, 1992) – reducing and possibly rethinking power in aid institutions by decentralising responsibility. During the years in which the GEF was taking its place in the world, authors like Robert Chambers (1993) were calling for a reversal in aid management to put people before things and, where necessary, for this to be done through challenges to dominant disciplinary and professional approaches with a 'new professionalism'.[32] Norman Uphoff (1990) advocated replacing aid projects with 'paraprojects', with agencies feeding small amounts of money to the ground level only after fieldworkers have spent years observing and participating in an area to discover who in any given community is most capable of using them fairly and effectively. Jules Pretty and Irene Gujit (1992) chimed in to promote 'primary environmental care', local conservation facilitated by 'para-professionals' using existing local knowledge and institutions where possible.

This kind of vision led one World Bank economist to avow 'I see the GEF as really a facilitator in a locally managed process of consultation, negotiation, hopefully reaching agreement and then implementing a collaborative way of managing these natural resources' (quoted in Howitt and Young, 2000). But for all its experimental promise, the GEF is hardly able to offer the tools, staff and accountability procedures needed for such bottom-up processes to actually work, largely it seems because the GEF's component agencies can or dare not face the political consequences of empowering citizens at the grass roots at the expense of governments, international consultants and aid project managers.

Perhaps surprisingly, it seems that other World Bank people have been more confident about trying out new approaches than the GEF's senior managers:

Mohamed El-Ashry is a conservative figure compared to Bob Watson and Andrew Steer [senior environmental figures] in the World Bank: they are radical thinkers, looking for real innovation.

32. Kuhn's (1970) definition of paradigm: universally recognised scientific achievements that – for a time – provide model problems and solutions for a community of practitioners to use unproblematically. Essentially conservative, 'normal professionalism' (Chambers, 1993) can be equated to 'normal science' as defined by Kuhn; 'new professionalism' like 'new science' responds with an emerging new paradigm incorporating real-world facts that do not fit in the old models.

But then, the World Bank is well established and has more money than it knows what to do with, while the GEF is new and fragile, always with an eye on the next donor replenishment, so it can't be seen to step out of line. (interview, CBD secretariat, 1997)

So whatever the public rhetoric, real justifications for the policies of the GEF, as of any development institution reliant on regular replenishments, have primarily to be aimed at donor agencies rather than their 'targets' in the South (Hobart, 1993). Better communication is then proposed to solve any obstacles to implementing the resulting policies, but this assumes that information 'transmitted' is received in the same state in which it was sent. *Ecodevelopment* and many other conservation programmes are described to donor governments as 'cutting edge' with unprecedented participation and innovation, but, for many of their 'targets', such projects are just another imposition by outsiders interested in local resources.

We saw above the limitations of democracy in the GEF's technocratic boardrooms. The NGOs aiming to represent 'civil society' in the GEF Council tend to be little more participatory, transparent, accountable etc. than the global institutions they criticise there. Formally democratic bodies, for example local government, seem to have little role to play in identifying, developing or overseeing GEF projects. At the GEF's Participants' Assembly, 'local government' was only one of the nine UN 'major groups' (along with 'youth', 'business', 'women', etc.), invited on the basis of the incomplete model of global participation used at the Rio Earth Summit.

With the admirable language of participation disguising the replacement of formal democratic structures with selected project partnerships, the World Bank can dismiss critical responses to their projects from the ground as extremism and/or jealousy of other groups winning World Bank money. And as Bourdieu and Passeron (1990) put it, the imposition of meanings as legitimate by concealing the power relations behind them adds symbolic force to those power relations, while also increasing their symbolic violence. In this context conditional aid is effectively used to buy certain forms of cooperation from selected poorer and/or politically weaker communities. People unwilling to consider 'selling' rights over their environment risk being ruled out of the GEF-hosted market for environmental solutions.

Environmental protection GEF style therefore comes to symbolise well-resourced, largely Northern-educated elites seeking to control poor and politically weaker people's access to environmental resources – paying them not to develop in the same way the Northern countries did. But without any mutually agreed and understood contract for individual transactions, even those willing to accept promised benefits can end up mistrusting the agents of global environmental management when fine rhetoric turns into broken promises (interview, NGO, 2002). This analysis seems to move the reality of GEF spending into a realm of shady commerce, with certain environments commodified in terms of 'global' value in fora largely inaccessible to the people who actually live, work and pray in those environments. And 'when locally distinct ecologies are left in the hands of global "anti-politics technocrats"', says Michael Goldman (1998), 'the terrain of struggle moves from the grassroots to the ... boardroom'.

The Science of the GEF

Engagement with the politics of institutions operating at the global level only becomes possible when internal functions as well as external actions are exposed to public scrutiny. The GEF is endowed with so many publications and NGO consultations that El-Ashry asked me rhetorically to 'define transparency, if the GEF is not transparent' (interview, 1997) but, other than the GEF's own evaluations and involvement of some interested NGOs, the scope of critical social scientific access has been effectively limited – partly by El-Ashry's opaque management from the centre.

An environmental engineer himself, El-Ashry certainly makes use of the scientific expertise available to him though the Secretariat and his SAP. Moreover, he has tried to raise the profile of the STAP's work in GEF processes. Yet the second Overall Performance Study recommended that GEF administrators 'make a special effort to use scientific analysis as a constant foundation in planning and implementation of new projects' and there have been numerous calls in the GEF Council and elsewhere throughout its history for more particularly social scientific expertise to be brought in. This agenda has tended to result in practice in ever more environmental economic analyses being commissioned, with a few anthropologists brought in alongside staff from scientific NGOs like the IUCN to make sure project documents contain the latest ideas and language. But this begs the question of why the GEF's allied scientific expertise is not directed towards more open-minded seeking of practical insights into why so many environmental protection initiatives have failed in the past, and how they could be done better using not just top-down 'command and control' or 'economic logic' but applied history, sociology, philosophy, psychology, geography, political analysis, and so on.

Involvement of such disciplines could help to bring a wider community to discuss existing and potential arrangements for managing nature 'globally', and help to design environmental initiatives taking diverse needs and conditions more fully into account. In particular, committed natural and social scientists could work together on action research initiatives to identify the problems and options of groups and communities who may lack technical know-how and tools for energy efficiency measures for example, or have lost resources they once managed sustainably to illegal impositions by more powerful economic interests. Applied science could then help environmental financiers to recognise and if appropriate connect with local urges to conservation – natural, social, individual and cultural – of people whose environments are threatened and/or threatening through no fault of their own.

But while consultants and scientists linked to the STAP and the Implementing Agencies do inspect GEF project sites and make recommendations, the emancipatory vision of engaged science set out above is scarcely on the agenda. These experts' jobs involve elaboration of 'global' environmental issues into policy advice at prestigious international scientific meetings, the production of reports and building of the network at the GEF's scientific edge. When projects directly support scientific priorities, it tends to be for the gathering of environmental data, for example when the IUCN and the World Conservation Monitoring Centre ran biodiversity planning and information management initiatives.[33]

> For the global scientist to be able to function, they require access to the whole globe and its data. No longer constrained by national or local politics, the global scientist uses the local as a site for data collection and the global as a site for knowledge production, legitimation and dissemination. (Goldman, 1998)

33. For example in a GEF–UNEP project for *Global Biodiversity Data Management Capacitation in Developing Countries and Networking Biodiversity Information*, which set up biodiversity plans in ten countries (see previous chapter).

Putting Knowledge in the Bank

The globalisation of science has contributed to the World Bank's growing aspiration to become an 'honest broker' for knowledge about the world's natural resources, their distribution and professional management for economic development. One of the World Bank president's more hubristic initiatives in the 1990s was to create a 'knowledge bank' (World Bank, 1998; Mehta, 2001; Wilks, 2001).[34] His staff are expected to centralise 'approved' information gathered worldwide on, for example, water, energy and genetic resources, and organise it to be accessible and useful to experts and investors both public and private.

The World Bank and GEF's *Costa Rica Biodiversity Resources Development* project for example uses the term 'participation' to mean information dissemination and the use of locals to feed their knowledge of Costa Rica's forest species into a computerised inventory. Labelled with a barcode, each species is thus rendered easily accessible to taxonomists and bio-prospectors from international pharmaceutical companies.

With biotechnology seen as a motor of economic growth in the 1990s, data on the genetic potential and distribution of rare or little known plant and animal species promises to be economically valuable in the right hands – as does information about the energy sectors of former communist and other privatising governments. Rare species and ecosystems often inhabit inaccessible regions remote from the eye of governments, and the information that scientists produce can be combined electronically with satellite data to create maps and models informing resource management policies. The same scientific decision tools can also feed the geographical information systems used by military strategists interested, for example, in wild areas where rebels may hide, and in the landscapes and ecological conditions that US forces may face (pers. comm., World Bank, 1997).

But any such use of environmental data in strategic military planning is not widely publicised compared with its use by development institutions seeking environmental improvements and

---

34. World Bank initiatives under this label include the Global Knowledge Partnership, the Global Development Network, Infodev, the web-based Development Forum and Development Gateway, and the African Virtual University.

legitimacy. In 1997 the governing bodies of the Biodiversity Convention and the World Bank agreed a Memorandum of Understanding. The CBD was to gain access to some of the World Bank's policy and funds, and the Bank was to send some of its own staff to work in the offices of the CBD's secretariat, and to participate in the latter's meetings, writings, and even 'concepts and ideas'. 'Leading' on some issues, and participating in CBD debates over the role of trade, investment, agriculture and indigenous rights to manage biological resources, the World Bank would apply its economic expertise to the management of biodiversity. In not only the CBD but numerous other international bodies, governments and NGOs seeking 'credibility', 'the World Bank's brand of assessment science has become virtually hegemonic, as scores of trainers, consultants, and engineering firms apply (more or less obligingly) ... strategic tools of economic rationality' (Goldman, 2001b).

At the same time however the very basis of this rationality was under fire, and not just from the Bank's usual critics but from a very senior level within the institution itself. Repeating a pattern set when Herman Daly left the World Bank in the early 1990s – citing its unjustified obsession with economic growth at almost any cost – by 1999 the Bank's chief economist, Joseph Stiglitz, was having doubts about some of the assumptions of the 'Washington Consensus'. But according to Greg Palast, 'He was not allowed quiet retirement; US Treasury Secretary Larry Summers,[35] I'm told, demanded a public excommunication for Stiglitz' having expressed his first mild dissent from globalization World Bank style.'[36] The World Bank therefore fired its chief economist in 1999, essentially for daring to deviate in public from the official neo-liberal dogma.[37]

Lacking faith in such a system and the national 'democracies' apparently powerless to act against it, members of what might be called the 'global justice movement' therefore find their own ways to exchange ideas and get their voices heard in their own terms: directly, sometimes confrontationally, with each other, through the vagaries

35. Earlier employed at the World Bank, Summers' views caused a furore when an internal memo he wrote was leaked. In the memo he pointed to the economic logic of exporting waste and pollution from the North to 'under-polluted' Southern countries where people don't usually survive long enough to be poisoned.

36. <www.gregpalast.com/detail.cfm?artid=78&row=1>

37. In 2001 Joseph Stiglitz was awarded a Nobel Prize for his work on the problem of incomplete information in economics.

of travel, media, socio-cultural exchange and the increasingly accessible internet – not channelled through any one agency. For example, the emerging Peoples' Global Action network of peoples' movements 'for humanity and against neo-liberalism' use their own knowledge and resources in 'joined up' campaigning for human-centred development worldwide.

Democratic Reform in the GEF System?

Many people in donor governments claim to be serious about using the GEF for institutional reform as well as effective conservation. But if so, given the World Bank's economic fundamentalism, perhaps they could help to free the GEF's expertise and resources from the grip of its 'Trustee' and allow it to be guided from the other end. Initiatives could flow less from boardrooms full of other agendas than from the places where environmental degradation mostly takes place and could, with well-targeted non-dogmatic assistance, be prevented.

Were this politically possible in Nagarhole, for example (see case study in Appendix IV), studies could be made of different communities' needs and impacts on nature, and aspects of indigenous culture proven useful in conserving local biodiversity could be supported through a strategy based on the indigenous 'Peoples' Plan' for Nagarhole forest.[38] In Zimbabwe (see case study in Appendix III), extensive participatory research could help local councils to identify rural energy needs, and the Zimbabwe Solar Industries Association could be assisted to overcome technical difficulties to extend their markets. Social science could be used to identify underlying politics so that interventions do not contribute to racial or other forms of oppression, but instead win support from as wide a constituency as possible for local conservation policies which, if effective, will be resisted by powerful established interests. If GEF's advocates really want it to be catalytic, experimental and lead by example, then they might do better to stop the flow of 'projects, projects, projects' and keep GEF's money for times and places where it can inspire the public by bringing people together to conserve their environment, even against the political odds.

Obviously this approach would demand a total shake out of the bureaucracies running the GEF, moving their staff away from project

---

38. 1998, produced by Adivasi organisations with assistance from local NGOs, see Appendix IV.

management to support local democratic planning. The 'global environment' restriction would have to be relaxed to allow GEF administrators to recognise local environmental needs and values. It would also not be easy for international professionals to subject their skills and ideas to democratic as well as scientific scrutiny – but some say they should have to, since the money they spend is taxes raised from people in 'democracies' ostensibly for the public good (pers. comm., NGO, 1997). As Cassen et al. (1994) observed, safety conscious aid achieves little, so aid administrators should take risks. And as international principles of democracy and human rights suggest, people whose lives are likely to be affected deserve a say in what risks are taken with their money and environments, and by whom.

CONCLUSIONS

For now the possibility of achieving democracy and justice – locally or globally – with the GEF remains limited by the political interests of its designers in the major 'democratic' donor powers and their preferred institution for global management, the World Bank. There are people within Northern environment and aid ministries who do want to move the GEF beyond simply spreading information and funds to people who already know how to use them and using less elite greens and locals for expertise and legitimation. But tackling old prejudices and 'normal professionalism' head on risks bringing the politics underlying the GEF's implementation into wider public view. So even most of those environment and other officials promoting more science and democracy in GEF operations, do not push for major alterations to the structure of a still fledgling international organisation whose grip on the priorities of its treasury paymasters remains fragile.

7 Can Anyone Save the World?

THE `BOTTOM-UP` APPROACH TO
SUSTAINABLE DEVELOPMENT

Revisiting Assessments; Sustaining Systems; Possible Alternatives to
Spending on a GEF; Final Thoughts

After years of exploring the character and context of governments'
ambitious international green funding efforts, I have discovered,
reported and considered only a small proportion of the GEF's story
so far. The GEF world is big and complex and does not invite clear
boundaries, so I have drawn a line where it seemed to me possible if
not appropriate.[1] The goal of this book was not simply to describe
international arrangements set up, as if their mere existence could
heal the world's damaged ecologies. Nor was it to comprise a
thorough exposé of imperfect projects, as if international interventions can be understood simply in terms of their impacts on the
ground. The book was not written by an 'insider' sharing confidences, nor was it commissioned by the subject institution, nor by
any body wishing to be better acquainted with it so as to access
policy and/or funding. The goal was not to advance any particular

---

1. Probably almost every reader will argue with where I drew lines and what
   I found within them. In response I would simply say that important institutions like the GEF deserve more, and better, committed social science
   and story-telling.

theory, nor disprove another. However, despite the fact that the research behind this book emerged from a University-based, English-speaking, Western-educated elite, as the author I did not aim to participate in 'the close affinity of mainstream academic discourse with the [neo-liberal] "Washington Consensus" on the global political economy' (McKinley, 2001).

Put simply, the goal of this book was to set out in one place what I have found out about the GEF, for an audience ranging from staff and watchers of international institutions to interested students, teachers, researchers, journalists, scientists, environmentalists and others concerned about 'our global future'. Having said all that, this final chapter steps back to review a unique Facility in its political context, summarising assessments – and alternatives – after a decade of operations.

REVISITING ASSESSMENTS

Ambitions and Limitations

For economic globalisers, environmental threats to sustainability seem to have two basic aspects. The first and most obvious is potential scarcity of the resources needed to keep physiological, agricultural and industrial processes functioning: including the risks of pollution affecting productivity, over-extraction of renewable resources like fish and wood, and the extinction of species with potentially lucrative genes. The other is the risk of environmentalists even more bothered by these trends gaining sufficient hold on society's levers to challenge the enclosing, extractive patterns of resource use currently being globalised.

The Western European donor governments' plan for a fund to finance environmental Conventions for 'global' benefit was therefore presented in some fora as a means to shape economic development to the needs of the global environment, elsewhere it seemed to shape environments and environmentalism to support global economic priorities. Thus were professionals in environmental protection and economic development to be brought together: each wanting the other to adapt to their own norms and conceptions of 'global' benefits, and neither fully able to enforce their priorities given real-world complexities.

It seems that the GEF's design was too ambitious and its procedures convoluted partly because it was entrusted with conflicting objectives, among them supporting the environmental

Conventions financially without threatening established patterns of economic development; using public money to price and privatise the global commons; making conservation 'businesslike' while opening up to participation of diverse NGOs and communities with different values; reforming both the 'efficient' World Bank and the 'democratic' UN agencies to give each more of the other's attributes – without undermining their comparative advantage. In this experimental context, risk aversion combined with the search for consensus and a good public image to mean that the GEF Council had more money than it was effectively able to spend according to its own demanding rules.

The second Overall Performance Study of the GEF released in January 2002 attempts to reach conclusions about GEF's real-world effectiveness. As with earlier evaluating teams (IEPP, 1994 and OPS-1, 1998), the consultants worked under tight time constraints and with restricted scope for enquiry. Under subtle social pressure to give a verdict that would help the GEF through its upcoming replenishment, they felt able to state that GEF funds have, to some extent, promoted energy efficiency and renewable technologies, improved management standards in protected areas, and supported agreements on international waters and reducing ozone depletion. Yet the evaluators also said that given the GEF's short life so far and limited funds, 'whether [they] have had an impact on the global environment is difficult to determine'. The report found that only 12 per cent of projects financed by the GEF since 1991 had yet resulted in completion reports or final evaluations. Perhaps damning with faint praise, the OPS-2 concludes that GEF operations so far have led to 'important project results … that can be considered important process indicators towards achieving future positive environmental impacts'.

While waiting for more substantive verdicts on the GEF's environmental performance, other participants and observers interpret the indicators so far to remain variously optimistic, pessimistic and cynical about its transformative as well as environmental potential. To return to the conflicting hopes and fears for the GEF expressed at the beginning of this book, perhaps they are all coming true to some extent.

'A Work in Progress'

As I write, the GEF remains in place, and, while the pace of change may have slowed since the restructuring in 1994, it is still evolving.

The agenda is still subject to pressure from participating governments, environmental Conventions, international agencies, NGOs,
scientists, and elements of the organised private sector. A second Participants' Assembly is due to consider the latest evaluation (OPS-2)
and confirm a third replenishment in Beijing in late 2002. The US
under Bush II is dragging its feet even more than usual, while the
European Union's priorities for the event are to 'replenish by 50%
the Global Environment Facility and broaden its mandate'.[2] NGO
and Southern governments' proposals to improve the GEF under its
third replenishment remain familiar: more transparency, technology
transfer, capacity-building and connection of environmental goals to
national development priorities.

'The Only Practical Thing to Come out of Rio'

The Conventions on Climate Change and Biodiversity have been
galvanised into action with the GEF's financial assistance – at least
compared to UN agreements lacking such a fund for implementation. Despite widespread suspicion, especially in the US, of their
implications, initial framework texts have been fleshed out and
begun to be implemented. The GEF has also proven more practical
in terms of getting things done than Rio's other products such as
Local Agenda 21 and the UN Commission for Sustainable Development which, lacking direct powers or access to large-scale finance,
have not moved far beyond discussion and reports. Given that the
tasks of these UN initiatives include overcoming political resistance
to sustainable development practices worldwide, the GEF's wordily
limited central purpose seems almost more achievable.

'A Mechanism for International Cooperation'

The GEF was described in the Operational Strategy as 'a mechanism
for international cooperation for the purpose of providing new, and
additional, grant and concessional funding to meet the agreed incremental costs of measures to achieve agreed global environmental
benefits in the areas of biological diversity, climate change, international waters and ozone depletion'.

2. 'Communication from the Commission to the European Parliament, the
   Council, the Economic and Social Committee and the Committee of the
   Regions – Towards a Global Partnership for Sustainable Development',
   Commission of the European Communities, Brussels, 2002.

This purpose has not however proved easy to realise, and, as the 1998 evaluation (OPS-1) confirmed, GEF funds are not sufficient for the massive scale of the interventions demanded under the Climate Change and Biodiversity Conventions. Meanwhile, to meet governments' need to announce ever more strategies and initiatives, new global environmental financial schemes have been emerging since Rio – many devised in association with the World Bank. They include engineered markets for carbon trading and the Clean Development Mechanism (CDM)[3] under the FCCC, as well as biodiversity investment funds and other developments which may sideline the GEF's role as primary mechanism to finance the Conventions. In addition, in 2001, the $21 million Millennium Ecosystem Assessment was launched by the UN and 1,500 scientists. According to the UN secretary general, Kofi Annan, the study was 'designed to bring the world's best science to bear on the present choices we face in managing the global environment': almost as if the 'science-based' GEF – let alone the IPCC, Global Biodiversity Assessment, etc. – had never existed.[4] There was also little sign in this study's terms of social science, which if applied more widely could almost certainly offer new insights into why previous conservation efforts have not worked as promised, and suggest more practical proposals for effective international cooperation on the environment.

At the global governance level, another big green idea is an international or world environment organisation (WEO, to parallel the WTO), initially suggested in 1997 by Germany, Brazil, Singapore, and South Africa. The US government in particular remains unconvinced however, not least since another environmental body might 'result in a possible duplication and multiplication of current institutional problems' (UNEP Report on Environmental Governance, in IISD, 2001).

'An Enormous Con'

The GEF received nowhere near the vast amounts of money (up to $600 billion) that speakers at the Rio Earth Summit had suggested would be needed to protect the global environment, and not even

3. The Clean Development Mechanism adopted certain elements of the GEF model of governance, notably the GEF Council's 'consensus practice' for the CDM executive board (Barathan, 1998).
4. Quoted in the *Seattle Times*, 6 June 2001.

all the sums advertised as committed to GEF replenishments have been spent in the years since 1992. Yet for many globally active environmental professionals – whether in government, international agencies, scientific bodies or NGOs – the potential for even the most limited multilateral green aid was reason enough to support the GEF. Cynical observers therefore point to the GEF's vague promises of institutional reform, consultancies and green deal-making to underfunded environmental professionals – who might otherwise be objecting to the encroachment of World Bank priorities into conservation management, let alone to the Bank's ongoing environmentally damaging projects in oil, coal, forestry, roads, ports, and so forth. GEF processes and project applications can tie up interested people and institutions in reams of detailed policy and paperwork, while maintaining their interest with the promise of institutional funding and a 'listening ear' for environmental concerns in the World Bank.

But only the project-based expectations of selected ministries, agencies and professional conservationists tend to be favoured for funding, and only selected professional voices tend to be heard. This dynamic can marginalise not only politically distant or problematic forms of knowledge, but also angrier and Southern voices seeking substantial action to go beyond mitigation to prevent environmental problems alongside the other negative impacts of structural adjustment, unfair global trade etc. By making partners and consultants only of those willing to be 'businesslike' and 'non-political' in the pursuit of narrowly defined 'global environmental benefits', the World Bank and its partners have apparently been able to channel selected environmentalist passion and expertise away from grass-roots ecological movements and into helping to spend the GEF's 0.5 per cent of total multilateral aid funds – funds which constitute themselves a declining fraction of international investment as a whole.

'A Green Virus in the Bretton Woods Software'

The World Bank is now held by many of its former critics to be honestly reforming: producing numerous good ideas and publications in response to the global environmental agenda. By 1995, Hilary French at the World Watch Institute reported a 30-fold rise in World Bank 'environmental' spending since 1989 (though warning that this may be due to 'changes in the type of project counted as "environmental"'). Even if it has not fully 'mainstreamed' all of GEF's global priorities, the World Bank certainly seems to be setting the pace with global financial institutions, advancing a particular style of environmental management and showing up its recidivist Bretton Woods twin, the IMF, in the process.[5]

However, it is not clear to what extent the GEF – as opposed to any of the Bank's other environmental initiatives – has created this new emphasis. Nor is it clear how deep any changes go into shaping the underlying values of the World Bank, especially given claims that reforms in the institution effectively involve the Bank's president, James Wolfenson, 'surrounded by yes men', running the bureaucracy on a 'Stalinist' basis and issuing endless new initiatives from above (Chatham House rules, 2001).

'Greenwash for the World Bank's Destructive Practices'

Whatever reforms the World Bank is or is not making on some fronts, its various arms still lend for road building, agribusiness, industrial fisheries and logging, not to mention GHG-releasing oil and coal developments, often with ineffective environmental safeguards and in the face of local hostility. The GEF pays separately for projects tackling the symptoms of selected associated environmental problems, but it has hardly addressed issues shaping World Bank lending and thereby the causes of many such environmental problems – for example energy supply politics, land, tax and subsidy reforms, intellectual property rights or planning laws.

'Helps the World Bank to Externalise Environmental Costs'

The GEF is differentiated from other financial institutions by its duty to create only global environmental benefits. By taking on responsibility for funding environmental components of development projects, the GEF risks encouraging the Bank – and its borrowers – not to worry about environmental concerns in their mainstream

5. IMF management refused demands that they too set up an environment department in 1991, and in the mid 1990s usually only three of the IMF's thousands of economists would be looking at environmental issues (French, 1995).

operations. Given that environmental concerns cannot effectively be tacked on to for example an agriculture project, donor governments' emphasis on 'mainstreaming' in the Implementing Agencies was meant to prevent this externalisation happening. But with incremental costs 'at the heart of the GEF' and the value of any resulting 'leverage' opaque (as seen in Chapter 5), this problem is unlikely to go away.

Haufler (1997) suggests an unusual perspective on the GEF's function – as an insurance policy. Pointing to international investors' use of financial institutions like the World Bank's Multilateral Investment Guarantee Agency and the European Bank for Reconstruction and Development to manage and underwrite their political and economic risks, she suggests that 'now [investors have] the GEF to underwrite environmental risks'. With major actors in the global economy often keen to avoid environmental regulation, perhaps governments' payments into the GEF can be seen as publicly financed insurance premiums against the risk of international investments causing global environmental damage.

But no body or institution, whatever their actuarial and other expertise, can fairly assess the distribution of environmental risks and liabilities for unsustainable development sufficiently to ensure that any related 'premiums' paid reflect real risks taken, and by whom. In the real world, lack of full information means that this kind of calculation is just not doable – even if anybody was really trying to connect payments, costs and benefits meaningfully. Yet the GEF's use of ostensibly technical 'incremental costs' analyses and formulae to assess 'global benefits' suggests that full and fair environmental costing is not only doable, but being done. This may be a problem for real-world conservation if it persuades people paying for GEF and the World Bank that they are helping the world's environments to be managed objectively and rationally for the greatest good, when in practice they are not.

'Sweetener for International Loans', 'Green Subsidy for Transnational Science and Investment'

The GEF's potential as a 'sweetener' for debt seems limited because private investors tend to be wary of involvement in the convoluted procedures attached to the GEF's relatively small amounts of 'transparent' and 'accountable' spending. However, in the World Bank especially, incentives to keep loans flowing can outweigh the promise to use consistent, clear criteria for appropriate use of the GEF's 'leverage' potential. As McNeely (1991) feared, the GEF's top-up to development finance therefore risks producing 'business as usual, only more so'.

Mohamed El-Ashry meanwhile observes expansively that 'the environment business is a new business' (interview, 1997). Under the headline 'Billions in Profits Predicted for Renewable Energies', in 2001 he stressed that: 'The opportunities for countries and for business are enormous ... If renewable energy captures just 3% of the market in developing nations within 10 years, investments could exceed $5 billion a year.'[6] Though such investment is widely needed and wanted in the South, the question of who controls and benefits from it remains contentious, not least when local democratic institutions and businesses face the World Bank, donor governments and the large-scale private sector engaging in what McAfee calls 'green developmentalism'. With help from the GEF to develop a knowledge infrastructure and extend credit lines for the transnational sector, the South provides not just raw materials but a test bed and new market for largely Northern investors, ideas and products. Looked at very harshly and without its green gloss, the GEF seems to involve a highly politicised transfer of Northern taxes to subsidise elite management of Southern resources, and to assist allied NGOs, firms and agencies to provide approved products and services in the South for global science and markets.

SUSTAINING SYSTEMS

Defending Enclosures

Looking at environmental management in the business world, Levy (1997) observes that institutional sustainability is often the primary goal of initiatives in environmental management. Assisting sustainable development is not a direct goal of the GEF, but staff of any publicly funded body have to sustain their own institutions' development, and that of the treasuries supporting their work, if they are to do their jobs. According to Acselrad (1996), environmental and other planners quite rationally make plans for a world in which there

---

6. *Financial Times* Information Environment News Service, 12 February 2001.

will always be a need and salaries available for their brand of professional planning. Therefore when the GEF's CEO and chairman told NGOs attending the 1998 Participants' Assembly that 'one key challenge is survival – will the GEF exist ten years from now?', his words suggested that, from where he sits, effective action depends on the continued existence of the GEF. This existence depends on the active support of governments, with whom NGO pressure can be a great help – if appropriately inspired and channelled in the GEF's service with the rhetoric of environmental protection through global sustainable development.

Insofar as donor governments designed the GEF to deal with environmental threats, there are similarities to how the IDA was supposed to deal with poverty – insofar as it could pose systemic and political threats to the expansion of Anglo-Saxon capitalist institutions. Yet uniquely for a Bretton Woods institution, the GEF differs from IDA in that it is also legally obliged to finance implementation of UN Conventions. Ostensibly tied to the UN system, the GEF must be seen to respond directly to their environmental instructions. But if it was actually to implement the grass-roots social and ecologically-based thinking advocated in many environmental communities and partially transmitted through the UNEP and UNDP as well as the Conventions, the GEF could be the first victim of its own success.

For instance, the GEF could theoretically have a role to play in promoting enforcement of environmental regulations, or creating infrastructure and conditions for what some call ecological modernisation, others industrial transformation. Ayres and Simonis (1994) suggest minimising resource throughput and hence environmental damage in modern economies by closing cycles in industry, adopting almost permacultural principles[7] to use waste outputs – perhaps heat or particular chemical compounds – as productive inputs elsewhere. But such approaches, if effective, could make the idea of bounded, specifically environmental projects redundant.

Saving Worlds – Within Limits

If environmentalism means 'saving the world', some wonder: whose world? The end of the world has long been nigh in cultures

---

7. Permaculture is a way of low-impact gardening, making use of natural processes to improve functional efficiency and minimise expensive inputs as well as externalities. See, for example, <www.permaculture.org>.

with millenarian tendencies – but in whose world, to which ecosystems, at what levels are threats perceived in a globalised world? The ecological niche and resource base of, for example, cockroaches, rats and viruses seems secure, while for some other species and habitats, the apocalypse has already happened. The same is true for human communities: some people are thriving in the global economy, others losing everything to environmental, economic and social transformations. But threats to which community take on the status of global issues, deserving of universal attention, finance and cooperation?

Just as those willing to listen will hear from forest-dwelling tribes that their world is about to end when logging, damming or mining interests set their sights on their lands, so we hear from global elites that the natural world is at risk when *their* territory and livelihoods seem fragile. And just as the environmental threats to the survival of forest peoples tend to come from 'outsiders' who do not respect their traditional rights and cultural values, so too do political threats to the global 'tribe' come from 'outsiders' who do not respect *their* economic values and rights to manage the globe accordingly. So to continue their development, the transnational capitalist class must – whether consciously or not – secure their own 'sustainable liveli-hoods' from the threat of not just specific resource shortages but also radical environmentalists demanding that other animals and peoples' (including, for example, traditional forest peoples') worlds be saved first.

In response, new experts may be employed at a global level to identify the sources of environmental risk and manage them 'pro-fessionally' to minimise the impacts on economic development. By calling for ever more participation by global civil society in their processes, they win collaborative allies who can help to drive more radical ideas and advocates from the 'terrain of political contesta-bility' (Gill, 1997). Selected environmental activists can be listened to – even hired – and the World Bank can 'vaccinate' itself against related critiques: strengthening its analyses and rhetoric and beefing up its staffing quotas against future environmentalist attacks.

Transformation in a Trojan Horse?

Accepting the Bank's 'partnerships' and adopting a kind of 'Trojan Horse' strategy for change from the inside seems like the only way to reform the Bank for many environmental NGOs[8] – indeed El-Ashry has appealed to NGOs saying the GEF itself is a Trojan Horse (or perhaps a pony, given its limitations) for their concerns inside the economic walls of the World Bank. But if NGOs, let alone the GEF, find this approach failing to make the necessary changes to development policy, can they choose to move away from cooperation with institutions like the Bank? The GEF probably would not be funded so well if removed from the Bank's effective legal control, so where else would big international NGOs find a similar level of credibility – and access to finance? In the end, even those who seek to represent 'outside' interests 'inside' can find that once effectively absorbed into an institutional ecosystem, they too depend on the status quo for influence and livelihood.

Yearley (1994), who is not an anti-environmental author, calls it 'ironic' that the very existence of a green campaigning class depends on the surplus of the capitalist system they criticise. Funded largely from major US charitable trusts, people working in big green NGOs may not be paid much compared to staff in the institutions they lobby and oppose, but they still make a living by arguing for a world where resources would not be concentrated enough to pay for their jobs at all. Like 'free market' economists, professional greens claim to aim for an idealised state of nature which would abolish their own profession – which can create a fundamental tension in their work between a belief in the necessity of political and economic change for the sake of the environment, and personal, political and economic sustainability in their organisations.

When independent scientists, businesses, farmers, fishers, hunter-gatherers, even governments become involved in environmental or economic activism, they cannot and largely do not deny having their own goals, sources of livelihood and worlds to save. 'Professional' economists, conservationists and civil servants charged with managing resources for the 'global good' have, however, to pretend that their own values – and searches for sustainable livelihoods – do not come first. Not only for this reason, Guha (1997) referred to some international environment professionals as 'green missionaries [who are] possibly more dangerous, and certainly more hypocritical than their economic or religious counterparts'.

8. Many big green NGOs have been developing their expertise in environmental economics to cope with the World Bank's approach (interview, NGO, 1997).

Buying up Nature

Whatever the realities of NGO activity around the GEF, World Bank and individual GEF projects are designed as if there is little or no structural basis to global problems, and the environment can be preserved with technocratic tinkering by professionals in 'partnership' with transnational capital. Meanwhile, in the ideological climate of recent decades, the 'global commons' – nature described by the UN as the 'common heritage of all mankind' – has been mapped, priced and privatised, that is, enclosed by technocratic resource managerialists on behalf of powerful political masters. According to Goldman (2001b),

> It is through what I call the 'green neo-liberal project' – in which *neocolonial* conservationist ideas of enclosure and preservation and *neo-liberal* notions of market value and optimal resource allocation find common cause – that institutions such as the World Bank have made particular natures and natural resource-dependent communities legible and accountable.

In the bigger picture, the GEF's work is part of the broad process of political and economic 'globalisation'. The World Bank's role in this process tends to extend the range and hegemony of mainly US and Western European interests and institutions into new areas, recolonising not only Southern economies but also new aspects of the global environment. To quote Goldman (1998) again,

> former socialist countries in Eastern Europe and the South … are rapidly integrating their economies into global capital circuits by following the ecological conditions for foreign loans established by the World Bank … 'getting the price right' on nature – that is, making one's natural garden suitably fit for capitalist integration.

Faced with inevitable local opposition to this agenda, the GEF's advocates have practised the art of green rhetoric as moral persuasion. They argue convincingly that without the World Bank's role there would be nothing to pay for the environmental Conventions and that, for all its faults, the GEF is of unique value because it is experimental, aiming innovatively to deliver global benefits, transfer technology, conserve species and ecosystems, reform institutions and enhance participation and accountability in aid. Anybody raising difficult questions about the political, economic, cultural and other conditions that may make or break these public goods, let alone contribute to any form of colonisation, can be asked whether they think poor people and countries don't deserve aid and an equal chance to participate in the GEF's global environmental partnerships.

Globalisation and its Discontents

For all the power of this language, the GEF's publicity does not stop some people seeing additional green aid as a little bit of sugar to help the neo-liberal medicine go down, and/or an irrelevance. The financial interests of the 'Dollar–Wall St regime' are still using the neo-liberal 'Washington consensus' as a political lever to deregulate and open economies worldwide to US goods, firms and speculative investments (Gowan, 1999), and in high-powered 'economic' trade and investment negotiations at the IMF and WTO, ecological claims are explicitly treated as protectionist obstacles to 'free' trade – as defined by the richest and best-represented governments (Ford, 2000), and violated by them apparently at will.

In this context, aid is certainly not used apolitically but as 'a third tool of foreign policy, between diplomacy and military action', according to Andrew Natsios, head of USAid. He is reported to have dismissed concerns about neutrality, impartiality and independence, saying 'I don't think American interests are evil.'[9] But the connections between aid funds coming out of Washington DC and the US government's mission to achieve military and economic (and perhaps also ideological) 'full spectrum dominance'[10] can only undermine the argument, necessary elsewhere, that aid is directed to serve the wider common good. The European and other governments involved in aid cooperation often therefore try to mitigate some of the more shortsighted elements of the US government's attitude.

This mitigation is seen as essential by more cosmopolitan capitalists because an untrustworthy empire creates resistance of many forms, violent in places but currently, for the most part, non-violent and in the shape of a more diffuse worldwide movement to put justice and security for people and planet before narrow advantage, and secure some recompense for the poorest for losses suffered

9. Speaking to the InterAction Forum (<www.alertnet.org/thefacts/reliefresources/251995>).
10. <www.defenselink.mil/news/Jun2000/n06022000_20006025.html>

from colonialisms to date (see, for example, <www.agp.org>, <www.indymedia.org>, <www.oneworld.net>, <www.twnpen.org>). This movement gained ground in the late 1990s partly because high-profile events like the Rio Earth Summit did not produce the promised effective solutions for managing ecological resources on a fair basis worldwide, but merely sought to stabilise the ground beneath a particular community's expansion of its market and investment model.

For senior capitalists like the head of Morgan Stanley (quoted in Gowan, 1999) economic globalisation has therefore remained 'a rather fragile creature dependent on the nurturing care of states'. Northern governments and their international agencies often do provide that care and whilst welcoming inside selected NGOs bearing constructive messages, send riot police to deal with massive protests outside the meetings of international financial institutions, as when the WTO met in Seattle in late 1999, and the World Bank and IMF in Prague, 2000, and regularly in Washington DC.

Demonising Dissent

One solution adopted has been to restrict the scale of summits or move them to largely inaccessible places like Qatar or the high Rocky Mountains, and, as ever with Northern 'colonialisms', divide and rule tactics can be used against most forms of opposition: offering a choice between participating (and risking co-option) or dissenting (and perpetuating exclusion or worse). Yet dissent is vital for both 'democratic' debate and the 'rational' discourses of science and management, indeed it was environmental scientists' and activists' unwillingness to accept official reassurances that brought about international attention to the importance of green issues, let alone the creation of a GEF, in the first place: 'Conflict is the essential core of a free and open society. If one were to project the democratic way of life in a musical score, its major theme would be the harmony of dissonance' (Alinsky, 1971). Experience suggests any society does well to keep this music playing free, since its suppression easily leads to the discordant noises of repression, guns and bombs.

In the wake of the 11 September 2001 attacks on symbols of US power in New York and Washington, dissent has not been made welcome in much of the mainstream US media, even academia. Several North American environmental groups immediately called off campaigns critical of the Bush administration, and cancelled their involvement in planned protests against the World Bank and IMF.[11] In the ensuing months, there was little effective opposition as the US and allied governments around the world imposed draconian new laws on their distracted populations – in addition to existing legislation – to 'protect freedom' by restricting it.[12] In the UK, for example, there has been a redefinition of terrorism to include key elements of peaceful protest, including non-violent direct action and support for resistance to repressive regimes abroad. In fact, the UK's Anti-Terrorism, Crime and Security Act 2001, seems to put in place 'powers characteristic of a police state' (<www.blagged.freeserve.co.uk>).

Now the so-called 'war on terror' seems to be involving a 'war on dissent', binding citizens' movements while so-called 'corporate citizens' – acting under a legal compulsion to profit[13] – are for the most part allowed to 'self-regulate'. For example the latest UN initiative to make the transnational private sector more responsible, the 'Global Compact' agreed in the late 1990s, has no teeth. Meanwhile the WBCSD[14] – claiming to represent what it terms 'enlightened' corporations who see the potential in sustainable development – is hosting preparatory committees for the UN's 2002 World Summit on Sustainable Development, just as it did for the Rio Earth Summit in 1992. Nitin Desai, secretary general of the WSSD, may call on major corporations to increase their involvement in sustainable development initiatives, but nobody is proposing any legally binding framework for corporate accountability.

This leads cynical observers to conclude that the WSSD will turn out like Rio and Stockholm before it, with lots of good words about

11. Among the groups believed to have self-censored in the aftermath of 11 September 2001 are the trade union AFL-CIO, the International Rivers Network, Rainforest Action Network, the Sierra Club, the Ruckus Society and Friends of the Earth – among them some players in organising the protests which shut down the WTO meeting in Seattle, 1999 (<www.counterpunch.org/giombetti.html>).
12. <www.indymedia.org>, <www.blagged.freeserve.co.uk/ta2000/atcsabriefing.htm>
13. The directors of an Anglo-Saxon model corporation have a legal 'fiduciary duty' to maximise their shareholders' profit – though as I write the Enron scandal may be shedding a new light on the interpretation of this duty as freedom to profit at any expense.
14. <www.WBCSD.org> website available in Arabic, Chinese, French, Russian, Spanish (more languages than GEF – let alone its critics – have the resources for).

tackling hunger, poverty and environmental protection – and some new initiatives to show for it – but no answer to the problems of excess wealth and whose development is to be sustained. People building fairer institutions and actively seeking answers to immediate problems of environmental, social and personal sustainability are unlikely to participate much in WSSD processes, not only because most will be politically unpalatable to established interests, but because they will be busy working, too far away, ill, poor and/or caring for relatives. Those able and determined to be heard may demonstrate, but risk arrest and worse. And probably meanwhile various representatives of mainstream NGOs, corporations and government bodies will continue to sit together and try to advance global sustainable development as they each see it, sometimes wondering why there is so little public participation in the important issues they discuss.

POSSIBLE ALTERNATIVES TO SPENDING ON A GEF

Official evaluations have pointed to problems resulting from GEF's impotence in the face of environmental destruction and democratic failures at the local, national, regional and global levels. But on these as with other fundamental difficulties facing the GEF, what the evaluators have not done is to discuss potential alternative uses for the money, expertise and time committed. Stepping for a moment outside the current global 'terrain of political contestability', the following sections follow on from the reforms proposed for GEF above, and skim some possible alternatives for expenditure on actually participatory, transparent, cost-effective, etc., environmental protection, looking at three levels – local, national and global – from the bottom up. This is not meant to be any sort of charter for worldwide environmental action, rather hints of ideas that could work in a slightly more ideal world and that have worked elsewhere. At every level, key issues for effective conservation seem to be learning from experience, democratisation and co-ordination for fair, clear and firm regulation and enforcement. Popularising conservation values also demands that rich, powerful and Northern-educated people should have no greater influence in these processes than anyone else – except perhaps where they can lead by example instead of bribery or bullying.

Local Conservation

In areas where 'global' environmental aid projects are perceived as an outside imposition with costs for local communities but no benefits, it is usually hard to get widespread agreement on new conservation initiatives, even those designed to avoid old problems and new enclosures. As the designer of the World Bank/GEF *India Ecodevelopment* project put it, 'To try and think that one can sit in Washington or Geneva or somewhere else, and try and form a global picture of what is required for conservation; it seems to be an impossible task' (interview, NGO, 1999).

More appropriate conservation emerges from and builds on local peoples' environmental knowledge, values and democratic organisations. Interested outside environmental professionals can support diverse local experts, activists and democratically accountable bodies trying to develop fair and sound conservation policies: providing observers and advice where local power corrupts and polluting interests resist, and offering appropriate financial assistance to build successful bottom-up initiatives using an honestly paraproject or similar approach (see Chapter 6). 'Let us work together, us and the Forest Department. Then we can save the forests. We want that duty!' (interview, Adivasi village councillor, 1999).[15]

National Conservation

As a body established by intergovernmental agreement, the GEF has to work with governments, even where they are weak, corrupt and/or repressive – or have simply not overcome the usual unbalanced conflict between finance and environment ministries' interests. In this context one interviewee observed, 'The GEF could do better by getting relevant ministers together at one table, but it was not giving money for this sort of thing' (interview, NGO, 1997). So, as the UNEP told ministers meeting to discuss global environmental governance in 2001, a 'crucial consideration' for 'sustainable development' remains the 'coordination of governance issues at the national level – in both developed and developing countries' (IISD, 2001).[16]

15. This demand featured in a video letter from the Nagarhole forest dwellers to the GEF and the World Bank, shown in our documentary *Suits and Savages* (Howitt and Young, 2000).
16. Summary Report from the UNEP Expert Consultations on International Environmental Governance, published by the International Institute for Sustainable Development.

The gathered environment ministers also indicated that 'future international environmental governance arrangements should be multi-layered, with functions specified at local, national, regional and global levels' (IISD, 2001). Perhaps with such a degree of subsidiarity, instruments of environmental governance could avoid what Kaur et al. (1999) call the 'jurisdictional gap' between 'a globalised world and national, separate units of policy-making'. This gap is one of 'three key weaknesses in the current arrangements for providing global public goods', another of which is 'the incentive gap', reflecting the fact that 'operational follow up to [multilateral] agreements relies too exclusively on the aid mechanism, ignoring many other practical policy options that could make co-operation a preferred strategy for both developing and industrial countries'.

Escaping 'the aid mechanism', people in Northern nations might take note of the example set by their own environmental practices, for example the fact that the UK wastes more heat from cooling towers than is used to heat every building in the country.[17] As Ridley[18] among others has concluded, emission reduction 'by policy' is far more cost-effective than 'by project', and conservationists have long stressed the importance of reforms to agricultural, marine and planning policies for the protection of biodiversity. Governments could therefore find that a cheaper option would be to examine the anti-environmental aspects of their policies at home, as well as for the wider political economy.

At the international level, powerful governments tend to

preach things that they don't do, which undermines the message on sustainable development – for example when the US president has lots of limos, offers unlimited support for the armed forces, things like that. The donors need to lead by example on sustainability because Southern governments are watching closely to imitate what is done in more powerful nations. (interview, GEF Secretariat, 1997)

Nick Hildyard reports[19] how, in 1998, the UK Export Credit Guarantee Department (which uses taxpayers' money to guarantee

17. The *Guardian*, 14 February 2002.
18. University College London PhD thesis quoted pp. 10–11, *JI Quarterly Newsletter*, July 1997, Groningen, NL.
19. 'Moral Dilemmas in International Investment – Whose Morals? Whose Dilemmas? A Political Economy of Ethics in the Export Credit Debate' Talk to Wilton Park Conference, 'International Investment and the Environment – What Role for Governments?' 30 May–2 June 2000.

huge amounts of private investment in risky Southern markets) complained that environment and development NGOs should stop criticising its activities since 'we are not a development agency'. Yet enforcing environmental controls on such publicly backed operations would be much cheaper than trying later to mitigate the environmental impacts of their ill-considered investments.

In the meantime, if governments could establish and adopt coherent, democratic and science-based environmental criteria for all uses of public money, perhaps they could also contribute to an increasingly widely desired 'decentralisation and democratisation of the state, and a disentangling of the state from the power of capital' (Paterson, 1995).

Global Conservation

At the global level, Kaur et al. (1999) identify a 'participation gap' created by 'the steady privatisation and concentration of political and economic power in recent decades' and, in solution, they suggest 'expanding the role of civil society and the private sector in international negotiations'. But perhaps action for the public good at any level could be informed as much by committed and independent science (natural and social) as by commerce, and could demand more effective accountability of not only international agencies and negotiators but also the private sector, their advisors and the self-appointed representatives of 'civil society'.

Back when the GEF was created and began making friends internationally, others were suggesting that higher and stable prices for Southern-produced cash crop commodities would enable Southern countries to afford their own environmental and other domestic initiatives without foreign aid (for example, Jacobs, 1991). Yet in the absence of fair trade rules, the theoretical appeal of the 'free trade' agenda promoted by hegemonic Bretton Woods institutions and the 'dollar–Wall St regime' is undermined by some (that is, richer) governments and firms being a lot freer than others to shape[20] the terms of trade demanded of others.[21] Whatever the potential benefits of

20. For example, the US government in 2002 contradicted its instructions to every other country to liberalise at all costs with its own steel tariffs and domestic agricultural subsidies (see press).
21. The 2001 WTO meeting in Doha, Qatar is said to have featured 'economic gunboat diplomacy ... Wealthy countries exploited their power to spin the agenda of big business.' Mark Curtis, quoted by John Pilger in the *New Statesman*, 17 December 2001.

an idealised and truly free exchange between people with different resources, information, skills and values, such exchange is surely impossible in any economy regulated beyond the enforcement of property rights. Eventually, cultivated ideological illusions about free trade and liberalisation will come to be dispelled, at which time a saner tactic would be for banks, made more accountable to non-elites, to forgive international debt incurred at their urging by often tyrannical and corrupt Southern leaders supporting global super-powers. Another tactic might be for social and environmental NGOs to work less on replacing the functions of weakened governments than on practical contributions to repair injustices and support democratic solutions.

Meanwhile, without the communication and commitment necessary for budget reforms, enforcement of environmental regu-lations and corporate accountability, funds like GEF will always be tinkering at the margins. Reports for the Rio + 5 intergovernmental meeting in 1997 estimated that $700 billion was spent annually on 'perverse' (that is, anti-environmental) incentives – compared to the GEF's c. $100 million per annum grants.[22]

FINAL THOUGHTS

Nevertheless, in international discussions about future global ecological governance, lessons can be learned from GEF: from its projects, processes and impacts, its cultures of interaction and governance and the fact that in its operations, 'global' benefits are defined as something separate from, and potentially in conflict with, 'national' or 'local' interests.[23]

22. Despite lacking a mandate to tackle politically loaded issues like corporate regulation, in 2001 the WSSD secretariat still noted pointedly that 'Subsidy reduction, tax reform and internalization of externalities in pricing [are] financial instruments for promoting sustainable develop-ment with limited funding' (Summary of the WSSD Prepcom Bureau's 6th meeting, Zehra Aydin Sipos, United Nations).
23. Might this mean that GEF's goals are presented more honestly than those of most multilateral aid? The World Bank and IMF's rules, policy and projects are similarly shaped by and favourable to certain globally active communities, but they are not specified as being only for 'global' benefit. Should a similar distinction be made between global and local benefits resulting from global development aid too, given the costs to local economies and communities of neo-liberal policies for international

Meanwhile, for all GEF's surface democracy, participation and science, agreements reached in 'economic' Bretton Woods institutions still take precedence over environmental and social agreements reached in the UN. As a result, governments trying to cooperate for sustainable development still produce more consultancies than action, so that as the GEF's own CEO recognised:

> What we have at present is duplication, fragmentation and competition for scarce resources – fundraising gimmicks if you will. And despite all the fancy brochures and reports that fill our shelves, the state of the world environment continues to deteriorate.[24]

For now however, the GEF may be still 'grossly inadequate' (Pernetta, 1996), but it is probably the most ambitious international environmental institution in the currently dominant world order, and it remains possible that it will turn out to be relatively effective, despite all the contradictions and flawed compromises that it embodies. Yet whatever GEF's efforts, the fate of (particularly human) ecology worldwide will not be held in so few hands.

To be fair and effective in saving people of many different worlds, not least from misunderstanding ecology and disrespecting each other, global environmental management would be best upended, designed to respond to the needs of grass-roots conservation and help collaboration between people with divergent values and constituencies. If the GEF cannot be fundamentally re-imagined and restructured for such tasks, its abolition might free up scarce environmental resources, expertise and political will for more appropriate reforms and initiatives. However, given the abandonment of most non-military and economic multilateral engagement by the current (illegitimate, according to Palast, 2002) Bush administration in the US, with the apparently tacit compliance of other Western governments, the necessary political will for substantial environmental action is unlikely to be forthcoming 'from above' in the near future.

---

investment? If Bretton Woods economic policy interventions were also restricted to serving the 'global' good, might this help to end the pretence that plans for growth through 'liberalisation' are good for us all?

24. El-Ashry speaking to an intergovernmental group of environmental ministers meeting on international environmental governance, Bonn, July 2001.

The GEF's major donor governments have little obvious reason to end or to change the shape of their multilateral creation. For the GEF is a *trust* fund – staff of its trustee, the World Bank, are generally trusted by donor governments to do their bidding with funds allotted. The GEF's guiding governments cannot trust poorer governments' peoples to follow their restricted agenda for action under the UN Conventions, and so try to pay them to comply. With the GEF, Northern governments have to some extent bought environmentalists' and Southern governments' trust in a top-down, Northern-led agenda for 'global' environmental management. But while many do warily participate in the deals involved, mutual trust is undermined by inequality in the relationship. If a more effective global commons regime is to emerge, it must surely be based on honesty and mutual trust which – like love – can be earned and shared, but not effectively bought.

Appendix I
Biographies of GEF Chairman/CEO and his Senior Advisory Panel of 1997

Mohamed El-Ashry

Chairman of the GEF since 1991, CEO of the Secretariat since 1994. Chief environmental advisor to the president and director of the environment department (1991–4) at the World Bank. Graduated in 1959 from Cairo University, and received a PhD in geology in 1966 at the University of Illinois. Held teaching and research positions at Cairo University, Pan-American-U.A.R. Oil Company, Illinois Geological Survey, Wilkes University and the Environmental Defense Fund. Senior vice-president of the WRI, and director of Environmental Quality at the Tennessee Valley Authority, senior environmental advisor to the UNDP, and special advisor to the secretary general of the 1992 Earth Summit (UNCED). Fellow of the Geological Society of America and the American Association for the Advancement of Science.

Maurice Strong – Canada

Born poor in Manitoba in 1929, began his career in the oil business, a millionnaire and president of the Power Corporation of Canada by his 30s. Became head of the Canadian International Development Agency and organised the first Earth Summit – the Stockholm Conference on the Human Environment, 1972 – then became first director of the new UNEP. In 1976 Strong gave up running Petro-Canada, the national oil company, for various business deals, including one with Adnan Khashoggi through which he ended up owning the 200,000-acre Baca ranch in Colorado – now a New Age centre run by his wife, Hanne. Member of the World Commission on Environment and Development (the Brundtland Commission), president of the World Federation of United Nations Associations, on the executive committee of the Society for International Development, the Commission on Global Governance, and advisor to the

Rockefeller Foundation and the World Wildlife Fund. Among many other senior roles, he has been a member of the Club of Rome; chairman of the World Resources Institute; co-chairman of the Council of the World Economic Forum; and head of UN relief efforts in Ethiopia in the mid 1980s. He was almost shut out of becoming secretary general of the 1992 Earth Summit by the US State Department, but because George Bush I knew him – Strong had donated some $100,000 to the Democrats and a slightly lesser amount to the Republicans in 1988 – the State Department was overruled by the White House. As chairman of the Earth Council, he earned the nickname 'Father Earth', and the *New York Times* called him the 'Custodian of the Planet'. As advisor to Kofi Annan, he is overseeing UN reforms. James Wolfensohn (whom Strong hired out of Harvard in the early 1960s to run an Australian subsidiary of one of his companies) appointed him his senior advisor on becoming president of the World Bank. A fellow of the Royal Societies of the UK and Canada, he helps direct the Business Council on Sustainable Development, and has 37 honourary doctorates. He is deeply mistrusted by the North American militia movement, who see him as an anti-democratic agent of encroaching world government through the UN. A slightly less paranoid environmental NGO person called him 'a slick-talking criminal' – but did not elaborate (interview, 1997).

Barber Conable – US

Born in rural New York, studied law at Cornell. Former congressman and president of the World Bank from 1986 to 1991, he reannounced the Bank's greening in 1987 while recommending a tripling in the amount of money the Bank spent for population control. He sat on the Commission on Global Governance and the Smithsonian Institution's Board of Regents; also a director of American International Group, Inc. In 1997 he said: 'As a former president of the World Bank, I find it hard to overstate the remarkable benefits the US receives from the World Bank. As the largest shareholder at the bank, the US has tremendous leverage at minimal cost.'

Emil Salim – Indonesia

Born in Indonesia, received a PhD in economics at the University of California, Berkeley, in 1964. Indonesian state minister for Population and Environment (1978–93) and member of the High

Level Advisory Board on Sustainable Development of the UN. A member of House of Representatives and People's Consultative Assembly since 1966, he advised Suharto and subsequent presidents on debt and development issues. Member of the Indonesian Academy of Sciences; lecturer to the Army Command Staff School; economics professor at the University of Indonesia; chairman of the board of trustees of leading Indonesian environmental organisations including the Indonesian Biodiversity Foundation, the Foundation for Sustainable Development and the Indonesian Ecolabelling Institute. Co-chairman of the World Commission on Forestry and Sustainable Development, president of the Governing Council of the UNEP, 1985–7, member of the World Commission of Environment and Development, 1984–7, vice-president of the Advisory Committee on Population of the Sea for South East Asia, on the board of the International Institute on Environment and Development and the Stockholm Environment Institute. When he stood for vice-president of Indonesia in 1998, stressing the need for more economic reform, he was forced to deny rumors that he was an espionage agent for the US because of his Berkeley education.

Henrique Brandão Cavalcanti – Brazil

Born in Rio de Janeiro in 1929, a civil engineer and former deputy minister of mines and energy, deputy minister of interior, and minister of environment and the Amazon in the federal government of Brazil. Lecturer in engineering and energy economics at Rio de Janeiro universities, delegate to the UN Conference on the Human Environment in Stockholm (1972), and to the World Population Conference in Bucharest (1974). From senior positions in the electric power and steel business he moved into the environmental field, holding positions such as managing director of the International Environmental Bureau in Geneva, chairman of the Third Session of the UN Commission on Sustainable Development, and president of the Intergovernmental Forum on Chemical Safety.

Istvan Lang – Hungary

Advisor to the president of the Hungarian Academy of Sciences. A member of the ICSU Advisory Committee on the Environment and member of the GEF's second STAP. Contributed to setting up the World Science Conference, 1999, in Hungary. Chairman of the first Hungarian 'Nature Expo' in 1996, which featured hunting showcases, a display of new BMW automobiles, exhibits from the Paks nuclear power plant, mobile phone providers and Hungarian petrol companies as well as Hungary's Ministry of Environment, the World Wildlife Fund and smaller green businesses. Laszlo Perneczky of the Regional Environment Centre reported that for the most part NGOs were disappointed with the event, since the high costs of exhibition space prevented most of them from participating: 'Clearly many of the exhibitors were commercial enterprises trying to "paint it green".'

Mostafa K. Tolba – Egypt

Graduated in botany from Cairo University in 1943, his PhD was from the University of London in 1949. President of the International Center for Environment and Development in Cairo, Egypt, and former executive director of the UNEP (1976–94). He has been professor of microbiology, Cairo University; Egyptian education minister; fellow of Imperial College, London; on the board of directors of the WRI, Aspen Institute of Humanistic Studies, International Conference on Genetics, International Institute on Environment and Development, the Egyptian Botanical Society, Institut d'Egypt, and other organisations including the Earth Council. A master of 'informal diplomacy', he forced through international agreements on ozone depleting chemicals and hazardous waste by 'pre-negotiating' with key international actors and then refusing to let negotiators leave the room until an agreement was signed.

Qu Geping – China

Born in 1930, studied the arts at Shandong University, and chemistry at Jilin University. In 1947 he joined the Chinese Communist Party. Held senior positions in the Baoding Film Factory, the Ministry of Chemical Industry, and the State Planning Commission. Member of the Ninth National People's Congress Standing Committee. Member of the CSD's High-Level Advisory Board. Attended the 1972 UN Conference on the Human Environment in Stockholm; served as China's representative to the UN Environment Programme from 1976 to 1977 and led the Chinese delegation to the Rio Earth Summit in 1992. He headed the China Society of Environmental Sciences from 1990 to 1996, has been a guest professor at Beijing, Qinghua, and People's Universities. He is quoted as saying:

The World Bank knows China very well, and if they state that the cost of environmental pollution in China is 6 percent of annual GDP, this figure should be trusted. Many Chinese policies, including pricing policies, are first proposed by the World Bank and then accepted by the central government.

Robert Lion – France

Born in 1934, graduated from the Paris Institute for Political Studies, the Law University of Paris, and the Ecole Nationale d'Administration. Formerly a banker, CEO of Caisse des Dépots, the main financial institution in the country, he became chief of staff of the prime minister of France and inspector general of finances of the Finance Ministry in Paris. Has been member of boards including Banque de France, Crédit Foncier, Crédit National, European Investment Bank, Eurotunnel, Club Méditerranée, Air France, Wagons-Lits, Havas, the Board of Agence pour les Economies d'Energie. Created the Comite d'Action Solaire (Solar Energy Committee); consultant to private sector companies (US and French), president of Energy 21, the energy arm of the Earth Council, dedicated to promotion of energy efficiency and renewable energy. A member of the Earth Council, he has been vice-president of the High Council for International Cooperation (advisory to the French government), senior counsellor, Bechtel, Andersen Consulting, ABN AMRO Capital Markets, and executive director of Eurotunnel, Compagnie des Signaux.

Thomas E. Lovejoy – US

Graduated with PhD in biology from Yale University. A tropical and conservation biologist, worked in the Brazilian Amazon since 1965 and initiated the controversial programme of 'debt for nature swaps'. A member of the US Council on Foreign Relations, he has been a member of the board of directors at WRI and at Resources for the Future; executive vice-president of WWF–US; assistant secretary for Environmental and External Affairs for the Smithsonian Institution; chief biodiversity advisor for the World Bank; president of the American Institute of Biological Sciences and Society for Conservation Biology; chairman of the United States Man and Biosphere Program. Founded the popular public television series Nature; fellow of the American Association for the Advancement of Science, the

American Academy of Arts and Sciences, the Linnaean Society of London, Royal Botanical Gardens at Kew, Wildlife Preservation Trust. A cautious advocate of genetic modification and proponent of carbon trading, he is a keen valuer of environmental costs and benefits, seeking, for example, the price of 'environmental services' provided by oysters filtering Chesapeake Bay, near Washington DC.

Birgitta Dahl – Sweden

Speaker, Parliament of Sweden; second in authority only to the president. Born 1937 near Göteborg, graduated at Uppsala University, 1960. Member of the Labour and Socialist International's Commission on Economy, Development and Environment, chairperson of the High-Level Advisory Board on Sustainable Development of the secretary general of the United Nations. Author on international relations, environment, gender, children's living conditions, social welfare policy, education, democracy and human rights. There are unconfirmed reports on the internet that while serving as chair of the Swedish Kampuchea society in the early 1970s, she was a supporter of Pol Pot, and refused to recognise the genocide carried out by his regime.

Thomas Odhiambo – Uganda/Kenya

PhD in physiology from the University of Cambridge. Founded and managed the International Center for Insect Physiology and Ecology in Nairobi. Professor of Insect Physiology at the University of Nairobi, founded the Departments of Entomology and Agriculture. Founder and first president of the African Academy of Sciences, vice-president of Third World Academy of Sciences, member of the Club of Rome. He argues that Africa, with its extensive collection of plants with known medicinal properties and biodiverse produce, could cash in on its genetic resources through commercialisation and agricultural biotechnology with the aid of the developed world. Showed interest in endorsing Monsanto PR letter 'let the harvest begin' to African public figures. 1998 patron of the International Service for the Acquisition of Agri-biotech Applications for dissemination of Northern companies' biotech developments: 'By arranging for senior policymakers from developing countries to share views with business leaders of private corporations, ISAAA helps to generate the trust, confidence, and cooperation that will integrate developing countries into the agri-biotech revolution.' Gave the keynote speech to the Summer Institute for African Agricultural Research at the University of Wisconsin, an intensive three-week programme funded by the Rockefeller Foundation to teach African PhD students to apply their technical training to research and development priorities.

Tomomitsu Oba – Japan

A former vice-minister for international affairs in Japan's Ministry of Finance, advisor to Japanese prime minister Ryutaro Hashimoto on Big Bang (the sudden liberalisation of all aspects of the Japanese financial regulatory system in 1996). As member of the G-5 Deputies, played prominent role in international policy co-ordination fora. Member of the Committee on Foreign Exchange and Other Trans-actions, trustee of the Institute for Global Environmental Strategies, on the board of trustees of the Toshiba International Foundation, advisor to management of Meijiseimei Finansurance life insurance, advisor to Ritsumeikan Asia Pacific University. In a keynote speech to the fifth environment congress of Asia and the Pacific (1996) Mr Oba mentioned that a recent meeting of futurologists in Japan confirmed that the biggest medium- to long-term threats to humanity are deterioration of the environment and rapid population growth.

Yolanda Kakabadse – Ecuador

Studied Educational Psychology in Quito. Executive director of Fundacion Natura in Quito, president of the IUCN, counsellor to the vice-president for environment and sustainable development of the World Bank, senior advisor to the Institute for Dispute Resolution Associates in Washington DC, on the boards of the World Resources Institute's Global Council, WWF-International, and the World Commission on Forests and Sustainable Development, and the advisory board of the Instituto Nacional de Biodiversidad. NGO Liaison Officer for the Rio Earth Summit in 1992. Briefly minister of environment for the Republic of Ecuador in a newly created envi-ronment ministry; in 2000 however Campana Amazonia Por La Vida Accion Ecologica claimed that Kakabadse had allowed oil companies in to protected areas, even though they did not make a major con-tribution to the Ecuadorian economy and in fact had to be subsidised by the government.

Select Sources of Biographical Information:

<www.aibs.org>
<www.afn.org>
<www.biodiversitynet.org>
<www.biotech-info.net>
<www.britannica.com>
<www.ecoaccord.cis.lead.org>
<www.ecouncil.ac.cr>
<www.gefweb.org>
<www.gene.ch>
<www.globalpolicy.org>
<www.igbp.kva.se>
<www.inforamp.net>
<www.jcif.or.sp>
<www.pubs.acs.org>
<www.riksdagen.se>
<www.thenewamerican.com>
(McConnell, 1996)

Appendix II
GEFOP Criteria

The GEF website provides the following list of criteria for approval of projects:

Projects will be reviewed by the GEFOP taking into account the following considerations, as appropriate:

(a) Country Eligibility:
(i) within the financial mechanism:
a. Party to Convention and
b. Developing country; or
(ii) outside the financial mechanism:
a. Eligibility under paragraph 9 (b) of the Instrument (UNDP/ World Bank criteria)
b. Where relevant, Party to Convention.

(b) Policy and Program Framework of the proposed project:
(i) Endorsement by recipient country operational focal point;
(ii) Consultation and co-ordination among Implementing Agencies;
(iii) Substantive eligibility: Consistency with GEF strategy and operational programs;
(iv) Linkages to:
a. Country/sector programs, national strategies, action plans;
b. Implementing Agencies in-country programmatic framework;
c. Pilot Phase activities;
d. Other focal areas;
e. Other programs and action plans at region/sub-regional levels.

(c) Technical review including:
(i) Specification of global benefits;
(ii) Thoroughness of technical reviews by experts from STAP roster;
(iii) Response to recommendations of technical reviewers;
(iv) Plans to make natural resource use sustainable;

240

(v) Environmental assessment and measures to prevent or mitigate potential damage;
(vi) Technology co-operation and transfer.

(d) Social assessment and consultation including:
(i) Demonstration of local participation/consultation in project preparations and measures for on-going participation and consultation in project implementation;
(ii) Role of local communities;
(iii) Role of indigenous people;
(iv) Resettlement plans if human populations are going to be resettled;
(v) Plans for public awareness, environmental education, and social communication;
(vi) Gender considerations.

(e) Capacity building:
(i) Training;
(ii) Institution building;
(iii) Planning and policy development;
(iv) Targeted research;
(v) Linkage of capacity building to enabling activities and to investment.

(f) Financial information:
(i) Funding and budget, including cost-effectiveness;
(ii) Overhead and management costs of Implementing Agencies and executing agencies;
(iii) Use of PDF resources;
(iv) Co-financing from other sources and the Implementing Agencies;
(v) Financial sustainability.

(g) Incremental cost (preliminary estimates):
(i) Correct application of methodology;
(ii) Procedures for estimation and agreement with recipient country;
(iii) Reasonableness of estimates and assumptions for baselines and projects;
(iv) Lessons of experience from comparable cases.

(h) Monitoring and Evaluation:

(i) Provision for monitoring and evaluation;

(ii) If continuation of previously funded project, requirement that evaluation has been completed and recommendations of evaluation have been taken into account in formulation of project being proposed.

Appendix III
GEF Climate Project: Spreading Solar Energy in Zimbabwe[1]

In 1992, UNDP initiated a GEF programme for the rural diffusion of solar photovoltaic (PV) technology in Zimbabwe. The aim was to reduce future carbon emissions by pre-empting fossil fuel based development – thereby creating a 'global benefit'. Yet despite the project's promise to develop a sustainable local PV industry, independent research suggests that the project had trouble meeting its own targets, supplied mostly wealthy customers who could have bought PV systems anyway, and to some extent undermined the local PV industry with cheap Northern imports.

Background

Given the sunlight available in much of Africa, PV technology promises to relieve a chronic lack of energy in rural areas where grid-based electricity is prohibitively expensive. Yet while a small-scale PV industry has existed in Zimbabwe since the 1960s, it will never meet the needs of big energy consumers in industry, mining and commerce. In rural areas PV has been used mostly for lighting, radios and televisions: luxuries for most families, who cook using fuelwood which PV can not replace. Meanwhile PV systems have been expensive to buy up front, so the technology was accessible only to the upper echelons of rural society, or those with relatives working in cities. In the 1990s, companies from the North began to view the South as a potentially huge market for PV. Access to these markets through aid projects also presented them with valuable research and development opportunities.

---

1. The case study presented here is an edited version of Ian Bacon's article 'Photovoltaics in Africa and the GEF: The Right Path to Sustainable Development?', 1998, in Energy and Environment, vol. 9, no. 3. Ian visited Zimbabwe in 1996 as a masters student from Hull University.

The Project

One of the first Southern governments involved in the GEF and among the first to ratify the FCCC, Zimbabwe was rewarded with early GEF funding. This project was jointly funded by the GEF and the government of Zimbabwe,[2] and concentrated on providing stand-alone PV systems for rural homesteads. Listed in the project document were five key objectives for the $9 million project fund:

- A minimum of 9,000 domestic solar electric systems in rural areas over three years (1993–6), as well as small community institutional lighting systems ... financed through revolving fund mechanisms.
- To build and develop training, delivery, financial and institutional infrastructures for rural solar electrification.
- To upgrade local technology and manufacturing capacity while strengthening the local solar industry and commercial sector.
- To create lasting public awareness ... of solar electric technology.
- To employ three approaches of programme implementation: a) commercial/private sector, b) utility, and c) local community development.

The project was to be 'market driven', and optimistically projected as many as 25,000 installations by the end of the funding period in 1997, served by a mature and sustainable PV industry. The Implementing Agency (UNDP) facilitated procurement of materials and equipment, while a Project Management Unit (PMU) was responsible for the running and operational planning of the project. This included a publicity campaign and training for PV installers, end users and others, and technical assistance to the industry from an international consultant.

Initial Outcomes

The project began slowly. In February 1996, the number of complete installations was put at 3,500,[3] and one interviewee said 'this is the

2. The foreign funds ($7 million) were for the procurement of solar merchandise, administration, consultancy and transport costs. The domestic funds (Z $2 million) were for baseline costs such as office space, furniture and communications.
3. *Zimbabwe Solar*, the quarterly newsletter of SEIAZ in association with GEF, 1996, vol. 1, no. 1.

first year that we are really making headway in the project' (interview, 1996). Many factors contributed to this underachievement. There was a shift in operations from the UNDP headquarters in New York to the national level. During the first few years of the project, drought damaged the rural economy. Meanwhile Zimbabwe's Economic Structural Adjustment Programme, imposed by the IMF in 1991, was reducing the wealth of many potential customers. In this context, the Zimbabwe Environmental Research Organisation (1995) estimated that 80 per cent of the rural population could not afford even the smallest system at the most basic, concessionary credit rates. Finally, the GEF project was competing with private enterprise to sell PV systems to the same consumer group.

Under the project, components were imported free from government taxes and customs duties, which would otherwise make up 41 per cent of the cost.[4] Local importing companies made orders through the UNDP, which had the foreign currency needed to bring components into the country (Zimbabwe was subject to strict currency controls at this time). PV panels, particularly from American companies (for example, Solarex) dominated imports. However, even when cheaper, internationally approved system components, such as deep cycle batteries, were available from a local supplier, the Project Management Unit also imported these items from abroad.

This led to people from the main importing companies stating that the PMU imported, stocked and sold PV components at landed cost (that is, duty free) in direct competition with the local industry. According to the PMU, if domestic installation companies were unable to honour their orders, components were warehoused until they could be sold on. Either way, all PMU overheads were paid for by the project, whereas others had to pay duty, staff, taxes and administrative overheads, and unlike the PMU, local installers had to sell at a profit. So to quote one industry figure, 'they are actually a funded competitor' (interview, 1996).

From only ten companies in the PV business at the start of the project in 1992, by 1996 there were at least 50 – almost all in Harare[5] and most of them small-scale operations formed purely in response

4. PMU, 'The Zimbabwe GEF Project', 1992.
5. *Zimbabwe Solar*, the quarterly newsletter of SEIAZ in association with GEF, 1996, vol. 1, no. 1.

to the project. Amongst the installing companies interviewed, their GEF-related business ranged from 60 per cent to close on 100 per cent. Some of these companies were reasonably successful but it was suggested that once the project came to an end with its guaranteed installations, the number of PV related companies in Zimbabwe would fall drastically – and it was not clear who then would maintain the systems they had installed (interview, 1996).

Learning Lessons from a Pilot Project?

Zimbabwean manufacturers were involved 'cursorily' in the identification of this project, they were not involved in its design – leading to local antagonism (Climate Network Europe, 1995). The project document assumed that provision of credit would stimulate the PV market. Yet the majority of potential customers would never meet the financial conditions required. Lending to people with little or no collateral is always a risk, but GEF project implementers could have learned from many examples of innovative financing schemes that more effectively targeted the poor in other Southern countries.[6] Yet despite a remit to be experimental and to ensure widespread participation, the Zimbabwe pilot project was subject to many of the same biases and inefficiencies implicit in traditional development projects.[7]

The United States – which accounts for 22 per cent of global carbon dioxide emissions – could have the largest PV market in the world, given its sunshine regime. Yet their energy market is dominated by the use of fossil fuels, so Southern countries became test beds and dumping grounds for Northern technologies, even where other forms of assistance might have better suited local conditions.

Certainly, the promotion of PV in Africa suited governments and industries of the North, lulling them into thinking they were alleviating the problems of both environmental protection and rural development in the South. The project also suited a national government keen to relieve national political pressures over rural electrification and show the North their willingness to tackle environmental problems in exchange for newly conditional aid. But insofar as this GEF project was not designed efficiently or effectively to promote sustainable solar development in Zimbabwe, it was dismissed as 'window-dressing' by some local NGOs.[8]

6. Yaron et al., 1994.
7. See, for example, Hobart, 1993; Cassen et al., 1994.
8. Climate Network Africa, 1992 (quoted in Gupta, 1995).

Appendix IV
GEF Biodiversity Project Case Study: *India Ecodevelopment*

In 1998 the World Bank's *India Ecodevelopment* project, to protect biodiversity in seven Indian national parks, received $20 million of its total $68 million from the GEF. The innovative project aimed to use participatory rural development to ease local communities' dependence on resources from the protected areas. Nagarhole National Park in Karnataka, Southern India, sometimes called the 'best park in India' due to the concentration of rare mammals found there, is one site of the *Ecodevelopment* project. With fierce opposition to the project coming from local people and NGOs and little evidence of environmental effectiveness, this site is generally seen as the most problematic of the seven. However, the issues and problems arising here appear to have arisen to some extent at other sites too.[1]

Background

At Nagarhole (literally 'snake rivers'), wild woodland, teak plantations and wetlands are populated by many endangered species including elephant, giant squirrel, slender loris, sloth bear, panther and up to 60 tigers. Also living in the forest are thousands of indigenous people known as Adivasi (literally 'original dwellers') who have lived self-sufficiently for centuries in settlements of airy thatched houses built from bamboo,[2] earth, dung and straw. Originally they gardened between the trees, hunted small animals and gathered fruits and roots, herbs for medicine and ritual, honey and soap nut to use or trade for oil, cooking pots etc. On the whole

1. For example at Gir in Gujarat, villagers were asked to leave the forest, despite *Ecodevelopment* rules on involuntary resettlement, see below and 'Gir encroachers asked to vacate forest', *Times of India*, 18 November 1999.
2. The Jenu Kuruba use bamboo already broken by elephants – traditionally they do not cut wood for timber.

the Jenu Kuruba ('honey gatherers') and other local tribes seek to sustain their indigenous forest-based culture and livelihood. Over the years some have chosen, and many were forced, to leave the shrinking forest and enter the encroaching mainstream society, but the social and economic conditions out the bottom of the caste system did not always appeal.[3] The land around Nagarhole's 643 sq. km protected area is under intense pressure from a dense and largely impoverished population. In recent decades much of the productive land has been turned over to tobacco, coffee and other cash crops grown by the wealthy with lower-caste labour, while people and wildlife were displaced for a World Bank-assisted dam and reservoir in the Kabini River, and thousands of Tibetan refugees have been granted land by the government.

In charge of Nagarhole Forest meanwhile is the Indian Forest Department (FD). Originally set up by the British to manage woodlands for maximum timber extraction, Indian forest management was structurally largely unchanged after independence. Since responsibility for nature reserves was added to the FD's brief, park areas have been policed by an armed and khaki-clad protection force. When the Wildlife Protection Act of 1972 banned all human habitation and productive activity from nature reserves, land rights were supposed to be respected and evictees resettled, but in India, with its large and increasing population, there is next to no productive land available for resettlement – if forest dwellers could even prove 'ownership' of the land they were losing.

Even when it came to run progressive sounding projects for 'joint forest management' with World Bank assistance, the FD did not recognise the shared status of a 'commons' managed through traditional common property regimes. Few Adivasi have land tenure documents – not least since they do not believe anybody can 'own' the life-giving forest. As a result, after Nagarhole was designated a national park in 1974, thousands of Adivasi were evicted, many violently. Seen as hardly human by some high-caste and landowning park managers, many of the indigenous people were rehoused in matchbox huts by the road and used as cheap labour by the FD and

3. Wherever India's Adivasi have entered the mainstream of Hindu society, historically they became *dalit*, 'untouchable'. With a right-wing government in power, Dalits as a group are still subject to widespread abuse by more powerful 'upper' castes.

nearby plantation owners, suffering the poverty, alcoholism and domestic violence that so often accompanies dispossession.

Despite these evictions, since the designation of Nagarhole National Park in 1974, there have been numerous encroachments by higher-caste settlers from outside the area and large-scale planters of coffee and tobacco.[4] Smugglers come from town with trucks to cut wood and shoot wildlife wherever they can bribe officials to let them pass unhindered, sometimes shooting their way to freedom and a large pay-off. Some Adivasi turn to helping these poachers for money to live, but most do not, treating wild animals with earned respect as fellow forest dwellers. However, being politically weak, Adivasi provide convenient scapegoats for damage caused to the forest by major smugglers, mismanagement and fires.[5] The most common forms of 'poacher' prosecuted at Nagarhole Forest are therefore from the community of 6,000-odd Adivasi still occasionally hunting and gathering inside park boundaries, along with local landless villagers from around the park who are still dependent on the forest for fuel and fodder.

These so-called poachers resent the forests' destruction as much as any professional environmentalist, to the extent that a local farmer called the Adivasi the 'real forest guards', as opposed to the 'fake forest guards' of the FD (interview, 2000). Yet for many local FD officials and wildlife conservationists[6] the Adivasi are the problem: too poorly educated to take part in 'scientific' work, they are 'all drunkards' who need 'rehabilitation' into the mainstream culture for their own good (interviews, FD and NGO, 1997).[7] With similar prejudices common across the country, Adivasi are organising to contest the governments' 'ownership' of India's forests, calling for culturally appropriate development and conservation initiatives respecting their human rights. With political attention focused on the Bank after mass protests against its role in the Narmada dams

4. Curing tobacco demands large amounts of wood to burn.
5. Some FD officials are said to set fires in their colleagues' areas of responsibility in order to damage their chances of promotion – they then blame the Adivasi, as well as sometimes local NGOs and journalists who support the Adivasi cause (interviews, 1998 and 1999).
6. Who, like me as a visiting researcher, motor around in jeeps.
7. In return the Jenu Kuruba call Ullas Karanth of the Wildlife Conservation Society 'tiger killer', after his scheme to monitor tigers with radio collars subjected the animals to damage from amateur sedation that disadvantaged them in fights. In addition the collars caught on branches, strangling some.

project in the early 1990s,[8] it has become harder to propose forced displacement for any project it funds. Yet still many environment professionals in India deem it necessary to separate poor people from nature in order to save it for posterity.

The Project

Ecodevelopment is a 'simple philosophy' (interview, NGO, 1998) that emerged in India during the early 1980s. Some conservation managers had found that providing the rural poor with alternative sources of fuel and income kept them from using resources from protected areas (Dang, 1991). This author was not alone in thinking that 'ecodevelopment needs massive amounts of capital to be meaningful', and when the Indian government proposed the concept for GEF funding, it soon became apparent that this was exactly the sort of initiative it needed to support. While Bank bio-diversity people were initially wary of getting mixed up with rural development and development people with biodiversity, they soon realised the innovative project's potential to improve the Bank's image in India after the Narmada debacle – as long as there was public participation and any resettlement would be strictly 'voluntary' (interviews, NGOs, 1998).

The World Bank–GEF project design was completed in 1996 by the Indian Institute of Public Administration (IIPA)[9] after two years of preparation and consultation with Indian NGOs including industry bodies,[10] resettlement professionals MYRADA,[11] WWF-

---

8. The World Bank eventually pulled out of the series of dams on the Narmada River in the face of opposition locally and globally to its forced displacement of many thousands of Adivasi without resettlement packages being in place and based on flawed assessments of the likely electricity and irrigation benefits of the dam. The GoI is continuing the project with other funds meanwhile, since (mainly urban) demand for the promised electricity and water remains stronger politically than the hundreds of thousands of mainly low-caste 'oustees' (Caufield, 1996).

9. An independent, largely academic institute, IIPA was set up in 1956 to provide training and expertise to the Indian civil service.

10. Society for the Promotion of Wasteland Development and Bharatiya Agro-Industries Foundation.

11. Created in 1968, MYRADA, the Mysore Resettlement and Development Association, initially worked for the government settling Tibetan refugees, and more recently ran micro-credit schemes in Karnataka. They aim to build appropriate popular institutions through participatory micro-planning, and 'exposing' the FD to joint forest management, etc.

India,[12] FD officials and the World Bank. *India Ecodevelopment* was to run from 1997 to 2002 in seven national parks, mostly tiger reserves.[13] The 'human beneficiaries' were to be the 'tribal peoples and forest fringe villagers, [who] belong to the poorest sections of society'. Five main headings for *Ecodevelopment* finance appear in the World Bank's 1996 staff appraisal report:

- Improved protected area planning and management: $13,911,700 for guards, watch towers, elephant ditches, solar-powered electric fences, metalled roads, jeeps and weapons for use against armed poachers; also incorporating protected area management into regional planning and regulation.
- Village ecodevelopment 'to reduce the negative impacts of local people on protected areas, reduce the negative impacts of protected areas on local people and increase collaboration of local people in conservation efforts': $33,835,500 for benefits identified by local people through 'participatory rural appraisal'; largely domestic animals, wells, village halls, bio-gas plants for cooking etc.
- Environmental education, visitor management, impact monitoring, research systems: $3,588,500 for expertise, computer systems, visitor centres and upgrading official guest houses inside parks.
- Overall project management: $5,276,800 to back up the operational finances of the FD providing project workshops for officials etc.

12. WWF was set up by, among others, princes worried about the dwindling numbers of their hunting trophies. Represented on the Trilateral Commission, WWF is a 'conservation partner' for governments around the world. The branch in Bangalore (the nearest major city to Nagarhole) is said to be made up of retired civil servants and military men, and the UK branch is rumoured to have distanced itself from WWF-India, partly over their role in the *Ecodevelopment project*.
13. Besides Nagarhole, the *India Ecodevelopment* sites are Periyar in Kerala, Buxa in West Bengal, Palamau in Bihar, Pench in Madhya Pradesh, Ranthambore in Rajasthan and Gir in Gujarat – the last remaining stronghold of the Asiatic lion. Simlipal, another tiger reserve, was included in the original plan, but cut out when local forestry department officials sought to pre-empt the strict resettlement guidelines involved in *Ecodevelopment* by trucking out people living inside the park before the project began.

- Preparation of future biodiversity projects including information, ex-situ conservation: $2,332,600 for studies of project impacts, and options for future resettlement.
  The remaining funds – $6,939,800 – went on the reimbursement of pre-project finance and contingency costs.

An unprecedented component of the project was no. 2 above: that about 60 per cent of the money remained unallocated, for priorities to be identified through 'micro-planning' during the project period. This included 'confidence building measures' for villagers living around the park, many of whom, like the Adivasi, are very distrustful of the Forest Department.

Early Impacts

I was shown around Nagarhole in 1998 and 1999 by FD officials in jeeps funded from the *Ecodevelopment* budget on roads soon to be resurfaced, and told of night viewers, motor boats and office refurbishments – 'all mirrors and everything' (interview, FD, 1999). A guest house inside the 192 sq. km 'core zone' of the park (off bounds for locals but served by 'tourist trails') was to be expanded and refurbished, and a science-based '3-D educational centre' developed in the 'tourist zone'. Elephant-proof trenches with solar-powered electric fencing had been constructed along park boundaries (officially, but not always, on request)[14] to keep big mammals inside the park – and people out.

Representatives of the FD had been to participatory rural appraisal workshops and were proud of their new role in 'uplifting' local people (interview, FD, 1998). *Ecodevelopment* committees were set up in 30-odd villages around the park and 'micro-planning' was underway to identify local uses for the project funds. To participate, villagers promise not to take wood and other resources from the forest, and I was introduced to people apparently delighted with the pump wells, bio-gas plants, goats, sewing machines and community centres they had received in return.

Using non-World Bank funds to avoid controversy, the FD was simultaneously building thousands of airless concrete houses[15] to

14. Residents of one Adivasi settlement alleged that a bulldozer ploughing through their paddy fields stopped only when they lay down in its way.
15. These houses were described to me as 'eco-friendly – no forest products used!' (interview, FD, 1999).

resettle forest dwellers on formerly reserved forest land outside the park. Stripped of trees, the soil was arid and rocky, the few people in residence looked miserable.[16] Meanwhile 'participation' in the project was not available for people still living in the park. When I revisited the area with people from local NGOs, I found that around 6,000 forest-dwellers – many already evicted from deeper forest – had not been consulted about the *Ecodevelopment* project, nor even about the type of house and livelihood to which they would be 'voluntarily' resettled.[17]

Local Verdicts

Most Adivasi therefore reject the project, saying the forest is not for sale, and that it should not be a playground of the rich and disrespectful. JK Kenchaiah, a human rights activist, said 'It's not fair if they make decisions outside of here that we have to give away the forests … Because you are asking us to leave the forest, and only then offering us help, we don't want any of your help.'[18] Speaking about the FD, Somayamma said 'If they get the money, it's like throwing rocks on our heads', because the FD want poor people out of the forest so that they 'cannot see what is happening there … If we had been doing this damage since the time of our forefathers, how would the forest still exist?' Subramani observed that if the World Bank and FD want trees and animals, they should let them grow in Delhi and Washington instead of stealing them from people who know how to live without destroying them.

Nagarhole-based organisations like the Budakattujanara Hakusthapana Samithi, through which the Jenu Kuruba spokespeople present their case to the outside world in their own terms,[19] were not consulted when the *Ecodevelopment* project was proposed. Two

16. Some of those who moved to the FD houses from the park were FD staff, many of them recent settlers in the area. A group of 50 Adivasi families were moved to the houses in 1999, but lacking employment or the skills, irrigation and tools for farming, most soon crept home (interview, NGO, 1999).
17. In solidarity, Kuruba settlements outside the park refused to participate with village *Ecodevelopment* committees.
18. Quoted in *Suits and Savages* (Howitt and Young, 2000).
19. Internally, the Jenu Kuruba of Nagarhole still govern themselves with the help of an elder or *yajamana*, who leads rituals and democratic group discussions.

World Bank consultations in Bangalore (most of a day away by bus), reportedly took no note of Adivasi concerns.[20] Several local NGOs supporting the Adivasi cause received an apology after the World Bank falsely claimed to have consulted them on the project.

In villages outside the park, *Ecodevelopment* committees (with quotas for women, landless, indigenous people, and so on) function in parallel to existing democratic institutions. Out of earshot of the men and officials, landless *Dalit* women said their village committee was dominated by powerful people, and wondered what they would do without access to the forest when project money ran out in a few years. Meanwhile, FD officials retain the power to 'supercede' an *Ecodevelopment* committee if they do not like its decisions. Local farmers report that officials will abandon project activities altogether in any village where the committee shows too much independence – if villagers choose, for example, to fund irrigation schemes (which they certainly need and hence would seek to control) rather than the cooking stoves or saplings for which FD officials' business contacts could overcharge the project (interview, farmer, 2000).[21]

Vocal wildlife activists meanwhile bemoan the use of 'trendy' community conservation rhetoric to disguise rural development aid of a kind – giving trees and animals to people without land – that has so far failed the worst off while doing nothing for the conservation of wild animals. Certainly very little scientific research into the inter-actions between local people and Nagarhole's ecologies had been conducted before the project got underway.

Despite a mutual antipathy, both local 'wildlifers' and 'social' NGOs supporting Adivasi rights agree that a sudden influx of large-scale funds – and the venal interests they can attract – is likely to increase destructive pressures on both society and ecology in places that remain wildlife rich largely *because* most locals have not been part of the money economy. Instead of starting from their culture and experience of using local nature sustainably, by promoting 'expert' management and resettlement the project tries to shift forest dwellers into a market-based mode of life to which they are ill-suited,

20. The story I heard several times was that there was no response to Adivasi points and questions, and when after half an hour the meeting ended, the World Bank task manager issued a pre-prepared press release about how well the meeting had gone.
21. Others claimed that new village halls were built around shrines to Ram: favoured god of the governing right-wing BJP (interview, NGO, 1999).

the project wastes the potential contributions of their unsurpassed local knowledge to scientific conservation. And while stoking local hostility to the unpopular FD, the project buys guns for its front-line guards, only adding to militarisation of highly contested park areas (interviews, NGOs, 1998–9). The situation is not unique to India – in 1999 indigenous people from South America told of similar situations with GEF projects in their own country (interview, NGO).

Faced with this barrage of criticism, the World Bank has argued that if both social development and wildlife NGOs object to India Ecodevelopment, the project must be 'about right'. The project's designer, who 'gave this line' to harassed Bank staff, stressed that while limited and imperfect, the project is at least trying hard to be participatory (interview, NGO, 1998). It is 'a self-correcting rocket' and 'a start, better made now than later', necessary to change 'hard-core bureaucracy'. He also suggested that for the next phase, the most critical NGOs should be invited into the project process. Critics thus brought 'inside' can be used both to improve projects and to defuse opposition (Young, 1999) but, in as divided a region as Nagarhole, will this be enough to save the tiger, or is a new approach merited?

Local Alternatives

In India, the world's self-professed 'largest democracy', some suggest conservation should be starting from the other end: not with the FD, experts and consultants – however unusual it may be that *Ecodevelopment* planning involved almost no foreign expertise – but with the people who have lived with nature sustainably up to now and need help to continue doing so in the face of social and commercial pressures. Not only have the Adivasi of Nagarhole been poorly served by their local government,[22] but neither the Bank nor the FD recognised their proposed 'Peoples' Plan' for managing the forest with practical help from the locals – rather than financial help from the World Bank.

Setting out Nagarhole's history and prospects from the Adivasi point of view, the Peoples' Plan advocates rural development in the native culture combined with conservation focused less on money than on realising local socio-ecological sustainability. Besides basic

22. In 1999 one *panchayat* was headed by a liquor dealer, who had a clear interest in Adivasi remaining as disempowered wage labourers – rather than a landed, self-sustaining community.

healthcare and education for all the community, the Plan proposes removing roads and concrete buildings from the park area. The Adivasi propose to host any visitors (scientific or otherwise) in traditional settlements and guide them on foot through the woods to see the wildlife undisturbed by vehicles and flash photography. Thus enabled to educate outsiders, locals would benefit and learn from them in return, and could with official support form a filter or 'social fence' around the deepest forest. With help from experienced elders of both cultures, individuals would then be able to choose a traditional forest-based life or to face outwards towards the towns and markets. However, with additional demands for no more aid projects (hence no large-scale taxable revenue) – the Peoples' Plan will probably always lack official support.[23]

Instead, from the mid 1990s the local FD collaborated with the developers of a high-class eco-tourist resort which promised international standards at $200 a night. Part of the Taj hotel chain (owned by Tata, one of India's largest corporations), the resort was to be based around some former FD buildings inside the park. All its laundry was to be driven 30 miles into town every day (to avoid polluting rivers in the park) and the hotel would employ Adivasi as guides, chambermaids etc. As noted by one local, the *Ecodevelopment* project 'only makes sense' in relation to the planned resort – providing its prospective guests with good roads and visitors' centres in return for their bringing money into the area. Unfortunately for the Taj and the FD however, the same law used to drive Adivasi from the park was invoked by locals – in alliance with people from the law department at Bangalore University – to have the building work stopped in the courts. The *Ecodevelopment* project however, supported by the national government in Delhi as well as the faraway GEF/World Bank, proved much harder to stop.

Protests Against the Project

Building hostility to the World Bank–GEF project led in 1998 to a visit by three Adivasi activists to the GEF Assembly in New Delhi. Sunita Narain of the Centre for Science and Environment told the World Bank at the GEF–NGO consultation that with *Ecodevelopment*

---

23. Allegedly one forest officer who supported the Plan was moved to a dead-end post elsewhere.

'you are creating a new process of alienation and you've only made the words more sophisticated, the actions don't meet the words'.

From GEF's point of view, the passionate debate in Delhi 'ventilated the issue' but made no impact on the project's backers (see Howitt and Young, 2000). Instead objectors were told by one member of World Bank staff that it was 'frankly ridiculous to say that the project is not working' at that early stage, and by another that they were only protesting because they weren't getting any of the money. Yet when JK Subramani of Nagarhole filed a request for inspection of the *Ecodevelopment* project at Nagarhole with the World Bank's Independent Inspection Panel, the visiting inspection team 'found merit' in the protesters' complaints. GEF guidelines on participation had been breached, indigenous people had no choice about whether to remain in the park, and no separate indigenous peoples' development plan was prepared (as required by World Bank Operational Directive 4.30).[24]

Nevertheless the chairman of the Inspection Panel also noted that 'our reports are necessarily controversial; no country wants to be investigated' (interview, 1999). Despite a six-month deadline for Bank management to respond to the Panel's findings passing without major changes made, the World Bank's governing board did not approve a full inspection, and the project continued apace amidst acrimony and agitations.

In September 1999 the leaders of local NGOs supportive of the Adivasi cause were jailed – ostensibly for their opposition to the project – then bailed after popular protests and hunger strikes. In early 2002 up to ten court cases are pending against them. Adivasi support groups have filed another complaint to the Inspection Panel – which is sympathetic to their plight but helpless in the face of World Bank procedures – and lacking the active support of a Washington DC-based NGO, the case has not yet got anywhere.

Meanwhile, the project continues to generate local hostility. Most of the gobar gas plants built in surrounding villages have allegedly broken down. In response to earlier protests some people inside the park have now been offered *Ecodevelopment* committees and benefits, but the process is apparently as bankrupt as outside the park – with

24. Memorandum to the Executive Directors and Alternates, 21 October 1998, Report and Recommendation of the Inspection Panel, IPN Request RQ98/1.

people selling on the solar lanterns, etc., which they have been given, and still facing relocation at any time. Though the FD has built huts for the resettlement of 1,500 families on 10,000 acres of cleared forest land, lacking farming tools and skills most of the oustees return to *coolie* work in the plantations, staying in farm buildings or constructing new settlements near the paid work. As a result forest officials are now watering the plants provided for the relocation sites, instead of protecting the rare animals from smugglers, while the clearance of so much forest outside the park for unwanted agriculture has increased pressure on the park from both wildlife and local people who once collected wood and grazed domestic animals in the lost forest (interview, NGO, 2002). With locals ever more alienated from park management by the broken promises of *Ecodevelopment*, there are few people to help the FD rangers when, for example, forests burn in the dry season. While future options for *Ecodevelopment* funding in India may promise to learn the lessons of Nagarhole and wherever else similar problems have arisen, it is unlikely that the current economically-based model can work in a messy real world laden with a history of conflicting knowledge systems, values, cultures and patterns of resource use.

Appendix V
Making an Independent
Documentary on the GEF

During my research, I found that very few people outside the GEF's constituent and target organisations even knew what it was supposed to be doing with their tax money – let alone the challenges it faces in practice. In this context I joined with Dylan Howitt, a film-maker, to produce a documentary about the GEF. Our aim was to make important but complex issues more accessible by reflecting the human elements of situations usually presented in purely procedural or economic terms. In the process we were to test the boundaries of the GEF's much lauded 'transparency'.

FILMING IN INDIA

We covered the 1998 Participants' Assembly in Delhi, and conducted numerous interviews with NGOs and officials in Washington DC. Time constraints meant that we visited only one GEF-assisted project – the World Bank's *Ecodevelopment* investments at Nagarhole forest in Karnataka, South India. Representatives from Nagarhole made their case against the project in the GEF–NGO consultation prior to the Participants' Assembly, and invited us to their forest to see at first hand a project which seemed (from a distance) to encapsulate much of what is both good and bad about the GEF's work (see Appendix IV and Young, Makoni and Boehmer-Christiansen, 2001). With persistence, I received permission to film at Nagarhole from the director of Project Tiger, which oversaw *Ecodevelopment* for the Indian government, and became the guest of the local forest department for a tour of Nagarhole. When we showed signs of staying in the area to meet locals, our hosts were suddenly keen to impress upon us the tourist value of nearby Mysore. But we stayed, and local activists were even more cooperative, accommodating us in their offices and taking us to impoverished Adivasi settlements in the park.

In Delhi our welcome from the GEF Secretariat was not so warm. El-Ashry (and his head of public relations) had earlier promised full transparency and cooperation with every aspect of our work, and El-Ashry's assistant had indicated by e-mail that I could film everything except the prime minister's speech to the meetings in Delhi. Despite some nervous looks from participants, we were able to shoot unhindered in the GEF–NGO consultation during passionate exchanges on the *Ecodevelopment* project. Yet at the Council meeting, I was bundled out of the chamber for discreetly filming the proceedings – despite ostensibly having been given permission to do so. When I queried my eviction with the Secretariat, I was told that the Council members needed confidentiality and had agreed not to allow any filming in the chamber. When asked, however, three Council members independently denied that such a decision had ever been taken, indicated that they had no problem with being documented and suggested that this ban originated within the Secretariat. Soon after this incident I was mysteriously removed from a list of NGOs invited to a formal dinner, apparently because someone somewhere had expressed a preference for only 'proper' NGOs to come along.

FILMING IN WASHINGTON DC

When filming in the US thereafter I feared being refused further interviews if I raised contentious issues in front of the camera – while still wanting to maintain a degree of academic independence. Yet it seems that I should not have worried, since several interviewees declined to answer even the most anodyne questions anyway.

Not only that, but we found that the GEF Secretariat's CEO, Mohamed El-Ashry, disliked an article that I had written a year or two earlier on the GEF's relationship with NGOs (Young, 1999; as a result of the ensuing outcomes, I became reluctant to share further drafts with informants, for which I must apologise to those whose responses would have been more open). When I sought clearance from El-Ashry to film at a GEF reception in the vast lobby of the World Bank's main building, he said I needed to check with Bank security. They said there was no problem, but when we started filming, a member of the GEF Secretariat stopped us, claiming that we were filming against El-Ashry's instructions. When I tried to find out from El-Ashry what the true situation was, he waved me away like an annoying fly.

Soon afterwards he seems then to have put the word out to people he works with against cooperation with our film. Eventually nobody in the GEF Secretariat or the UNDP would speak to us (though none of them would come out and say why not), and at least one person lied shamelessly to escape a pre-arranged interview on camera. Only some of the more confident (mainly British) people in the World Bank would appear in the film, having apparently retorted to those who would lean on them that it is better to be upfront about the good things they are trying to do than to invite suspicion by hiding away.

Once the film was completed back in the UK, I sent copies to all those who appeared in it, and arranged various screenings. I received no reply from the World Bank or GEF Secretariat (in fact I have had no response to any e-mails sent to the World Bank or GEF since, – with the exception of the Bank's Independent Inspection Panel). For his part, the UK Council member – employed in Clare Short's Department for International Development – declined to participate in any screening or discussion. When I took the film to India to get it translated into the local language and shown to project-affected people,[1] Karnataka state forest officials set up road blocks as I toured settlements in and around Nagarhole Forest with a TV and VCR, and threatened to arrest me if I went to their compound. Their justification was that I was filming illegally inside the forest. Needless to say, I did not arrange a screening with the Forest Department – although my arrest on this issue might have contributed to the debate about the *Ecodevelopment* project and the Adivasi's situation.

Elsewhere the film has been welcomed by diverse audiences. Nagarhole Adivasi said it represented them fairly; they only wished for more details of their lives and plight. Universities around the world have put copies in their libraries for use in courses, and NGOs, consultants and others have bought copies for their own use. Screenings at conferences and festivals always seem to generate discussion, often including the question: 'why don't more people know about this fund?'

1. One of the Adivasi interviewees in the film said after the screening that 'the spirit in which I spoke to you is there. I never thought that my voice would be heard in all those places, at the state level, national, even the World Bank ... Now I feel that in my lifetime I have gone beyond this place, made some difference to the world.'

References

Books and Articles

Acselrad, Henri, *Sustainability, Territoriality and Social Sciences*, 1996, Institute of Urban and Regional Planning and Research, Federal University, Rio de Janeiro.

Agarwal, Anil, Sunita Narain and Anju Sharma, *Green Politics*, 1999, Global Environmental Negotiations 1, Centre for Science and Environment, New Delhi.

Aggarwal-Khan, Sheila, *Promoting Coherence*, 1997, UNEP and IUCN-NL, Amsterdam.

Alinsky, S.D., *Rules for Radicals: A Practical Primer For Realistic Radicals*, 1971, Vintage Books, New York.

Andersen, Stephen O., Madhava Sarma and Jimin Zhao, *The Montreal Protocol Multilateral Fund – Lessons for Co-operation and Sustainable Development*, 2001, mimeo, US Environmental Protection Agency, Washington DC.

Athanasiou, Tom, *Slow Reckoning: The Ecology of a Divided Planet*, 1997, Secker and Warburg, London.

Aylward, Bruce A., Jaime Echeverria, Liza Fendt and Edward B. Barbier, *The Economic Value of Species Information and its Role in Biodiversity Conservation: Costa Rica's National Biodiversity Institute*, 1993, IIED Discussion Paper Series DP 93–06, London Environmental Economics Centre.

Ayres, Robert U., 'Limits to the Growth Paradigm', 1996, in *Ecological Economics*, vol. 19, pp. 117–34.

—— and Udo E. Simonis (eds), *Industrial Metabolism: Restructuring for Sustainable Development*, 1994, United Nations University Press, Tokyo.

Bacon, Ian, 'Photovoltaics in Africa and the GEF: The Right Path to Sustainable Development?', 1998, in *Energy & Environment*, vol. 9, no. 3, pp. 257–78.

Banuri, T. and E. Spanger-Siegfried, *Strengthening Demand: A Framework for Financing Sustainable Development*, 2000, RING of Sustainable Development Institutions.

Barathan, Sharmila, 'CDM Executive Board Based on GEF Model', 1998, in *Joint Implementation Quarterly*, vol. 4, no. 3.

Beck, Ulrich, Anthony Giddens and Scott Lash, *Reflexive Modernisation: Politics, Tradition and Aesthetics in the Modern Social Order*, 1994, Polity Press and Blackwell, Cambridge.

Becker, David G., Jeff Frieden, Sayre P. Schatz and Richard Sklar, *Postimperialism: International Capitalism and Development in the Late Twentieth Century*, 1987, Lynne Rienner, Boulder.

Bello, Walden, *Dark Victory: The United States, Structural Adjustment and Global Poverty*, 1994, Pluto Press with Food First and the Transnational Institute, London/Amsterdam.

Bhaskar V. and A. Glyn (eds), *The North, the South and the Environment*, 1995, UN University Press, London.

Binswanger, Hans, *Money and Magic: A Critique of the Modern Economy in the Light of Goethe's Faust*, 1994, University of Chicago Press, Chicago.

Block, Fred L., *The Origins of International Economic Disorder: A Study of United States International Monetary Policy from World War II to the Present*, 1977, University of California Press, Berkeley.

Boehmer-Christiansen, Sonja, 'Uncertainty in the Service of Science: Between Science Policy and the Politics of Power', 1997, in Gunnar Fermann (ed.), *International Politics of Climate Change: Key Issues and Critical Actors*, Scandinavian University Press, Oslo.

——, 'Climate Change and the World Bank: Opportunity for Global Governance?', 1999, in *Energy and Environment*, vol. 10, no. 1, pp. 27–50.

—— and Zoe Young, 'Green Energy Facilitated? The Uncertain Function of the Global Environment Facility', 1998, in *Energy and Environment*, vol. 9, no. 1, pp. 35–59.

Bourdieu, Pierre and Jean-Claude Passeron, *Reproduction in Education, Society and Culture*, 1990, Sage, London.

Bowles, Ian A., 'The Global Environment Facility: New Progress on Development Bank Governance', 1996, in *Environment*, vol. 38, no. 3, pp. 38–40.

—— and Glenn T. Prickett, *Reframing the Green Window: An Analysis of the GEF Pilot Phase Approach to Biodiversity and Global Warming and Recommendations for the Operational Phase*, 1994, Conservation International and Natural Resources Defence Council, Washington DC.

Brentin, Tony, *The Greening of Machiavelli: The Evolution of International Environmental Politics*, 1994, Earthscan and RIIA EEP, London.

Brundtland, Gro Harlem, *Our Common Future*, 1987, World Commission on Environment and Development, Oxford Paperbacks, Oxford.

Bryant, Raymond L., 'Power, Knowledge and Ecology in the Third World: A Review', 1998, in *Progress in Physical Geography*, vol. 22, pp. 79–94.

Cahn, Jonathan, 'Challenging the New Imperial Authority: The World Bank and the Democratisation of Development', 1993, in *Harvard Human Rights Journal*, vol. 6, Spring, pp. 159–94.

Cahn, Robert, *An Environmental Agenda for the Future*, 1985, Island, Covelo, California.

Carey, Jim, 'The President's Favourite Terrorists', 2002, in *Red Pepper*, no. 93.

Cassen, Robert and associates, *Does Aid Work?*, 1994, Clarendon Press, Oxford.

Caufield, Catherine, *Masters of Ilusion: The World Bank and the Poverty of Nations*, 1996, Pan, London.

Centre for Science and Environment, 'GEF Comes to Town', 1998, in *Down to Earth* supplement on Global Environmental Governance, New Delhi.

Chambers, R., *Challenging the Professions: Frontiers for Rural Development*, 1993, Intermediate Technology Publications, London.

Chatterjee, Pratap and Mathias Finger, *The Earth Brokers: Power, Politics and World Development*, 1994, Routledge, London.

Chatwin, Mary-Ellen, *Strange Happenings: GEF and the Georgian Case*, 1996, mimeo, NACRES, Tbilisi, Georgia.

Chomsky, Noam, *Year 501: The Conquest Continues*, 1993, Verso, London.

——, *Keeping the Rabble in Line (interviews with David Barsamian)*, 1994, AK Press, Edinburgh.

Climate Network Europe, *Getting the Right Mix: Participation in GEF Climate Change Projects*, 1995, CNE, Brussels.

—— and IUCN, *An NGO Guide to the Global Environment Facility (Letters to Nani G. Oruga)*, 1996, CNE, Brussels.

Cockett, Richard, *Thinking the Unthinkable: Thinktanks and the Economic Counter-Revolution 1931–83*, 1994, Harper Collins, London.

Commission on Global Governance, *Our Global Neighbourhood: The Report of the Commission on Global Governance*, 1995, Oxford University Press, Oxford.

Commoner, Barry, *The Closing Circle: Nature, Man, and Technology*, 1971, Beekman, New York.

Conca, Ken, 'Environmental NGOs and the UN System', 1996, in T.G. Weiss and L. Gordenker (eds) *NGOs, the UN and Global Governance*, Lynne Rienner, Boulder.

Cox, Robert W. with Timothy J. Sinclair, *Approaches to World Order*, 1996, Cambridge Studies in World Order, Cambridge University Press, Cambridge.

Croll, Elizabeth and David Parkin, *Bush Base: Forest Farm – Culture, Environment and Development*, 1989, Routledge, London.

Crozier, Michel, Samuel P. Huntington and Joji Watanuki, *The Crisis of Democracy: Report on the Governability of Democracies to the Trilateral Commission*, 1975, New York University Press, New York.

Curtis, R., C. Schmidt, A. Steiner, A. Sarmac, C. Monico, L. Zahno and S. Overall, *Partners or Hired Hands: Procurement Reform for Effective Collaboration Between NGOs, and Multilateral Institutions – the Case of the GEF*, 1997, TNC and IUCN, Washington, DC.

Daly, H. and K.N. Townsend,, *Valuing the Earth – Economics, Ecology, Ethics*, 1993, MIT Press, Cambridge, MA.

Dang, Himraj, *Human Conflict in Conservation: Protected Areas – the Indian Experience*, 1991, Har-Anand Publications with Vikas Publishing House Pvt. Ltd. Sustainable Development Series, New Delhi.

Davies, Paul, *The New Physics*, 1992, Cambridge University Press, Cambridge.

de Senarclens, Frédéric, *Obtaining Funds from the Global Environment Facility: Recommendations to the European Bank for Reconstruction and Development*, 1996, unpublished masters thesis, University of Sussex, Brighton.

Devall, Bill, *Simple in Means, Rich in Ends: Practising Deep Ecology*, 1990, Greenprint, London.

Douglas, Mary, *How Institutions Think*, 1987, Routledge and Kegan Paul, London.

——, *Dominant Rationality and Risk Perception*, 1994, Political Economy Research Centre, Occasional Paper no. 4, Sheffield.

Dosi, Giovanni, Chris Freeman, Richard Nelson, Gerald Silverberg and Luc Soete, *Technical Change and Economic Theory*, 1988, Pinter, London.

Draffan, George, *The Corporate Consensus: A Guide to the Institutions of Global Power*, 2000, Blue Mountains Biodiversity Project, Fossil, OR.

Dudley, Eric, *The Critical Villager: Beyond Community Participation*, 1993, Routledge, London.

Dunbabin, J.P.D., *The Post-Imperial Age – the Great Powers and the Wider World*, 1994, Longman, London.

The Ecologist, 'Whose Common Future?', July/August 1992, vol. 22, no. 4.

Edwards, M. and David Hulme, *Making a Difference: NGOs and Development in a Changing World*, 1992, Earthscan, London.

—— (eds), *Non-Governmental Organisations – Performance and Accountability: Beyond the Magic Bullet*, 1995, Earthscan, London.

Escobar, Arturo, *Encountering Development*, 1995, Princeton University Press, Princeton.

——, 'Constructing Nature: Elements for a Post-Structuralist Political Ecology', 1996, in R. Peet and M. Watts (eds) *Liberation Ecologies: Environment, Development, Social Movements*, Routledge, London.

Esteva, G. and M. Suri Prakash, 'Grassroots Resistance to Sustainable Development', 1992, in *The Ecologist*, vol. 22, no. 2.

Fairman, David, 'Increments for the Earth: The GEF', 1996, in Marc A. Levy (ed.) *Institutions for Environmental Aid: Pitfalls and Promise*, MIT Press, Cambridge MA.

Finger, Mathias, 'Environmental NGOs in the UNCED Process', 1995, in P. Princer and M. Finger (eds), *Environmental NGOs in World Politics*, Routledge, London.

Flitner, Michael, 'Biodiversity – of Local Commons and Global Commodities', 1998, in M. Goldman, (ed.) *Privatising Nature – Political Struggles for the Global Commons*, Pluto Press, London.

Ford, Lucy H., *A Critical Analysis of the Discourse of Global Environmental Politics*, 1995, MA Dissertation, International Relations, University of Sussex, Brighton.

—— *Global Enclosures: A Critical Analysis of Environmental Governance, Trade and Social Movements*, 2000, DPhil thesis, University of Sussex, Brighton.

Foucault, Michel, *Power/Knowledge: Selected Interviews and Other Writings 1972–1977*, 1980, edited by Colin Gordon, Harvester, London.

Fox, Jonathan and David Brown, *The Struggle for Accountability – the World Bank, NGOs and Grassroots Movements*, 1998, MIT Press, Cambridge, MA.

French, Hilary F., *After the Earth Summit: The Future of Environmental Governance*, 1992, WorldWatch Paper 107, Washington DC.

——, *Partnership for the Planet: An Environmental Agenda for the United Nations*, 1995, WorldWatch Paper 126, Washington DC.

Gadgil, Madhav, Fikret Berkes and Carl Folke, 'Indigenous Knowledge for Biodiversity Conservation', 1993, *Ambio*, vol. 22, no. 2–3.

Gan, Lin, 'Global Environmental Policy and the World Bank', 1992, paper for 'Symposium on Current Developments in Environmental Sociology', The Netherlands.

——, 'The Making of the GEF', 1993, in *Global Environmental Change*.

George, Susan, *A Fate Worse than Debt*, 1988, Penguin, London.

—— and Fabrizio Sabelli, *Faith and Credit: The World Bank's Secular Empire*, 1994, Penguin, London.

Gibson, James Jerome, *An Ecological Approach to Human Perception*, 1979, Houghton Mifflin, Boston MA.

Gill, Stephen, *American Hegemony and the Trilateral Commission*, 1990, Cambridge University Press, Cambridge.

——, 'Gramsci, Modernity and Globalisation', 1997, paper presented to 'British International Studies Association Conference', Leeds, UK.

—— and David Law, *The Global Political Economy: Perspectives, Problems and Policies*, 1988, Harvester Wheatsheaf, Hemel Hempstead.

Globalization Challenge Initiative, 2001, World Vision, Bank Information Center, Bread for the World.

Goldman, Michael, *Privatising Nature – Political Struggles for the Global Commons*, 1998, Pluto Press, London.

——, *The birth of a discipline – Producing Authoritative Green Knowledge, World Bank-Style*, 2001(a), University of Illinois at Urbana-Champaign, US. Working draft chapter for a forthcoming book: *Imperial Nature: The New Politics and Science of the World Bank*.

——, 'Constructing An Environmental State: Eco-governmentality and other Transnational Practices of a "Green" World Bank', 2001(b), in *Social Problems* (special issue on globalization).

Gowan, Peter, *The Global Gamble: Washington's Faustian Bid for World Dominance*, 1999, Verso, London.

Greenpeace International, *The World Bank's Greenwash: Touting Environmentalism while Trashing the Planet*, 1992, Greenpeace, London.

Griffen, Jeff, *Biodiversity, International Waters and the GEF: An IUCN Guide to Developing Project Proposals for the Global Environment Facility*, 1997, IUCN, Gland.

Groombridge, Brian (ed.), *Global Biodiversity: Status of the Earth's Living Resources*, 1992, Chapman and Hall, Norwell MA.

Grove, Richard H., *Green Imperialism: Colonial Expansion, Tropical Edens and the Origins of Environmentalism 1600–1860*, 1995, Cambridge University Press, Cambridge.

Gudynas, Eduardo, 'The Fallacy of Ecomessianism – Observations from Latin America', 1993, in Wolfgang Sachs (ed.), *Global Ecology*, Zed, London.

Guha, Ramachandra, 'The Authoritarian Biologist and the Arrogance of Anti-Humanism: Wildlife Conservation in the Third World', 1997, in *The Ecologist*, vol. 27, no. 1, pp. 14–20.

Gupta, Joyeeta, 'The Global Environment Facility in its North-South Context', 1995, in *Environmental Politics*, vol. 4, no. 1, pp. 19–44.

Haas, Ernst B., *When Knowledge is Power: Three Models of Change in International Organisations*, 1990, University of California Press, Berkeley.

Haas, P.M., 'Obtaining International Environmental Protection through Epistemic Consensus', 1990, in *Millennium Journal of International Studies*, vol. 19, no. 3, pp. 347–64.

——, Robert O. Keohane and Marc A. Levy (eds.), *Institutions for the Earth: Sources of Effective International Environment Protection*, 1993, Centre for International Affairs, Harvard, MIT Press, Cambridge MA.

Harker, Richard, Cheleen Mahar and Chris Wilkes (eds.), *An Introduction to the Work of Pierre Bourdieu: The Practice of Theory*, 1990, Macmillan, London.

Haufler, Virginia, 'Financial Regulation and Global Insurance', 1997, in Geoffrey R.D. Underhill (ed.), *The New World Order in International Finance*, Macmillan, London.

Hayter, Theresa, *Aid as Imperialism*, 1971, Penguin, London.

Henry, Reg, 'Adapting UN Agencies for Agenda 21: Programme Co-ordination and Organisational Reform', 1996, in *Environmental Politics*, vol. 5, no. 1, pp. 1–24.

Hertz, Rosanna and Jonathan B. Imber (eds), *Studying Elites Using Qualitative Methods*, 1995, Sage, London.

Hewson, Martin, 'Historical Sociology of Global Governance', 1996, in *Review of International Political Economy*, vol. 3, no. 1, pp. 186–93.

Hirsch, Fred, *Social Limits to Growth*, 1978, Routledge, London.

Hirst, Paul, *Globalisation in Question*, 1992, PERC Occasional Paper, University of Sheffield.

Hobart, Mark (ed.), *An Anthropological Critique of Development: The Growth of Ignorance*, 1993, Routledge, London.

Hodgson, Geoffrey M., *Economics and Institutions*, 1988, Polity Press, Cambridge.

Hoggett, Paul, *Partisans in an Uncertain World: The Psychoanalysis of Engagement*, 1992, Free Association Books, London.

Holling, C.S., L.H. Gunderson and G.D. Peterson, *Comparing Ecological and Social Systems: Draft*, 1995, mimeo, Dept of Zoology, University of Florida, Gainsville, US.

Horta, Korinna and Scott Hajost, *Breakdown of GEF Talks in Cartagena ...*, 1993, EDF note, Washington DC.

Howitt, Dylan and Zoe Young, *Suits and Savages – Why the World Bank Won't Save the World*, 2000, video produced by Conscious Cinema, London.

Hulme, David and Paul Mosley, *Finance Against Poverty, vol. 1*, 1996, Routledge, London.

Imber, Mark F., 'The United Nations' Role in Sustainable Development', 1994, in Caroline Thomas (ed.) *Rio, Unravelling the Consequences*, Frank Cass, London.

Indigenous People's Representatives, *Group Evaluation of the UNEP/GEF Indigenous People's Consultation Meeting*, Geneva, 29–31 May 1996.

International Institute for Environment and Development, *Whose Eden? An Overview of Community Approaches to Wildlife Management*, 1994, Report to the UK Overseas Development Agency, London.

International Institute for Sustainable Development, *Summary Report from the UNEP Expert Consultations on International Environmental Governance*, 2001.

Jackson, P.M., *The Political Economy of Bureaucracy*, 1981, Philip Allan, Oxford.

Jacobs, Michael, *Environment, Sustainable Development and the Politics of the Future*, 1991, Pluto Press, London.

Jordan, Andrew, 'Financing the UNCED Agenda: The Controversy over Additionality', 1994(a), in *Environment*, vol. 36, no. 4.

——, 'Institutions for Global Environmental Change: The Global Environment Facility', 1994(b), in *Global Environmental Change*, vol. 4, no. 3, pp. 265–7.

Juma, Calestous, *The Gene Hunters: Biotechnology and the Scramble for Seeds*, 1989, Zed Books, London.

Kahneman, D., P. Slovic and A. Tversky (eds), *Judgment Under Uncertainty: Heuristics and Biases*, 1982, Cambridge University Press, Cambridge.

Karanth, Ullas, *Comments on the Indicative Plan for Biodiversity Conservation in Indian Nature Reserves by Indian Institute of Public Administration for GEF*, 1994, Wildlife Conservation Society, New York.

Kardam, N., 'Development Approaches and the Role of Policy Advocacy: The Case of the World Bank', 1993, *World Development*, vol. 21, no. 11, pp. 1773–86.

Kaur, Inge, Isabelle Grunberg and Marc A. Stern (eds), *Global Public Goods: International Co-operation in the 21st Century*, 1999, Oxford University Press, Oxford.

Keohane, Robert O., 'International Institutions: Can Interdependence Work?', 1998, in *Foreign Policy*, no. 110.

Kingdon, J.W., *Agendas, Alternatives and Public Policies*, 1984, Little Brown, Boston.

Kjorven, O., 'The Challenge of Organisational Adjustment: How is the World Bank Incorporating the Global Environmental Concerns?', 1991, in *International Challenges*, vol. 11, no. 3, pp. 31–43.

Kolk, Ans, *The World Bank and its Role in International Environmental Politics*, 1996, University of Amsterdam International Studies, Working Paper no. 41.

Kolko, Joyce and Gabriel Kolko, *The Limits of Power: The World and United States Foreign Policy, 1945–1954*, 1972, Harper and Row, New York.

Kuhn, T.S., *The Structure of Scientific Revolutions*, 1970, University of Chicago Press, Chicago.

Lafferty, William M., *The Politics of Sustainable Development*, 1996, mimeo, Norwegian Academy of Science and Letters, Oslo.

Lake, Rob, *New and Additional? Financial Resources for Biodiversity Conservation in Developing Countries 1987–1994*, 1997, BirdLife International, UK.

Langdon, Steven, *Transnational Corporations and the State in Africa*, 1979, Harvester Wheatsheaf, Brighton.

Levy, David, 'Environmental Management as Political Sustainability', 1997, *Organisation and Environment*, vol. 10, no. 2, pp. 126–47.

Lewis, Martin, *Green Delusions: An Environmentalist Critique of Radical Environmentalism*, 1992, Duke University Press, Durham NC.

Lindqvist, Sven, *'Exterminate all the Brutes' – One Man's Journey into the Heart of Darkness and the Origins of European Genocide*, 1996, the New Press, New York.

Lipton, M., and R. Longhurst, *New Seeds and Poor People*, 1989, Unwin Hyman, London.

Litfin, Karen, *Ozone Discourses: Science and Politics in Global Environmental Co-operation*, 1994, Columbia University Press, New York.

Lohmann, Larry, *Whose Common Future? Reclaiming the Commons*, 1993, Earthscan, London.

——, *Forest Cleansing: Racial Oppression in Scientific Nature Conservation*, 1999, The Cornerhouse Briefing no. 13, Sturminster Newton.

Lumsdaine, D., *Moral Vision in International Politics*, 1993, Princeton University Press, Princeton.

Lustig, Sandra and Ursula Brunner, 'Environmental Organisations in a Changing Environment – Major US Environmental Organisations in the 1990s', 1996, *Environmental Politics*, vol. 5, no. 1, pp. 130–9.

Machiavelli, Nicolo, *The Prince and Other Political Writings*, 1981, Everyman's Library, London.

McAfee, Kathleen, *Biodiversity and the Contradictions of Green Developmentalism*, 1999, PhD Dissertation, University of California, Berkeley.

McConnell, Fiona, *The Biodiversity Convention – A Negotiating History*, 1996, Kluwer Law International, London.

McKinley, Michael, 'Triage: A Survey of the "New Inequality" as Combat Zone', 2001, paper presented to the International Studies Association Conference, Chicago.

McManus, Phil, 'Contested Terrains: Politics, Stories and Discourses of Sustainability', 1996, *Environmental Politics*, vol. 5, no. 1, pp. 48–74.

Macmillan, John and Andrew Linklater, *Boundaries in Question: New Directions in International Relations*, 1995, Pinter, London.

McNeely, Jeffrey A., 'The Global Environment Facility: Cornucopia or Kiss of Death for Biodiversity?', 1991, *Canadian Biodiversity of Nature*, vol. 1, no. 2, pp. 4–7.

——, 'Economic Incentives for Conserving Biodiversity: Lessons for Africa', 1993, *Ambio*, vol. 22, no. 2–3, pp. 144–50.

——, Conserving Biodiversity: The Key Political, Economic and Social Measures, 1996, in F. di Castri and T. Younes (eds), *Biodiversity, Science and Development: Towards a New Partnership*, CAB International, Wallington.

Majone, Giandomenico, *Evidence, Argument and Persuasion in the Policy Process*, 1989, Yale University Press, New Haven.

Marchak, M. Patricia, *The Integrated Circus: The New Right and the Restructuring of Global Markets*, 1991, McGill-Queens University Press, Montreal and Buffalo.

Mathur, Ajay, *Priorities of the Developing Countries on the Environment and Development*, 1992, mimeo, OPEC Seminar on the Environment, Vienna, pp. 78–102.

Matthews, Robert, 'On Reforming the Global Environment Facility', 1995, in Eric Fawcett and Hanna Newcombe (eds), *United Nations Reform: Looking Ahead after 50 Years*, Science for Peace, Toronto.

Mayne, John and Eduardo Zapico-Goni (eds), *Monitoring Performance in the Public Sector: Future Directions from International Experience*, 1997, Transaction, New Brunswick.

Mehan, H. and H. Wood, *The Reality of Ethnomethodology*, 1975, Wiley Interscience, New York.

Mehta, Lyla, 'From Darkness to Light? Critical Reflections on the World Development Report 1998–99', 2001, in *Journal of Development Studies*.

Middleton, N. et al., *Tears of a Crocodile: From Rio to Reality*, 1993, Pluto Press, London.

Midnight Notes Collective, *The New Enclosures*, 1990, Jamaica Plain, MA.

Milton, Kay (ed.), *Environmentalism: The View from Anthropology*, 1993, Routledge, London.

Mittermeier, R.A. and I.A. Bowles, 'The GEF and Biodiversity Conservation: Lessons to Date and Suggestions for Further Action', 1993, in *Biodiversity and Conservation* 2, pp. 637–55.

Moiseev, Alex, 'The Global Environment Facility – Aspects of Purpose, Formation and Change', 1996, Unpublished Masters Thesis, Faculty of Graduate Studies, University of Guelph.

Morgan, R. et al., *New Diplomacy in the Post-Cold War World*, 1993, St Martin's Press, New York.

Mosley, Paul, *Overseas Aid: Its Defence and Reform*, 1987, Methuen, London.

de la Mothe, John and Gilles Paquet, *Evolutionary Economics and the New International Political Economy*, 1996, Pinter, London.

Munasinghe, Mohan and Jeffrey McNeely (eds), *Protected Area Economics and Policy: Linking Conservation and Sustainable Development*, 1994, World Bank for IUCN, Washington DC.

Myers, Norman, 'The Biodiversity Challenge: Expanded Hotspots Analysis', 1990, in *The Environmentalist*, 10, pp. 243–56.

Najam, Adil, 'An Environmental Negotiation Strategy for the South', 1995, in *International Environmental Affairs*, vol. 3, no. 3, pp. 249–87.

Nelson, R.R. and S.G. Winter, *An Evolutionary Theory of Economic Change*, 1982, Belknap Press, Cambridge, MA.

Neumann, Roderick, *Imposing Wilderness – Struggles over Livelihood and Nature Preservation in Africa*, 1998, University of California Press, Berkeley.

New Economics Foundation, *Dangerous Curves: Does the Environment Improve with Economic Growth?*, 1996, New Economics Foundation report for WWF International, London.

Ngugi wa Thiongo, *Petals of Blood*, 1977, Heinemann, London.

Oliver, Robert W., *Early Plans for a World Bank*, 1972, Princeton Studies in International Finance no. 29, New Jersey.

O'Riordan, Tim and Jill Jäger, *Politics of Climate Change: A European Perspective*, 1996, Routledge, London.

Ostrom, Elinor, *Governing the Commons*, 1991, Cambridge University Press, Cambridge.

Page, Martin, *The Company Savage – Life in the Corporate Jungle*, 1972, Cassell, London.

Palast, Greg, *The Best Democracy Money Can Buy*, 2002, Pluto Press, London.

Paterson, Matthew, 'Radicalizing Regimes? Ecology and the Critique of IR Theory', 1995, in John Macmillan and Andrew Linklater (eds), *Boundaries in Question: New Directions in International Relations*, Pinter, London.

Payer, Cheryl, *The World Bank: A Critical Analysis*, 1982, Monthly Review Press, New York.

Payne, Roger A. 'The Limits and Promise of Environmental Conflict Prevention: The Case of the GEF', 1998, in *Journal of Peace Research*, vol. 35, no. 3, pp. 363–80.

Pearce, David, *Blueprint 4: Capturing Global Environmental Value*, 1995, Earthscan, London.

—— and Scott Barrett, 'Incremental Cost and Biodiversity Conservation', 1993, mimeo, GEF participants' workshop on incremental costs, Washington DC.

—— and Dominic Moran, *The Economic Value of Biodiversity*, 1994, Earthscan with IUCN, London.

Peet, R. and M. Watts (eds), *Liberation Ecologies: Environment, Development and Social Movements*, 1996, Routledge, London.

Peoples' Plan for Preservation of Adivasi and Nagarhole Forests in Karnataka, 1998, mimeo, Nagarhole Hadi, India.

Perkin, Harold, *The Third Revolution: Professional Elites in the Modern World*, 1996, Routledge, London.

Pernetta, John C., 'An Overview of the Global Environment Facility in International Waters with Reference to Marine Capacity Building', 1998, in *Marine Policy*, vol. 22, no. 3, pp. 235–45.

Peters, Mike, 'The Bilderberg Group and the Project of European Unification', 2001, *Lobster*, issue 32, Hull.

van der Pijl, Kees, *The Making of an Atlantic Ruling Class*, 1984, Verso, London.

Pimbert, Michel M. and Jules N. Pretty, *Parks, People and Professionals: Putting 'Participation' into Protected Area Management*, 1995, mimeo, UNRISD Discussion Paper 57, with IIED and WWF.

Plater, Zygmunt J.B., 'Damming the Third World: MDBs, Environmental Diseconomies and International Reform Pressure on the Lending Process', 1983, in *Denver Journal of International Law and Policy* 121, 136.

Plumwood, Val, 'Has Democracy Failed Ecology?', 1995, in *Environmental Politics*, vol. 4, no. 4, pp. 134–63.

Pretty, Jules N. and Irene Gujit, 'Primary Environmental Care: An Alternative Paradigm for Development Assistance', 1992, in *Environment and Urbanisation*, vol. 4, no. 1. pp. 22–36.

Redclift, M., *Sustainable Development: Exploring the Contradictions*, 1987, Wheatsheaf, Brighton.

Reed, David (ed.), *The Global Environment Facility: Sharing Responsibility for the Biosphere, Vol. I*, 1991, WWF International Institutions Policy Program, Washington DC.

——, *The GEF: Sharing Responsibility for the Biosphere, Vol. II*, 1992, WWF International Institutions Policy Program, Washington DC.

RESOLVE, *Progress on Incremental Costs Issues Assessment: Incremental Cost determination for GEF-Funded Projects*, 1998, GEF/C.12/Inf.4. Washington DC.

Rich, Bruce, *Mortgaging the Earth: The World Bank, Environmental Impoverishment and the Crisis of Development*, 1994, Beacon, Boston MA. and Earthscan, London.

Richter, Judith, *Engineering of Consent – Uncovering Corporate PR Strategies*, 1998, The Cornerhouse Briefing no. 6, Sturminster Newton.

Rowbotham, Michael, *Goodbye America: Globalisation and the Debts of the Developing Nations*, 2000, Jon Carpenter, Charlbury, Oxfordshire.

Sachs, Wolfgang (ed.), *The Development Dictionary: A Guide to Knowledge as Power*, 1993, Zed, London.

——, *Global Ecology*, 1993, Zed, London.

Sand, Peter H., 'Trusts for the Earth', 1994, Josephine Onoh Memorial Lecture, University of Hull Press, Hull.

——, 'Institution Building to Assist Compliance with International Environmental Law', 1996(a), in *Heidelberg Journal of International Law*, vol. 56, no. 3.

——, 'The Potential Impact of the Global Environment Facility of the World Bank, UNDP and UNEP', 1996(b), in R. Wolfrum (ed.), *Enforcing Environ-*

mental Standards: Economic Mechanisms as Viable Means?, Springer Verlag, Heidelberg.

Schmidheiny, Stephan, *Changing Course: A Global Business Perspective on Development and the Environment*, 1992, with the Business Council for Sustainable Development, MIT Press, Cambridge MA.

—— and Federico J.L Zorraquin with the World Business Council for Sustainable Development, *Financing Change: The Financial Community, Eco-efficiency and Sustainable Development*, 1996, MIT, Cambridge MA. and London.

Sheehan, James M., *Global Greens: Inside the International Environmental Establishment*, 1998, Capital Research Center, Washington DC.

Shiva, Vandana, *Monocultures of the Mind: Perspectives on Biodiversity and Biotechnology*, 1993, Zed and Third World Network, London, New Jersey and Penang.

——, 'The Enclosure of the Commons', 1997, in *Third World Resurgence*, no. 84, TWN Penang.

Sklair, Leslie, *The Sociology of the Global System*, 1991, Prentice Hall/Harvester Wheatsheaf, Hemel Hempstead.

Sklar, Holly (ed.), *Trilateralism: The Trilateral Commission and Elite Planning for World Management*, 1980, South End Press, Boston.

Steinberg, Paul F., 'Consensus by Design, Policy by Default: Implementing the Convention on Biological Diversity', 1998, in *Society and Natural Resources*, 11, pp. 375–85.

Stewart, F., *Technology and Underdevelopment*, 1978, Macmillan, London.

——, H. Thomas and T. de Wilde, *The Other Policy*, 1990, IT Publications, London.

Stirling, Andy, *Addressing Ignorance, Path Dependency and Discord through Diversification in Research Strategies*, 1995, mimeo, Science Policy Research Unit, Brighton.

Strange, Susan, *States and Markets. An Introduction to International Political Economy*, 1988, Pinter, London.

—— and S. Tooze, *The International Politics of Surplus Capacity: Competition for Market Shares in the World Recession*, 1981, Allen & Unwin, London.

Strathern, M., *The Gender of the Gift*, 1988, University of California Press, Berkeley.

Strong, Maurice, *Hunger, Poverty, Population and Environment*, 1999, The Hunger Project Millennium Lecture, Madras, India.

——, *Where on Earth are We Going?*, 2000, Texere, New York.

Teivainen, Teivo, *The International Monetary Fund: A Modern Priest – the Politics of Economism and the Containment of Changes in the Global Political Community*, 1994, paper presented at the XVIth World Congress of the International Political Science Association, Berlin.

Third World Network, *Earth Summit Briefings*, 1992, Third World Network, Penang.

Thomas, Caroline (ed.), *Rio – Unravelling the Consequences*, 1994, Frank Cass, London.

Tickell, O. and Nick Hildyard, 'Green Dollars, Green Menace', 1992, in *The Ecologist*, May/June, vol. 22, no. 3, pp. 82–3.

Tomaševski, Katarina, *Development Aid and Human Rights Revisited*, 1993, Pinter, London.

Toulmin, S., *Cosmopolis: The Hidden Agenda of Modernity*, 1990, Free Press, New York.

United Nations, Agenda 21, 1992(a), UNCED, UN, Geneva.

——, Rio Declaration, 1992(b), UN, Geneva.

Uphoff, Norman, 'Paraprojects as New Modes of International Development Assistance', 1990, in *World Development*, vol. 18, no. 10, pp. 1401–11.

Visnavathan, Shiv, 'Mrs. Brundtland's Disenchanted Cosmos', 1991, in *Alternatives*, vol. 16, no. 3, pp. 377–84.

Vogler, John, *Taking Institutions Seriously: How Regime Analysis Can be Relevant to Multilevel Environmental Governance*, 2002, given at the International Studies Association Convention, New Orleans.

—— and Mark F. Imber (eds), *The Environment in International Relations*, 1996, Routledge, London.

Wade, Robert, 'Japan, the World Bank, and the Art of Paradigm Maintenance: *The East Asian Miracle* in Political Perspective', 1996, in *New Left Review*, 217, pp. 3–36.

——, 'Greening the Bank: The Struggle over the Environment, 1970–1995', 1997, in Devesh Kapur, John P. Lewis and Richard Webb (eds), *The World Bank: Its First Half Century*, vol. 2, Perspectives, Brookings Institution Press, Washington DC.

Walker, R.B.J. 'On the Possibilities of World Order Discourse', 1995, *Alternatives*, vol. 19, no. 2, pp. 237–45.

Walton, John and David Seddon, *Free Markets and Food Riots: The Politics of Global Adjustment*, 1994, Blackwell, Oxford.

Webb, Anna L., *Establishing Linkages Between National and International Policy-Making for Sustainable Development: A Case Study of the United Nations Environment and Development UK Committee (UNED-UK)*, 1998, MSc. Dissertation, University of Hull.

Weiss, Thomas G. and Leon Gordenker, *NGOs, the UN and Global Governance: Emerging Global Issues*, 1996, Lynne Rienner, Boulder.

Wilks, Alex, *A Tower of Babel on the Internet? The World Bank's Development Gateway*, 2001, Bretton Woods Project, London.

Williams, David and Tom Young, 'Governance, the World Bank and Liberal Theory', 1994, in *Political Studies*, XLII, pp. 84–100.

Williams, Marc, 'Re-articulating the Third World Coalition: The Role of the Environmental Agenda', 1993, in *Third World Quarterly*, vol. 14, no. 1.

——, 'Institutions for Global Environmental Change', 1997, in *Global Environmental Change*, vol. 7, no. 3, pp. 295–8.

Wolf, Amanda with David Reed, *The Global Environment Facility: Sharing Responsibility for the Biosphere, Vol. III Incremental Costs Analysis in Addressing Global Environmental Problems*, 1994, WWF, Gland.

World Resources Institute, *Natural Endowments: Financing Resource Conservation for Development*, 1989, Report of the International Conservation Financing Project Commissioned by the UNDP, Washington DC.

——, *National Biodiversity Planning: Guidelines Based on Early Experiences Around the World*, 1995, WRI in cooperation with UNEP and IUCN, Washington DC.

Worldwide Fund for Nature – International, *The Southern Green Fund: Views from the South on the GEF*, 1993, WWF, Gland.

Worldwide Fund for Nature – UK, *Review of the WWF Network's Experiences with the Global Environment Facility (GEF)*, 1999, WWF, Godalming.

Yaron, Jacob, Marc Gurgand and Glen Pederson, *Outreach and Sustainability of Six Rural Finance Institutions in Sub-Saharan Africa*, 1994, World Bank, Washington DC.

Yearley, Stephen, 'Social Movements and Environmental Change', 1994, in Redclift, Michael and Ted Benton (eds), *Social Theory and the Global Environment*, Routledge, London.

Young, Oran, *International Cooperation: Building Regimes for Natural Resources and the Environment*, 1989, Cornell University Press, Ithaca.

Young, Zoe, 'Friendly Foes? NGOs and the Global Environment Facility', 1999, in Chris Rootes (ed.) *Environmental Movements: Local, National and Global*, special issue of *Environmental Politics*, Frank Cass, London.

——, George Makoni and Sonja Boehmer-Christiansen, 'Green Aid in India and Zimbabwe – Conserving Whose Community?', 2001, in *Geoforum*, 32, pp. 299–318.

Websites

<www.agp.org>, Peoples' Global Action network for humanity and against neo-liberalism.

<www.alertnet.org/thefacts/reliefresources/251995>, *British Minister Hitting the Wrong Targets*, Nick Cater, August 2001.

<www.autisme-economie.org> and, for English text, <mouv.eco.free.fr/movementtext.htm>, French economics students challenge neo-liberal assumptions.

<www.bilderberg.org/bildhist.htm#The>, Mike Peters, *The Bilderberg Group and the Project of European Unification*.

<www.biodiv.org>, The UN Convention on Biological Diversity.

<www.blagged.freeserve.co.uk/ta2000/atcsabriefing.htm_>, Information on the new UK terrorism laws and campaign for their repeal.

<www.brettonwoodsproject.org>, network of UK NGOs, monitors the World Bank and IMF.

<www.caat.org>, Campaign Against Arms Trade, monitors military expenditure etc.

<www.consciouscinema.co.uk>, Independent video production including the documentary on the GEF: *Suits and Savages*.

<www.counterpunch.org/giombetti.html> *Enviros in the Bunker – Has the Left Unilaterally Disarmed?*, Rick Giombetti, September 2001.

<www.defenselink.mil/news/Jun2000/n06022000_20006025.html>, *Joint Vision 2020 Emphasizes Full-spectrum Dominance*, Jim Garamone, American Forces Press Service, June 2000.

<www.gefweb.org> The Global Environment Facility homepage.

<www.gefweb.org/gefloss.html>

<www.gefweb.org/Operational_Policies/Eligibility_Criteria/Funding_Options/funding_options.html>, Criteria for GEF funding.

<www.gefweb.org/Operational_Policies/Eligibility_Criteria/Incremental_
Costs/incremental_costs.html>, Details of GEF incremental costs criteria.
<www.gefweb.org/Operational_Policies/Public_Involvement/public_
involvement.html>, Guidance for public involvement in GEF projects.
<www.gefweb.org/Outreach/outreach-PUblications/outreach-
publications.html>, List of GEF publications.
<www.gregpalast.com/detail.cfm?artid=78&row=1>, *The Globalizer Who
Came In From the Cold*, October 2001, the *Observer*, London.
<www.indymedia.org>, Globally distributed, open-access independent media
centre.
<www.permaculture.org.uk/whatis/whatisindex.htm>, Explanation of per-
maculture.
<www.schnews.org> Brighton-based weekly independent news sheet.
<www.thecornerhouse.org.uk>, Briefings on a variety of environmental and
political issues.
<www.transnational.org/features/chossu_worldbank.html>, Chossudovsky,
Michael, 1999.
<www.unctad.org/en/pub/poiteiiad3.en.htm>, Data on foreign direct
investment in the poorest Southern countries.
<www.unfccc.int>, The UN Framework Convention on Climate Change.
<www.wadsworth.com/humanity/ch18/>, *Humanity, an Introduction to
Cultural Anthropology*, James Peoples and Garrick Bailey, on Balinese water
management.
<www.wbcsd.org>, The World Business Council for Sustainable Develop-
ment.
<www.wild.org>, International Wilderness Leadership Foundation.
<www.worldbank.org>, The World Bank.

World Bank Documents

Funding for the Global Environment: The Global Environment Facility, 1990,
World Bank discussion paper, Washington DC.
Effective Implementation: Key to Development Impact. Report of the World
Bank's Portfolio Management Task Force (Wapenhams Report), 1992,
World Bank, Washington DC.
World Bank Submission to Independent Panel on GEF Evaluation, 22 November
1993.
*Statement of the World Bank in its Role as an Implementing Agency, Review of the
GEF Evaluation at the GEF Participants' Meeting*, Cartegena, 6 December
1993.
Guidelines for Procurement: Procurement under IBRD Loans and IDA Credits, 1995,
World Bank, Washington DC.
Knowledge and Information for Development, 1998, World Bank World Devel-
opment Report, Washington DC.
The World Bank and Civil Society, 2000, World Bank, Washington DC.
Internal World Bank memorandum, 1993.

GEF Documents

El-Ashry, Mohamed, *Opening remarks on Decision-Making in the Restructured GEF*, Beijing Participants' Meeting, 27 May 1993.
Statement by UNEP's representative to Beijing meeting of GEF participants, May 1993.
World Bank Submission to Independent Panel on GEF Evaluation, November 1993.
The GEF and the Evaluation: Learning from Experience and Looking Forward, GEF/PA.93/97.
El-Ashry, Mohamed, *Background Note for the GEF Participants Meeting*, Cartagena, Colombia, December 1993.
NGO statement to the GEF Participants Meeting, Cartagena, Colombia, December 1993.
DRAFT Instrument for the Establishment of the Restructured Global Environment Facility GEF/PA.93/6/Rev.1, 9 December 1993.
DRAFT Instrument for the Establishment of the Restructured Global Environment Facility, GEF/PA.93/6/Rev.4, 4 March 1994.
Independent Evaluation of the Pilot Phase (IEPP), World Bank, UNDP, UNEP, 1994.
Instrument for the Establishment of the Restructured Global Environment Facility, Washington DC, 1994.
Sjöberg, Helen, *From Idea to Reality: The Creation of the GEF*, GEF Working Paper No. 10, Washington DC, 1994.
Rules of Procedure for the GEF Council, Washington DC, 1995.
The GEF Project Cycle, Washington DC, 1996.
GEF Operational Strategy, Washington DC, 1996.
GEF Strategy for Engaging the Private Sector GEF/C.7/12, 2–4 April 1996.
GEF Procurement Report GEF/R.2/Inf.2, First Meeting on the Second GEF Replenishment, 2 May 1997.
Draft CEO Report on Policies, Operations and Future Development of the GEF, GEF/C.11/5, 1998.
Note on the Reconstitution of STAP for the Second Phase of the GEF, GEF/C.11/Inf.4, 6 March 1998.
Funds and Trust Funds, GEF/C.12/inf.5, 2 October 1998.
Annual Review of the STAP Roster of Experts, FY98, GEF/C.12/Inf.15, 2 October 1998.
Keeping the Promise – Actions and Investments for a 21st Century, GEF, Washington DC, 1998.
GEF–NGO Newsletter, June/July 1998.
Overall Performance Study, 1998.
Overall Performance Study, 2002.

Project Documents

GEF Small Grants Programme, Project Summary, July 1991.
Republic of Congo – Wildlands Protection and Management Project, Grant and Project Summary, 1992.

Global Data management Capacitation in Developing Countries and Networking Biodiversity Information, Project Document, UNEP/GSF, 1994.

Cost Rica Biodiversity Reources Project, GEF Proposal for Review, World Bank/GEF, 1996.

Zimbabwe Photovoltaics for Household and Community Use, Project Document, UNDP.

India Ecodevelopment, Staff Appraisal Report, World Bank, 1996.

Index

Compiled by Sue Carlton

Page numbers followed by n indicate footnotes

Implementing Agencies *continued*
  project development training
    147–8
  project initiation 143–6, 152
  and project preparation 146–8
  RDBs and 138–9
  relations between 185–92
  and STAP 111, 142
  transparency 146, 179
  and trust funds 166
  see also UN Development
    Programme (UNDP); UN Envi-
    ronment Programme (UNEP);
    United Nations, agencies;
    World Bank
incentive gap 227
incremental costs 84, 116–18,
    128–9, 133–4, 147, 148–52
  and global environmental
    benefits 14, 178, 212, 216
  and national priorities 97n
  PRINCE 78, 118
  Small Grants Programme and 167
  see also global environmental
    benefits
Independent Evaluation of GEF
    Pilot Phase (IEPP) report 82,
    84–6, 88–9, 176
India 20, 55, 73n, 102, 104
  and Small Grants Programme
    projects 167n, 169
  solar energy project 166n
India Ecodevelopment project 202,
    226, 247–58
  background 247–50
  and documentary about GEF 259
  impacts of 172, 252–3
  local alternatives 255–6
  local verdicts 253–5
  participation 195, 196–7,
    199–200, 252–4, 257
  protests against 256–8
  resettlement 248–50, 252–3, 254,
    258
Indian Forest Department (FD)
    248–9, 252–6, 258
Indian Institute of Public Adminis-
    tration (IIPA) 250

indigenous people 196–8, 207, 248,
    253–5
  see also Adivasi
Indonesia 23, 25, 55, 73n
industry
  energy conservation 162
  and permaculture principles 218
Infodev 205n
innovation 58, 61, 83, 128, 165,
    173, 177
institutional sustainability 217–18
Instrument for Establishment of
    Restructured GEF 81, 91, 97,
    102, 112
Inter-American Development Bank
    138
Intergovernmental Panel on
    Climate Change (IPCC) 42, 43,
    77, 117, 213
International Bank for Reconstruc-
    tion and Development (IBRD)
    23
International Centre for Settlement
    of Investment Disputes (ICSD)
    23
International Conservation
    Financing Program (ICFP) 49,
    51, 52
International Council of Scientific
    Unions (ICSU) 50, 78n
International Development Associa-
    tion (IDA) 23–4, 52, 218
International Finance Corporation
    (IFC) 23, 137–8, 162, 166
International Geosphere–Biosphere
    Programme (IGBP) 77
International Monetary Fund (IMF)
    2, 3–4, 21, 22, 215n
  and carbon dioxide emissions 43
  Structural Adjustment
    Programmes (SAPs) 25, 245
  supporting US foreign policy 23
  and Third World debt 24
International Parliamentary Confer-
    ences on Environment 34
International Rivers Network 224n
international waters 40, 117, 212
  GEF projects 60, 83n, 114n, 168,
    171

procurement contracts 158
scientific research 77
United Nations 18, 21–2, 51, 188,
    230
  agencies 10, 58–60, 185, 188–9,
    211
    see also Implementing
    Agencies; UN Development
    Programme (UNDP); UN Envi-
    ronment Programme (UNEP)
United States (US) 53–4, 72–3,
    142–3, 165, 212, 230
  carbon emissions 246
  and contributions to GEF 131
  environmental movement 3, 35
  foreign aid 53–4, 71
  and international financial
    institutions 4
  and NGO participation 75, 85
  procurement contracts 158
  and World Bank 21, 71
  and world domination 5, 222
Unocal 68
Uphoff, Norman 201
Uruguay 125
US Agency for International Devel-
    opment (USAid) 30, 118, 120
US Environmental Protection
    Agency (EPA) 115
US National Forum on Biodiversity
    (NFB) 44

van Bolhuis, Frederik 51
Vienna Convention 41
Vietnam, biodiversity project 82–3,
    142n
Vogler, John 163n
Voluntary Fund, GEF 99

Wade, Robert 29n
Wapenhams, Willi 24, 71
war on terror 5, 224
Washington, protests in 223
Washington Consensus 4, 206, 209,
    222
waste, exporting to Southern
    countries 206n
water 7, 33, 38
Watson, Bob 78n, 110n, 201
Werksman, Jake 123

Western Europe
  interests 5
  and international financial insti-
    tutions 4
Western European and Others
    Group (WEOG) 64, 90
whales 125
White, Harry Dexter 21
Wilderness Society 35n
Wildlife Protection Act (1972),
    India 248
Wilson, E.O. 44
wind power 138
Wolfenson, James 21nn, 162, 194,
    215
Wood, Alex 60, 82
Woods, John 110n
World Bank 2, 3–4, 15, 108–10
  accountability 7, 123, 124
  and biodiversity 134
  calls for abolition of 71, 98
  and civil society 72, 98, 144
  and control of UN Conventions
    64, 66, 72, 87
  creation of 20–1
  criticism of IEPP 85–6
  criticism of 2, 24, 62, 71, 83, 202,
    206–7
  development agenda 11
  Economic Development Institute
    28
  and efficiency 188–9
  and enabling activities 164
  and environmental damage 39,
    62, 71, 136, 214, 215
  and establishment of GEF 5–6,
    18, 52
  external relations 185
  fiduciary duty 108–9
  Financial Management Unit 109
  and focal point system 139–40
  and forest exploitation 61–2
  and G77 55n, 64
  and GEF projects 62, 63, 144,
    145–6, 153
  and GEF Secretariat 105, 106,
    109, 185–6
  and GEFOP 153
  and global environmental
    benefits 178, 179